Computer Electrical Power Requirements

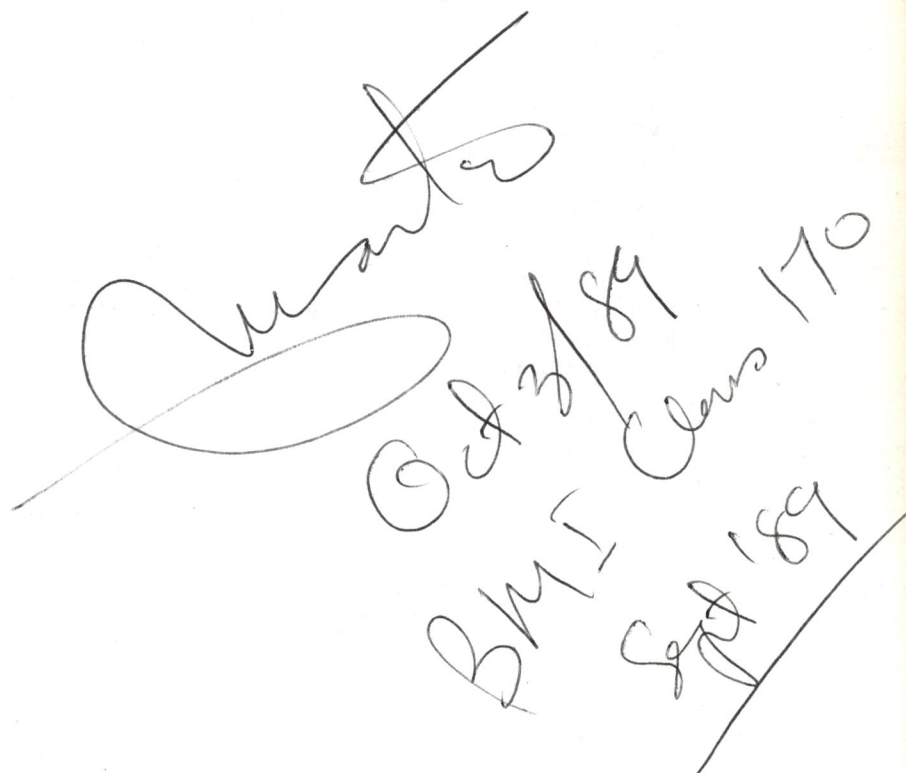

HOWARD W. SAMS & COMPANY/HAYDEN BOOKS

Related Titles

Understanding Fiber Optics
Jeff Hecht

Understanding Microprocessors, Second Edition
Cannon and Luecke

Understanding MS-DOS®
O'Day and Angermeyer, The Waite Group

Understanding Security Electronics
Joseph J. Carr

Understanding Solid State Electronics, Fourth Edition
Hafford and McWhorter

Understanding Telephone Electronics, Second Edition
Fike and Friend

Understanding Computer Science, Second Edition
Roger S. Walker

Understanding Computer Science Applications
Roger S. Walker

Understanding Data Communications, Second Edition
Friend, Fike, Baker, and Bellamy

Understanding Digital Electronics, Second Edition
Gene W. McWhorter

Understanding Digital Troubleshooting, Second Edition
Don L. Cannon

Understanding Electricity and Electronics Circuits
David Heiserman

Understanding Electricity and Electronics Principles
David Heiserman

Understanding Advanced Solid State Electronics
Don L. Cannon

Understanding Artificial Intelligence
Henry C. Mishkoff

Understanding Automation Systems, Second Edition
Farwell and Schmitt

Understanding Automotive Electronics, Second Edition
Ribbens and Mansour

Understanding Communications Systems, Second Edition
Cannon and Luecke

Understanding CAD/CAM
Bowman and Bowman

For the retailer nearest you, or to order directly from the publisher, call 800-428-SAMS. In Indiana, Alaska, and Hawaii call 317-298-5699.

Computer Electrical Power Requirements

Mark Waller

Power Management Associates
P.O. Box 875
Montrose, CA 91020–0875

HOWARD W. SAMS & COMPANY
A Division of Macmillan, Inc.
4300 West 62nd Street
Indianapolis, Indiana 46268 USA

© 1987 by Mark Waller

FIRST EDITION
FIRST PRINTING—1987

All rights reserved. No part of this book shall be reproduced, stored in a retrieval system, or transmitted by any means, electronic, mechanical, photocopying, recording, or otherwise, without written permission from the publisher. No patent liability is assumed with respect to the use of the information contained herein. While every precaution has been taken in the preparation of this book, the publisher and author assume no responsibility for errors or omissions. Neither is any liability assumed for damages resulting from the use of the information contained herein.

International Standard Book Number: 0-672-22561-1
Library of Congress Catalog Card Number: 87-61778

Acquisitions Editor: *James S. Hill*
Editor: *C. Herbert Feltner*
Word Processor: *Kim Clark*
Illustrator: *Don Clemons*
Indexer: *Ted Laux*
Cover Graphic: *Keith J. Hampton*
              Visual Graphic Services, Indianapolis
Compositor: *J. Jarrett Engineering*

Trademark Acknowledgements

All terms mentioned in this book that are known to be trademarks or service marks are listed below. In addition, terms suspected of being trademarks or service marks have been appropriately capitalized. Howard W. Sams & Company cannot attest to the accuracy of this information. Use of a term in this book should not be regarded as affecting the validity of any trademark or service mark.

IBM is a registered trademark of International Business Machines Corporation.
Univac is a registered trademark of Burroughs Corp.

Printed in the United States of America

Contents

Preface ix

Acknowledgments xiii

Introduction xv

1 Utility Power 1

    Transmitting Power *1*
    Math Mysteries *2*
    Creating AC *2*
        Ohm's Law 4
        Definitions 8
    Transformers *9*
    City Power *10*
        How Hydro Works 11
        How a Steam Plant Operates 11
        Transmission and Receiving 11
        The Basics 13

2 A Closer Look at Utility Power 15

    Definitions *16*
    Power-Line Monitors *19*
    Computer Tolerances *22*
    Ride Through *25*
    Power Quality *25*
        The IBM Survey 26
        The Bell Telephone Survey 26
        Recent Surveys 27
    Interaction Between a Computer and Its Source *27*
        Inrush 27
    A Step Back *29*

3 Inside the Building 31

    Two Shocking Stories *31*
    Voltage Considerations *32*
        Voltages Defined 33

Buildings Big and Small *34*
    Large Vertical Buildings *35*
    Tall Buildings *35*
    Large Horizontal Buildings *35*
    Groups of Small Buildings *35*
    Industrial Plants *35*
    Small Commercial Buildings and Homes *36*
Service to the Computer *36*
The Culprits *37*
    Capacitors *38*
    Motors *38*
    Air Conditioners *38*
    Arc Equipment *38*
    Other Culprits *38*
Some Solutions *39*

4 Lightning, Static, and Noise   41

Lightning *41*
    The Electrical Effect of Lightning *45*
    Lightning Frequency *45*
    Protection *46*
    Transient Overvoltage *48*
Static *49*
Noise *51*
    Kinds of Noise *51*
    Power Supplies *52*
    Isolation, Shielding, and Grounding *53*

5 Grounding   55

Safety *56*
    Shielding *56*
    Codes *58*
    Grounding Myths *59*
Proper Grounding Techniques *60*
    Signal Reference Grids *62*
    Transient Suppression Plates *63*
    Theory Versus Real World *63*
    A Few Tips *63*

6 Personal Computers and Office Electronic Equipment   67

Utility Power *67*
Inside Your Building *68*

Grounding *69*
 Networks 71
 Telecommunications 71
The Office *72*
Wiring for Data *72*
Prewire for Data *74*
 Cable Types 74
 Other Considerations 77
The Smart Building *78*

7 Transient Suppression **79**

Transients *79*
Transient Suppressors *82*
 Crowbars 82
 Clamps 84
 Failure 86
 Multistage Protection 87
 Suppressor Installation 88

8 Isolation and Distribution **91**

Isolation Transformers *91*
 Noise Coupling 93
 Computer Grade Isolation Transformers 95
Distribution *97*
 Conventional Wiring 97
 The PDU 99

9 Voltage Regulation **103**

Filters *103*
Line Voltage Regulators *104*
 Variable-Ratio Transformers 104
 Variable-Induction Regulators 105
 Saturable Reactors 106
 Magnetic Coupling Controlled Regulators 106
 Isolation Regulators 107
Ferroresonant Transformers *107*
Tap-Switching Regulators *111*

10 M-G Sets, RUPS, and UPS **117**

M-G Sets *117*
 Induction Motors 118
 Synchronous Motors 119
 Overall Considerations 119

RUPS *120*
UPS *123*
   UPS Building Blocks *123*
   On Line Versus Standby *127*
   Transfer Switches *129*
   Redundancy *130*
   Batteries *131*
MTBF & MTTR *132*

11 Batteries for UPS Systems — *135*

Battery Types *136*
   Lead Acid *136*
Three Kinds of Batteries in Use *137*
   Nickel Cadmium *138*
   Gel Cells *139*
Outages *140*

12 PC Power — *141*

UPS *141*
   Transfer Time *143*
   Making Waves *144*
   Synchronicity *144*
   A Battery of Questions *146*
Backup Power Systems *147*
   Conditioning *147*
Power Conditioners *148*
Surge Protectors *149*

13 Conclusion — *151*

The Representative *152*
The Environment *153*
   Power and More *153*
The Future *154*

Glossary — *157*

Bibliography — *163*

Index — *167*

Preface

Like so many people, I was bit by the computer bug in the mid-1970s. We called them microcomputers then. How many of us stayed up night after night with a soldering iron and a magnifying glass putting memory chips on pc boards? Terror was running the "memtest" program only to find that some chip in high memory was bad.

All programs came on cassettes. So the next project was to build a cassette interface for my semibreadboard computer. I used a little radio frequency generator to drive an old black-and-white TV. It usually took three or four tries to load a program.

Each program had several bugs, it seemed. Or a glitch while loading would render certain portions of the program unusable.

My eyes burned, my back hurt, and my wife missed me. But I loved every minute of it. I learned a new technology. I made new friends. And by the time the TRS-80 Model 1 was released I was ready.

What a beauty! It had 64k of memory and two disk drives. Word processing was my main use for the machine. It didn't take long for me to learn the value in saving my work to disk every so often. Typically, I would be several hundred words into a project when my disk drive would suddenly "fire up." The screen would freeze. The keyboard would lock up. All my work would disappear.

Next were a few bitter lessons in the need to back up disks. More often than I care to remember I would hear the motor go into a retry. I would pray while I listened. Finally, the words "Disk Read Error" would pop up on the screen. Disk zapping, directory fixing, and hash index coding became my pastime. Relief was knowing that my backup disk just read properly.

Years later I got the chance to upgrade to a hard disk system. Sure, I learned to back up critical files, but I had nearly half of a 20 meg drive full of unduplicated material when I left that fateful weekend. Sunday night, as we drove home through a lightning storm, I thought of my trusty computer. I had done some writing on my portable and was eager to download it into the main system.

It was drive D that wouldn't read. At least not on the first try. It took several read errors before the directory on drive D would come up. For days I worked on the problem. I tried zapping, fixing, and praying. No luck.

So, two full days and two boxes of 94 TPI disks later I had backed up everything and was ready to format my hard disk. I wasn't happy.

The computer was turned off. What went wrong? The lightning storm, I thought. A spike of some kind must have gotten into the system and hit the hard disk. Hmmm, could power disturbances explain all my reruns and false starts? I knew one thing. Every time my wife turned on the iron, my screen shrank to half its normal size. Then as the thermostat turned on and off my screen would jump, wiggle, and wobble. That had to be a power problem.

It all came to me then. No wonder experts take such precautions with big computers. Imagine losing data from a lightning strike in a large computer facility. It could be catastrophic. It could even ruin the equipment.

By this time, I was working for a company that made power distribution equipment for major computer manufacturers. I began studying the world of power and its interaction with the devices that are connected to it. I got the shock of my life, excuse the pun. There was no way I should have expected my PC to withstand all the variations it was subjected to.

From micro to mainframe, the need for an understanding of the electrical environment for computers is critical. It's a vast electrical wasteland out there, but fortunately there are a number of strategies as well as devices to deal with the situation.

There are experts on power, and there are scholarly publications that deal with the subject of computers and their power sources. This book is an effort to combine and simplify the available knowledge.

A fundamental understanding of the problem is necessary. The first portion of this book deals with the electrical environment. The three demons of destruction are

- Lightning

- Static

- Noise

In the second part of the book, we discuss

- Isolation transformers

- Power distribution

- Voltage regulation

- M-G sets

- RUPS

- UPS

and an array of other techniques and devices available to solve power problems. It is not intended that the reader be an engineer to understand the concepts explained here. Everyone who operates a computer, whether it's a huge mainframe or a small PC, faces the vagaries of electricity. A proper understanding, therefore, sets the stage for the devices used to solve various problems.

This book is meant to fill a void that exists between the computer user and the power expert. The principles explained apply to micros, minis, and mainframes. The devices, in one form or another, are common to the home or the office.

As a result of writing this book, I don't worry anymore. The power for my hard disk system and all its peripherals comes from a state-of-the-art device that provides a complete, friendly, portable, electrical environment. I call it insurance against a rainy day.

MARK WALLER

Acknowledgements

I would like to thank Brad Little, Gary Grandbery, Richard Bowyer, and Diane Bullen for their help in providing photographs for this book. To Milton Hanson, Bob Erickson, Dick Bowyer, and Jack Pouchet for on the spot technical assistance, thank you. Much thanks goes to Art Behnke for his technical review. Most importantly, I would like to acknowlege Fred Kalbach and Warren Lewis for their life-long contribution to the computer power industry. Also, this book would not have been possible without the contribution of Bill Coleman. A special note of gratitude goes to the team at Howard W. Sams & Company, especially Jim Rounds who guided me and encouraged me to go the extra mile. Finally, I must mention the patience of Jan, Petra, and Abigail, who did without me all those many weekends of writing.

Introduction

They say the computer age started in 1946 when the ENIAC digital computer produced its first useful results. Actually, the basic concepts behind computing machines go way back to Charles Babbage, who put forth the principles that can be found behind even the most sophisticated digital designs of today.

The modern computer industry traces its roots to the Univac 1 in 1950. Made out of vacuum tubes, the Univac 1 filled an entire room (Fig. I-1). Strange as it my seem to us, it had less computing power than today's desktop computers.

Although the principles of computing have remained relatively stable for over a generation, the technology that puts those concepts to work has changed dramatically. By the early 1960s, prices and performance had reached a level where general-purpose data processing was available to most large corporations. Almost 15 years from the lab to the office, computers had become an integral part of the future plans of most businesspeople.

That first jump of 15 years was forgotten when only 5 years later the PDP-8 was introduced, and the minicomputer industry was born. Now managers could control a production line or crunch numbers in a laboratory. Prices fell dramatically. The size of internal CPU components underwent the most drastic change of all. Enter solid-state devices: AND Gates, OR Gates, EXCLUSIVE ORs, NAND Gates, and inverters. The physics of computing would never be the same.

The next leap forward came when gates were grouped together on a single chip, the integrated circuit. The first family of chips to incorporate four gates on one wafer were known as the 7400 series. Four gates soon became 100, then 1000, and were classed as medium scale integration. Over 1000 gates per IC became known as LSI (large scale integration).

In 1969, Datapoint Corporation decided it was time to move ahead yet again. It contracted two IC makers (Intel and Texas Instruments) to produce a relatively simple computer on a single chip. Intel was able to produce the chip, but to Datapoint's frustration the microcomputer executed instructions nearly ten times slower than what had been specified.

Intel faced a dilemma. Should they junk the project, or could the little computer become a viable product to the market place? Intel called it the 8008 and launched another era in computer development.

Fig. I-1.
Univac 1, the world's first commercial electronic computer, is shown at the Eckert-Mauchly Computer Corp. plant in Philadelphia. After Remington Rand purchased Eckert-Mauchly in 1950, the first Univac (Universal Automatic Computer) was delivered to the Bureau of Census in 1951.
(Courtesy Sperry Corporation)

Of course, during this time mini and mainframe technology didn't just stand still. Each year found a new group of smaller, faster machines capable of doing an ever increasing array of tasks the likes of which could only be found in the books of science fiction writers a couple of decades earlier.

While the computer industry exploded, changing the lives of virtually every man, woman, and child, one industry stayed frozen in time—the electrical power industry. In 1950 when Eckert and Mauchly first developed the Univac 1, it was necessary for the manufacturer, Remington Rand, to get intimately involved with the utility company to make sure the engineering of the computer's power source was correct. We would never think of such a thing today. We merely plug in the computer and turn it on.

Since those early days, the power available has not change significantly from that used by Univac 1. Meanwhile, clock speeds that were slow became nanoseconds. Signal levels high enough for vacuum tubes became logic levels of a few volts. Big, slow, and insensitive became small, fast, and critical. Unlike the behemoths of 30 years ago, the machines of today require a steady flow of high-quality power to function within their operating specifications. We will see that computers and the power that supplies them have been on a collision course for many years.

Because of this situation, an entire industry has grown up to serve the power needs of computers and related peripherals. In the early days of computing, the technology of power regulation and conditioning was primitive. A regulator might have used motor driven taps to adjust to voltage fluctuations. This technology worked slowly, approximately at a ten cycle correction time. So large were the current requirements that battery backup systems were cost prohibitive to all but a few.

But as computers became smaller and faster, the technology behind power products improved. Old methods were streamlined using solid-state controls and components. The cost of protection began to fall in line with more DP (data processing) budgets. Today, we find a variety of power devices in nearly every computer installation.

The world of electrical power remains a mystery to most field engineers, data processing managers, and weekend hobbyists. Even most digitally trained engineers know little or nothing of the subject. And to make matters worse, many DC power supply design engineers know little or nothing about "real world" AC power.

On the other hand, we have the electricians. Better than 60 percent of all computer installations will get their power from conduit, wiring, and receptacles installed by electricians. Many of these guys know nothing about computers—what's best or what's disastrous. They are only concerned with satisfying the minimum requirements of the electrical code.

Lest some take immediate umbrage at our sweeping belittlement of electricians, let's acknowledge that many do a fine job and are true students of their craft. Most, however, get a work order to install a certain number of outlets and could care less what is going to be plugged into them. This leads to no end of problems in the computer room.

The world of electrical power, as it relates to computers, is a hostile place indeed. That's why we have devoted the first part of the book to the electrical environment. We discuss the unique characteristics of utility power and see what factors inside the home or office affect the quality of power that the computer sees. The three demons of destruction will be exposed for what they really are: lightning, static, and noise. Although, the key to proper computer operation is grounding, it is one of the least understood and most abused topic in the electrical environment. We shed enough light on the subject so that the average person can make some sense out of proper grounding techniques. Finally, we take a look at how all this might relate to the personal computer and other electronic office equipment.

In the second part of the book, we discuss the array of techniques and devices available to solve power problems. Each technology may be applied at the micro, mini, and mainframe level. The function, advantages, and disadvantages of all common devices will be explored, from MOVs to MG-Sets.

The use of power products is on the rise. Analysts say industry growth will be 20 percent for the foreseeable future. This eclipses the projected growth of computers and peripherals by almost double during the same time frame. We are likely to be confronted with this strange alternating current technology more and more often. Knowledge of power and power products is critical in buying decisions, protection of data, and ease of operation.

This book provides everything needed to cut through sales hype and help protect the investment we all have in computing.

1

Utility Power

When I was 14 I toured Grand Coulee Dam. It was awesome. Huge generators were turning at unthinkable speeds, driven by the churning force of the Columbia River. So that was where electricity was made. It's strange that what was such an overpowering discovery for a young man is seldom even contemplated by most adults. AC power is a mystery even to the well educated, even though it is always there when we need it.

Transmitting Power

Like Grand Coulee Dam, most power generating plants are located well away from populated areas. Nuclear plants need large amounts of water for cooling. Hydroelectric plants must be near rushing water. Other fuel burning facilities must be located away from cities and near available resources, like coal or oil.

Because of the vast distances and tremendous costs involved in bringing power to people, utilities use high-voltage, low-current transmission techniques. Voltages of 345,000 and higher are common on most long distance power lines. This is achieved by stepping up the voltage coming from the generator, which may be 18,000 volts. Were this not done, radiation and heat losses due to line dissipation would be enormous, and the cost of our electricity would be considerably higher.

When the lines are near the users, substations are used to step the voltage back down to levels of 13,800 volts. This stepping down of the voltage continues until levels such as 208 volts appear at transformers near homes and offices.

The 120-volt service that we use to power our household appliances and office equipment comes from the standard three-phase transformer. We'll see how that is done in a moment.

Math Mysteries

One of the truly strange things in life is the mathematical relationships that exist. For example, a three-phase wiring system delivers 1.73 times as much power as a single-phase two wire system. And if that's not mystical enough, it's all tied into the fact that 1.73 is the square root of three—three because it's three-phase. We will look into this more later.

Three-phase power is popular for a number of reasons. First, it delivers more power than a single-phase system, all things being equal. Second, machines, rectifiers, and motors operate on three-phase power better.

The rotating field produced by three-phase power is useful in some machine applications. Three-phase power has a lower ripple amplitude, which means it requires less filtering when rectified. The performance and economic advantages are readily clear in the area of motors. Three-phase motors are cheaper to build and are physically smaller. They have better starting torque, run more quietly, and have better efficiency. The larger the motor the greater the benefits of using three-phase power.

Creating AC

What really is the difference between single- and three-phase power? As taught in high school physics, when a conductor cuts through a magnetic field a current is induced in that conductor. The electrical generator uses this principle (Fig. 1-1). When the conductor cuts through the maximum number of flux lines, maximum current flows. When the conductor is between lines of flux, therefore not cutting through the field, no current flows (Fig. 1-2). As the conductor rotates the next quarter turn, it begins to cut through again. But since the conductor is now 180 degrees from where it started, current flows in the opposite direction (Fig. 1-3).

If we plotted the flow of current through the 360 degrees travel of the conductor, we would find the curve looking like the one in Fig. 1-4. Each 360-degree cycle through the flux lines gives us an identical sine wave. And by some mathematical twist of fate this curve matches the sine function in trigonometry—that's how it got its name.

By adding two more conductors and applying the same principle, we end up with three sine waves. In a standard generator, these added windings are designed so that the peak currents occur 120 degrees from one another. Since each cycle has three peaks and portions of three sine waves, we can draw it in a diagram like the one shown in Fig. 1-5. The vector diagram shows three phases: A, B, C and a neutral connection, N.

The voltage between points A and N, neutral, of the generator might

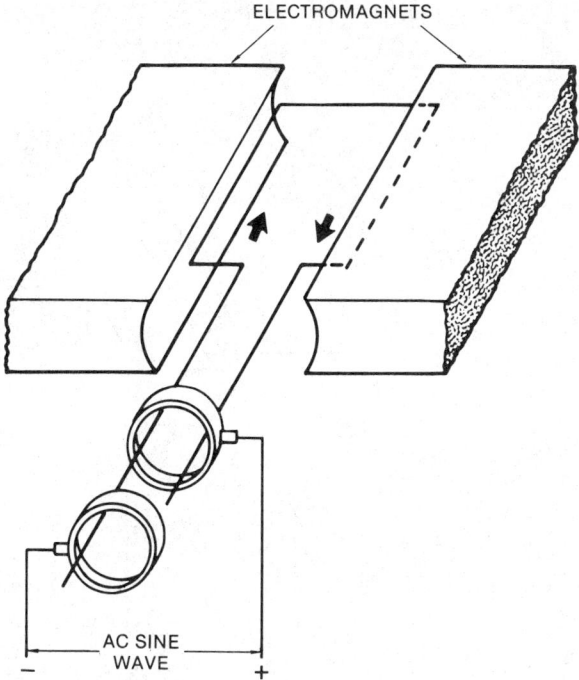

Fig. 1-1.
A conductor cuts through a magnetic field and induces voltage in the rotating conductor.

be 2400 volts. The phase-to-phase voltage (between points A and B) is 1.73 times the line to N. If the vectors were drawn to scale, we would find this relationship by measuring the distance AN against AB. The terms phase to phase and phase to neutral are common in the world of three-phase power. We are referring here to a "Wye" wound generator. The other armature connection method most common is the Delta system. The previous discussion also applies to a Delta system except it is the phase-to-phase current and not the voltage that is 1.73 times line to neutral. We will discuss Delta and Wye systems later.

Obviously, this is not a complete discussion of three-phase power generation. Nor have all the combinations of generator windings and outputs been discussed. The object is to get a feel for three phases as it applies to subjects that will be discussed later. It is not necessary to become an expert in order to understand the how and why of the power that appears at the building service entrance. We see what that connection might look like in Fig. 1-6.

Does the preceding describe every situation? No, but with few basic differences this is how power enters all our homes, factories, and offices. Notice that the neutral is grounded. This neutral-to-ground bonding will come up again.

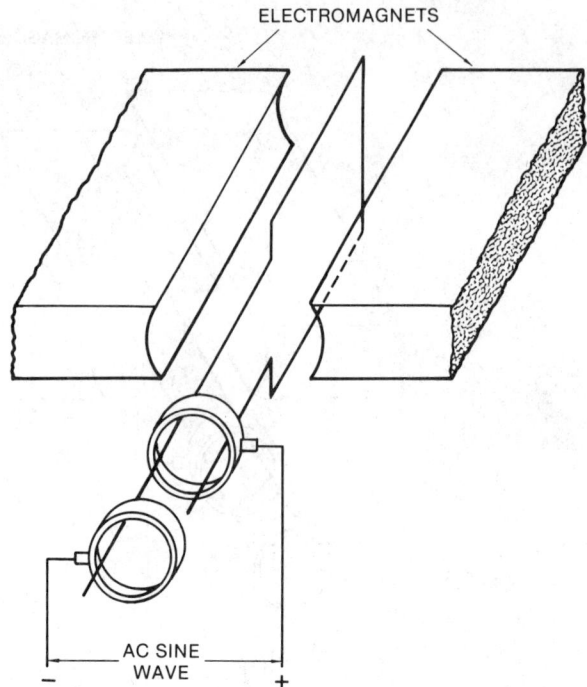

Fig. 1-2.
*When the conductor is between lines of flux,
no current flows.*

One might ask how the utility takes the power from the generator and steps it up for cross country transmission then steps it all the way down so we might use it to run a personal computer. To prepare to tackle the subject of transformers, we must go over a basic mathematical relationship that most of us know well, but some may have forgotten.

Ohm's Law

Ohm's law explains the relationship between current, voltage, and resistance.

$$I = \frac{E}{R}$$

From this we can derive two more equations: $IR = E$ and $R = E/I$ where
I is current in amperes,
E is voltage in volts,
R is resistance in ohms.

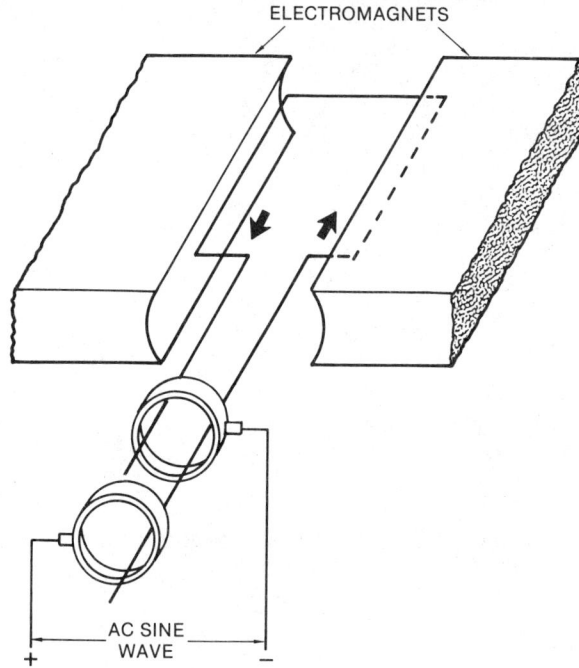

Fig. 1-3.
Current flows in the opposite direction since the conductor is 180 degrees from where it started.

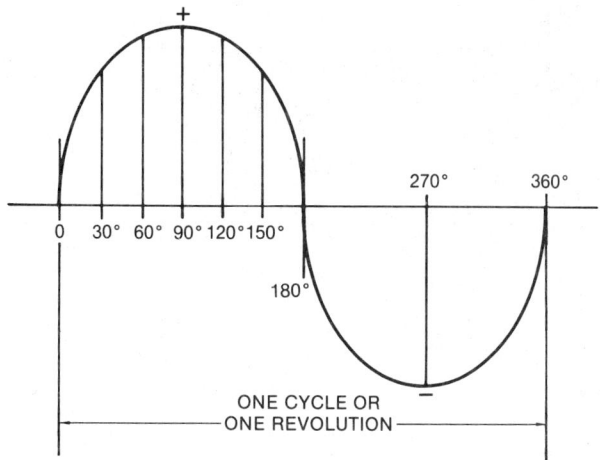

Fig. 1-4.
As the conductor turns through 360 degrees, the flow of current, when plotted, traces a sine wave.

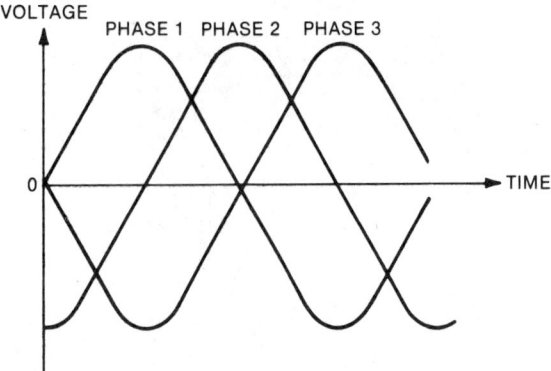
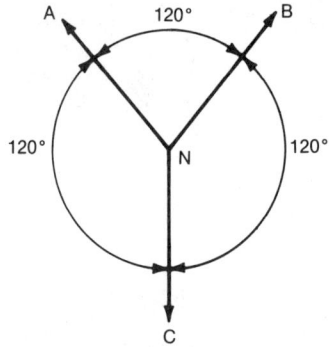

(A) Three-phase generation produces three sine waves with peaks 120 degrees from one another.

(B) Vector diagram of three-phase generation.

Fig. 1-5.
Three-phase generation produces three sine waves.

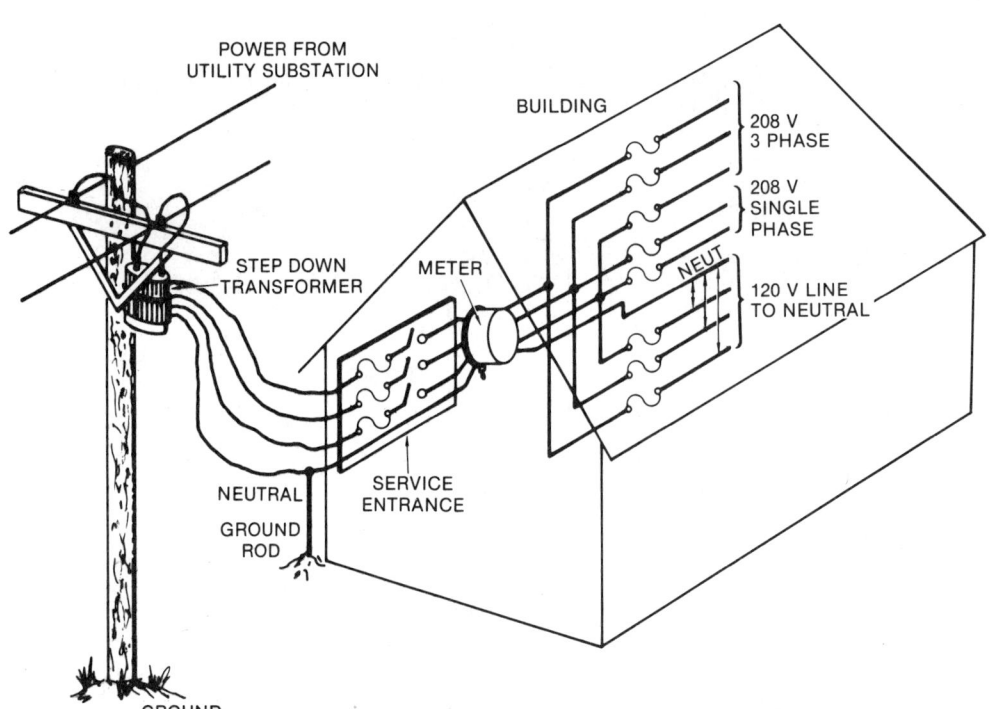

Fig. 1-6.
How power might appear at the building service entrance.

Looking at $R = E/I$, we see that with R constant, a variation in I will cause a direct change in E. Or a change in E will cause a change in I.

For example, if our house has voltage at an outlet of 120 volts and we plugged a 10-ohm resister into the socket it would draw 12 amps (amperes).

R in the formula can get complicated. A load of pure resistance is a relatively simple thing to deal with. Even the ohmic value of inductors and capacitors, called impedance, can be calculated without getting a headache. But when you apply AC to a load that is mostly inductive or mostly capacitive, the calculations get more complicated. Possibly you've heard of impedance (opposition to current flow that is not purely resistive) caused by capacitors and inductors in a circuit. Unfortunately, inductive reactance and capacitive reactance cause voltage and current to shift in relationship to one another. Now that's complicated. For the most part, we'll ignore reactance in our discussion of R, but remember it is always there. Every load has characteristics that affect R in Ohm's law.

Suppose we changed our example and used a 1-ohm resister. Now the current drawn would be 120 amps. In the real world, the first thing that would happen would be a circuit breaker would trip. But let us assume that we actually wanted our house circuit to carry 120 amps. What would have to change? Wire size!

As the current capacity of our line increases, its physical size must increase also—the reverse is also true. Ah, possibly you are ahead of me at this point. Since current in amperes affects sizing, then raising line voltage while holding resistance (the load) steady would mean less current flows through the line, thus smaller wire size. That's one good reason for stepping up generator voltage to hundreds of thousands of volts. Unless power engineers did this, the size of the wires would be such that if one broke and fell you might be crushed instead of electrocuted.

There is a more practical reason for transmission voltages being so high. To explain this we need one more equation.

$$P = EI$$

where

P is power in watts,
E is voltage in volts,
I is current in amperes.

We know from an earlier discussion that $E = IR$. So if we combine the equations we get:

$$P = (IR)I$$

or

$$P = I^2 R$$

All conductors have resistance, and the power lost due to resistance to current flow is heat. We can see that if we step voltage in a line down, the current will increase. If current doubles, the loss, according to our power formula, will not double it will quadruple. If we increase I 10 times, we get 100 times the losses. This I squared relationship is the reason for stepping up transmission voltage because losses are related to current flow rather than potential (voltage).

The other side of the coin is voltage drop. $E = IR$ tells us that the voltage drop from the generator to our house, for instance, is the current times the resistance. If we step the voltage up, we reduce the current carried in the line. Therefore, at higher voltages, our IR loss is considerably less. In other words, if we reduce the line-carrying current by a factor of three, we will reduce the voltage drop by the same factor. This is yet another reason for high transmission voltages.

Definitions

A reader with a solid technical background can see that we have omitted many variables to keep the story simple. AC power is much more complex than the brief space allowed here. We hope, however, that the newcomer can glean a rudimentary understanding of power generation and distribution. Here is a summary of definitions that have and will be used.

$$
\begin{aligned}
I &= \text{Current in amperes} \\
E &= \text{Electrical potential in volts} \\
R &= \text{Resistance in ohms} \\
P &= \text{Power expressed in watts} \\
kV &= 1000 \text{ volts} \\
kW &= 1000 \text{ watts} \\
kVA &= 1000 \text{ volt amperes (apparent power)} \\
PF &= \text{Power Factor (kW/kVA)}
\end{aligned}
$$

Power Factor—Inductive and capacitive reactance in a load cause real power consumed in watts to differ from apparent power as shown by a measurement of volts and amperes. What this means is that if we took a meter and measured the volts and amperes used by our computer and compared that reading to the number of watts used, we would see two different numbers. Inductive reactance causes current to lag voltage, and capacitive reactance causes current to lead voltage. These impedances cannot be added arithmetically—they must be added algebraically.

It would be simple if the leading and lagging currents always equaled one another—they would cancel out. Most computer systems present a complex load to the source such that the apparent power (kVA) exceeds real power (kW)—this results in a PF (power factor) of less than unity. This means that not all the volt amperes are consumed by the load as watts. Some power is not used by the load but is circulated between the load and the source as the inductive and capacitive elements interact. These leading and lagging characteristics of AC circuits cause the typical computer system to have a power factor of less than unity (1). This can also be due to rectifiers and SCR switching elements which interrupt the load current for a portion of every cycle.

This effect means that the load current will increase without transferring the additional energy to the load. This net current increase must be dissipated in the load. Thus, larger capacitors and conductors must be used.

kVA, then, must be the critical number we deal with when we size the power requirements for a computer installation larger than a few thousand watts. As the power requirements of an installation increase, the difference between kW and kVA due to PF can be substantial.

The serious student can find many reference books that explore this area in detail. It is not our intent to provide a rationale either through vectors or equations as to why all this happens. As we move into the jargon and practice of computer power, it is enough to know that AC power has its own set of rules that dictate safe and effective methods of computer operation.

Transformers

Stepping voltage up and down from the generator to the user is done using transformers. Most of us know that a transformer consists of a primary winding of wire and a secondary winding of wire and a core of iron or steel. It was discovered many years ago that magnetic flux lines go through iron or steel 10,000 times better than through air.

A transformer uses the principles of electromagnetism. A magnetic field builds up and collapses about a conductor carrying AC power every half cycle. This moving magnetic field will induce a voltage in any other wire that is within the field. The induced voltage follows the expansion and collapse of the AC current in the primary conductor.

We can increase the inductive effect if we link the two wires with a steel core. We can again increase the effect by making our core of many sheets of steel. The input, or primary, winding is insulated from and wrapped around the core. The magnetic flux in the core will induce a voltage counter to the primary voltage, keeping current flow relatively low. When we add a secondary winding, this same flux induces current in the secondary. As load is added to the secondary, current flow produces a new magnetic field that opposes the flux in the core. When the flux tries to drop off, counter voltage in the primary decreases. This results in more current being pushed through the transformer to fill up the flux gap. Current in the primary builds up the flux in the core, compensating for the increased load. The result is that the watts output of the transformer equals the watts in the primary. As the secondary load changes, primary current is fixed by the counter voltage that is induced by secondary current flow. Load changes, therefore, are reflected back to the primary while the flux in the core remains constant.

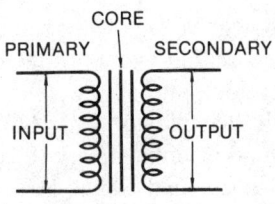

Fig. 1-7.
With a transformation ratio of 1 to 1, secondary voltage equals primary voltage.

Figure 1-7 shows the effect of transformation ratio. If we place the same number of turns on the secondary and the primary, a voltmeter would show the same potential on the output as on the input. Remember our formula for power, $P = EI$.

If we double the number of turns (Fig. 1-8) on the secondary winding, our voltmeter will show twice the potential at the output. What about current in amperes? $P = EI$ tells us that current will be one-half that of the primary. We can ignore losses since they are very small. The same principle applies to stepping voltage down. If the secondary had one-half the windings of the primary, one-half the voltage would appear and twice the current would flow. Power in equals power out is the transformation ratio. If power in equals power out, we can adjust the winding ratio to get virtually any combination of voltage and current we need. We can step the voltage up for cross-country transmission and step it down to distribute power to homes and offices. And we can use this principle in our own devices to manipulate the transformation ratio.

City Power

Let's look at a mythical city. We will use our mythical city to further explore power generation and distribution. We'll call our city Metro. It's one of the largest cities in the country. Where does it get its power, and how is it distributed?

Metro's electric utility annually generates over 18 billion kilowatt-hours of electricity. Its electric energy comes from a variety of generating

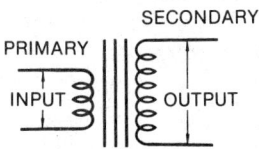

Fig. 1-8.
With twice as many turns on the secondary winding, the transformation ratio is 1 to 2.

plants including hydroelectric, coal fired steam plants, and nuclear steam plants. A dozen different facilities contribute to the power supply. In addition, Metro purchases significant power from the Bonneville Power Administration dams along the Columbia River. These include Bonneville, The Dalles, John Day, and Grand Coulee. This power is delivered by a 500,000 volt DC line of nearly 850 miles. The capacity of this line is a staggering 1,800,000 kW.

Another huge hydro project that delivers power to Metro is Hoover Dam. Its rated capacity is 1,450,000 kW. Typically, Metro can use about 500,000 kW of Hoover's output.

How Hydro Works

Water is collected and stored in a forebay, or reservoir. Then it is fed through a pipeline, sometimes called a penstock, to a lower level. The force of the forebay through the penstock turns a hydraulic turbine. The force of the water on the turbine provides the power for huge electric generators. The water then flows into what's called a tailbay.

As the turbine rotates, a shaft connects this rotation to electromagnets mounted on a rotor inside the generator. Electricity is generated in the coils of the stator, the stationary cylinder of the generator, by the motion of the rotor. The electricity flows to a bus (conductor) which carries it to step-up transformers for its journey to the user. Hydro power is often the most economical method of electrical generation.

How a Steam Plant Operates

Water is heated in a boiler and converted into steam. Burning coal or a nuclear reaction may supply the heat. This steam turns a turbine which turns the generator. The steam, now expended, goes to condensers where it is cooled and becomes water again. Depending on location, either fresh water or sea water may be used for the cooling process.

As Metro has grown, its demand for electricity has grown. Steam generating plants have filled the gap created by growth in the grid.

Transmission and Receiving

Metro gets power from various generating sources over a highly reliable, although complex, system of transmission and distribution. The electricity is sent over high-voltage lines to receiving stations where the voltage is stepped down. Then it is delivered to distributing and customer stations. The voltage is again stepped down to user levels.

The city receives power over lines from all the various generating plants at voltages of 500 kV, 287.5 kV, 230 kV, 138 kV, and 115 kV. Often the kV level is nearly equal to the transmission distance in miles (500 miles, 500 kV). Each line terminates at a receiving station designed to handle great quantities of power. These stations, located throughout Metro, are linked together in radial fashion ensuring a high degree of reliability. Figure 1-9 shows how this is done. Since voltage is fed in loops or rings it is easy, by throwing switches, to isolate problem areas and back-feed the rest of the grid. That is why a blown transformer or circuit breaker at one substation

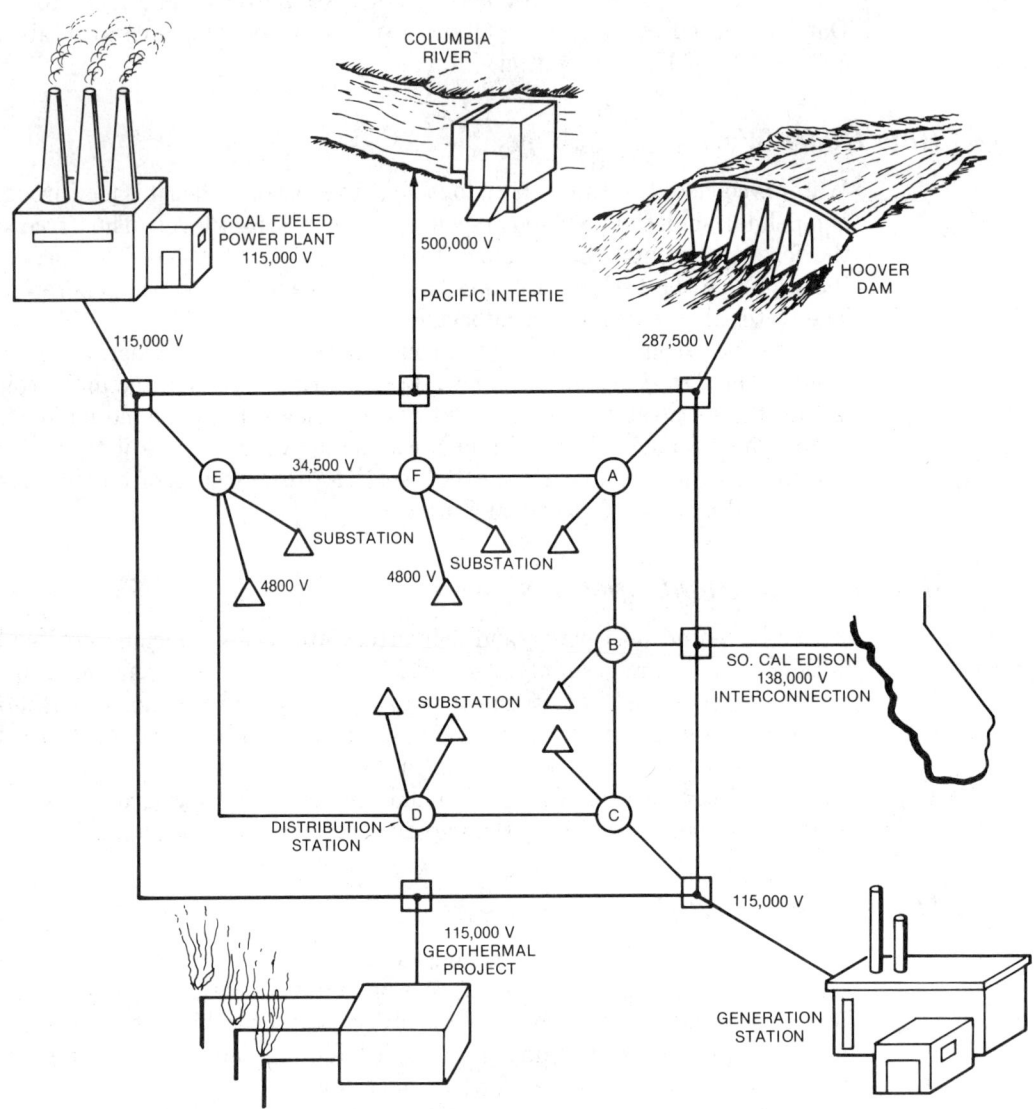

Fig. 1-9.
Metro's power supply system.

might only cause the lights to flicker while power is fed in from the other direction.

Each receiving station is the center point serving a large part of Metro. The power is fed over 34,500-volt sub transmission lines to distribution stations. Voltages are then stepped down to 4800 volts and sent over primary distribution lines to neighborhoods where the level is stepped down again to secondary voltages. Metro now has over 170 distribution stations, and more are planned in the near future.

Many large users are serviced directly from substations located on their premises. These voltages are usually 34,500 or 4800.

We have made Metro a little easier to understand than the real thing. However, the principles we see at work in the Metro power distribution system apply to most cities in the country. Radial distribution, receiving and distribution stations, and levels of voltage in use are common to all utilities.

The Basics

This overview of utility power is not meant to fill any gaps or presume to provide vast amounts of new information. It does serve as a frame of reference to what comes next and later. The computer's electrical environment is tied directly to the things we have discussed thus far. The causes of power problems find their foundation in things like power factor and radial distribution. We will see in the next chapter that an incompatibility exists between computers and the power that magically appears at the building service entrance.

Now that we have seen the building blocks of utility power, let's move on into the dark side of the force.

2

A Closer Look At Utility Power

In 1984, Con Edison of New York published a pamphlet entitled *Electric Power and the Computer*. On the first page they state that their power is adequate for sensitive electronic equipment. They go on to say that voltage fluctuations can cause problems with computers if

> The electronic equipment is designed to operate only within narrow voltage limitations.
>
> The internal wiring in the customer's building is inadequate to supply the electronic equipment.
>
> The electronic equipment does not have buffering systems.

This list probably describes every potential computer installation in the nation.

It might be easy to, at some point, blame the utility companies for all computer problems. After all, we are building a case for the incompatibility of modern data processing equipment and utility power. Pointing the finger at the utility companies is futile for several reasons.

First, they produce an amazingly clean, reliable product. When you consider the exposure a utility has from weather, errant motorists, birds, animals, and even terrorists, it's hard to fault the job they do. Sure, they could build in more redundancy, get a little fancier, perhaps add filters and the like. But the cost to the consumer would be staggering. The tradeoff between power quality and affordable rates is one where the consumer has the upper hand. Don't forget—utilities are regulated by governmental authority.

According to an article in the November issue of the *Electrical Power Research Institute* (EPRI) *Journal*, utilities are spending over 1 billion dollars each year to prevent power interruptions. Projects range from installing more lines underground to moving poles further back, away from traffic. The use of tree growth inhibitor near power lines is another method. Separate transformers may be used to serve sensitive loads. This might isolate a major computer installation from an arc furnace that might have been on the same feeder line.

To make matters even worse, some common solid-state devices like variable-speed motor controls or light-dimmer switches can feed back harmonic distortion into lines that not only confound computers but put stress on utility power equipment. Harmonic distortion causes excess heat buildup that affects the useful life of transformers, motors, and capacitors by as much as 30 percent.

Those who produce the power are sensitive to the growing complaints of their customers, and while it would be nice to find some simple solution, there is no quick fix in sight. The power industry along with computer manufacturers have recognized the need to identify the issues, research the problems, set standards, and implement solutions. Some utilities have started programs of recommending various problem-solving products to their customers. Others are providing more information and education. Most are cooperative when dealing with individual customers in resolving their problems. In short, this is not a good guy versus bad guy issue.

The standards set for various measurements and conditions emanate from two organizations: the ANSI (American National Standards Institute), and the IEEE (Institute of Electrical and Electronics Engineers). Before we go further in our discussion of power quality, we must define those power anomalies that affect computer operations. Of course, we will consult ANSI and IEEE for our definitions. But more importantly, we will consult with those people who make a living from identifying power-line disturbances, the makers of power-line monitors.

The oldest manufacturer of power-line monitors is Dranetz Technologies of Edison, New Jersey. They have defined certain power disturbances somewhat differently than IEEE. This is probably because they actually measure an event and report on it. In order to report on an event, a definition must be sufficiently precise to differentiate it from other events.

Definitions

We used no less than five recognized sources for our definitions here. None agreed. However, these definitions combine the common elements of those found in most industry documentation. Variations, euphemisms, and jargon do exist that differ.

> *Blackout*—A widespread planned or accidental loss of power. Storms, catastrophic system failures, and major automobile accidents are often causes of blackouts.

Brownouts—A long duration undervoltage condition usually hours or days in length. Brownouts can be caused by heavy usage during peak hours, or they may be planned as an energy conservation strategy.

DIP—Another term for sag.

Dropout—A total loss of voltage for a short period of time, say 1 millisecond up to 1 second (Fig. 2-1). Utility switching operations are a typical cause of dropout. Computer-based equipment will usually go down if the supply voltage drops to zero for a very few milliseconds.

Impulse—A disturbance of the voltage waveform that is about 1 millisecond or less (Fig. 2-2). Voltages can rise to hundreds or even thousands of volts in a very short period of time. It is not unusual to have nanosecond range impulses of 400 or 500 volts on an AC line. An impulse may be additive or subtractive (sometimes called a notch). Typical causes of impulses include utility switching, switching power supplies, SCRs firing, welding equipment, and lightning.

Notch—Slang for a negative or subtractive impulse.

Outage—A long-term loss of voltage resulting from a localized utility failure. In this case, long term means 1 to 5 minutes. Usually this type of condition is caused by an occurrence in the neighborhood—a local transformer failure would be an example.

Sags and Surges—A short term RMS voltage increase or decrease that exceeds established upper or lower limits for less than 2.5 secponds (Fig. 2-3). Some literature states that a surge is a 10 percent

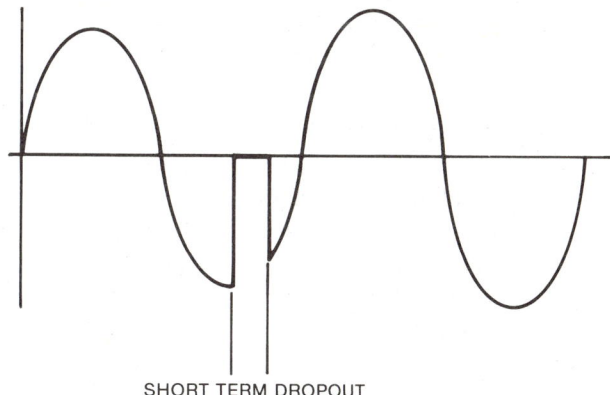

Fig. 2-1.
Dropouts are a total loss of voltage for a short period of time.

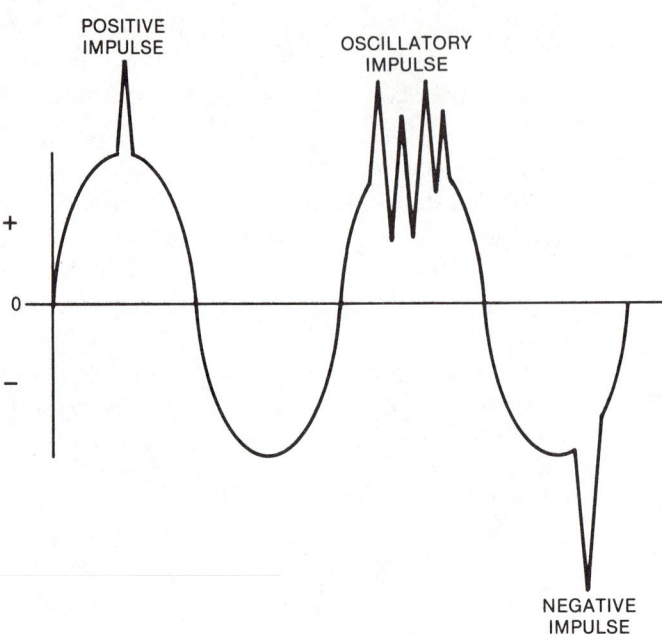

Fig. 2-2.
An impulse is a waveform disturbance that is about 1 millisecond or less.

variation above or below standard limits. Sags and surges can cause computer memory loss, data transmission errors, power supply damage, and even shutdown if equipment confuses a sag with a power failure—typical causes are load switching. Air conditioners, disk drives, transformers, and anything else that draws large amounts of instantaneous current can cause a sag when switched on or a surge when switched off.

Spike—Slang for a positive or additive impulse.

Transient—A transient is an event of nonrepetitive nature. Strictly speaking, a transient should not be used in association with impulses, but it often is. In the jargon of power, transient and impulse may be used interchangeably. However, the term transient relates more to the intermittent occurrence of surges and sags.

Undervoltage and Overvoltage—Like a sag or surge but for a longer period of time, over 2.5 seconds. We measure undervoltage and overvoltage conditions as a function of slow averaged RMS (root mean square) voltage. This is a normal measurement of line voltage over a time of 1 to 5 seconds.

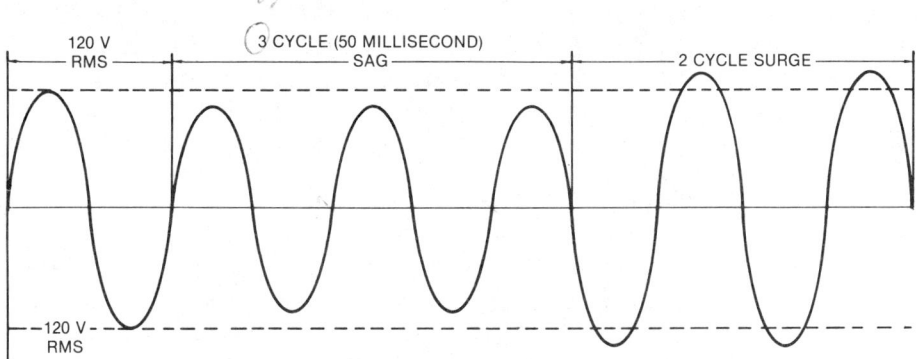

Fig. 2-3.
Sags and surges are short term voltage decreases or increases.

Power-Line Monitors

Before we go on to a more detailed look at the quality of power, we must look at the most common device for sensing, analyzing, and reporting disturbances. Power-line monitors are sensitive instruments that detect electrical disturbances. They are used to perform what is sometimes called a power or site survey. This can be done over a short period of time, but it is recommended that most surveys last at least two weeks.

To protect computer equipment, a precise profile must be obtained of the kind of power that exists at the point where the equipment will be or is installed. In order to gather the details of sometimes random occurrences, an extended period of monitoring may be necessary. It may even be desirable to purchase a power-line monitor to continuously record the electrical environment. The point is that while the kinds of disturbances appearing on power lines may be predictable, the particular set of circumstances that create the events are not. The monitoring period should be long enough to ensure that every specific event that might occur at the site is recorded by the monitor, so that the most cost effective cure might be found for the problem. Without the proper information, the cost of solving a particular problem with the wrong device may be an entire order of magnitude, as we will see in the second half of this book.

Changes in the computer load can create problems, or adding or deleting loads on the same feeder could have an effect. Wiring might be altered in a manner that suddenly produces undesirable effects. Monitoring during different seasons might prove beneficial. The electrical environment changes radically at many sites as winter turns to summer.

As strange as it seems, computer equipment itself often introduces garbage into the electrical environment. Other nonutility related causes of problems can be within the same building: X-ray equipment and CAT scanners, copiers, and air conditioners. All of these conditions can be detected, analyzed, and printed out by a power-line monitor.

Some of the major computer manufacturers have studied their field-service reports and found that over 50 percent of the "no trouble found" calls are power related. After a thorough check of the hardware and software, the application of a power-line monitor can show if any electrical disturbance is occurring at the same time the computer malfunctions. If so, it becomes a matter of exploring the power side of the environment to isolate the problem area. Too often field-service personnel are not trained in power and overlook simple sources of problems.

Those that are aware of how computers interact with their electrical environment are often untrained on the use of power-line monitors. The application of a monitor to look for a power problem is a lot like programming a computer—GIGO (garbage in garbage out). If the monitor is not connected properly or adjusted properly to measure what is actually desired, GIGO occurs. FEs (facilities people) and electricians may say they know how to use a power-line monitor but may never have been trained nor have read the instructions.

This is an important point since an improperly installed monitor can show events that aren't really important or any number of false or misleading readings that will help no one in solving a performance problem. Also, one must be trained in order to accurately interpret the reporting of a monitor. A Dranetz meter, for example, produces a printed tape of recorded events. While the tape may seem straightforward enough, it takes an experienced, trained technician to translate the taped information to the site specific events that relate to it. Many of these problems were resolved by Basic Measuring Instruments (BMI) with the introduction of their power monitor (Fig. 2-4). It is easy to use, hookup, and interpret.

Power-line monitors can look at a wide variety of conditions and report on them. Single- and three-phase power can be monitored on both the load side and the source side. Separate readings are given for each phase. Monitors report on overvoltages, undervoltages, sags, surges, impulses, and frequency changes. They can look at a wide range of DC voltages, too. A monitor may even be connected to look at variances in temperature and humidity.

Some tips on the best circumstance for power-line monitoring are as follows:

1. Preinstallation site survey permits a comparison between the disturbance profile and the load specifications. Installation of corrective equipment can be planned in advance.

2. Simultaneous correlation is a better way of handling an erratic site. Monitor power conditions, both line and internal points, while hardware and software evaluation are underway, and look for a correlation between equipment failures and power disturbances.

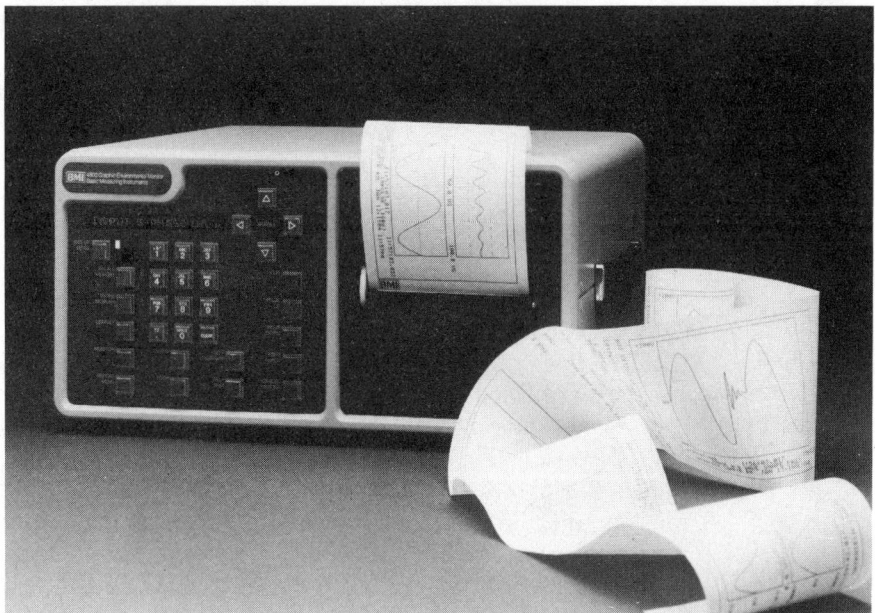

Fig. 2-4.
This Basic Measuring Instruments (BMI) power monitor is self prompting and has a "help" feature. But more importantly it actually prints a graph of the power disturbance.

3. One-for-one monitoring is a good rule of thumb. Put a separate monitor on each load installed on a common feeder when impulses are being generated on the load side.

4. Simultaneously monitor the input and output line conditioners. Line conditioners or uninterruptible power supplies may be a source of dirty power, or they may not be shielding the load from line disturbances. Monitoring of both input and output will determine proper operation of these devices.

One final point to keep in mind is that faulty power conditions can put tremendous stress on internal computer components. Even after a power-line monitor has located the problem and corrective action has been taken, failures and disruptions may not stop immediately. These parts must be replaced as they fail until stability is gradually returned to the site.

These are the four functions performed by power monitors:

1. Separating intermittent failure caused by power disturbances from those caused by software bugs, defective connections, hardware failure, or user errors

2. Determining the location and cause of power-line disturbances so they may be eliminated at their source

3. Assigning responsibility for correcting problems that cannot be eliminated at their source
4. Selecting power conditioning solutions for uncorrectible site specific problems

Computer Tolerances

So far we have mentioned ANSI and IEEE. Another scholarly group is CBEMA (Computer and Business Equipment Manufacturers Association). CBEMA does not set standards; however, their work is often accepted as standard or picked up and used in publications of the IEEE.

One of the concerns of this group was to quantify the typical range of input power quality and load parameters of major computer manufacturers. Figure 2-5 shows this in graph form. While not a standard, this can be considered to be basic computer design criteria for power conscious hardware engineers.

Standards for voltages are covered in ANSI C84.1. This publication describes the commonly used nominal voltages and anticipated normal variations. We have shown this in Fig. 2-6. If we superimpose the CBEMA graph on the ANSI graph, we see areas of concern (Fig. 2-7). Even standard voltage ranges do not always meet the design criteria for most computers.

One area of power not mentioned often is frequency. Utility power is a very steady source of 60 Hz power. Line frequency is so closely regulated

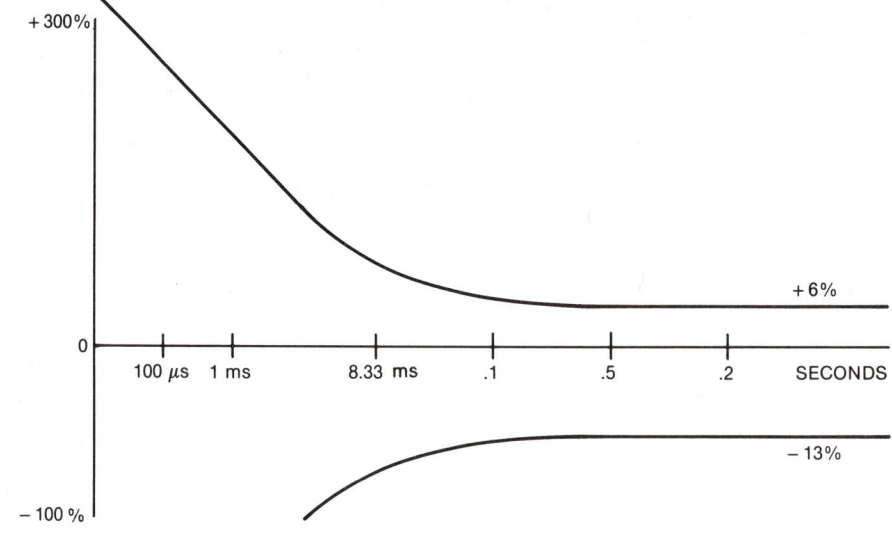

Fig. 2-5.
CBEMA design criteria for hardware engineers.

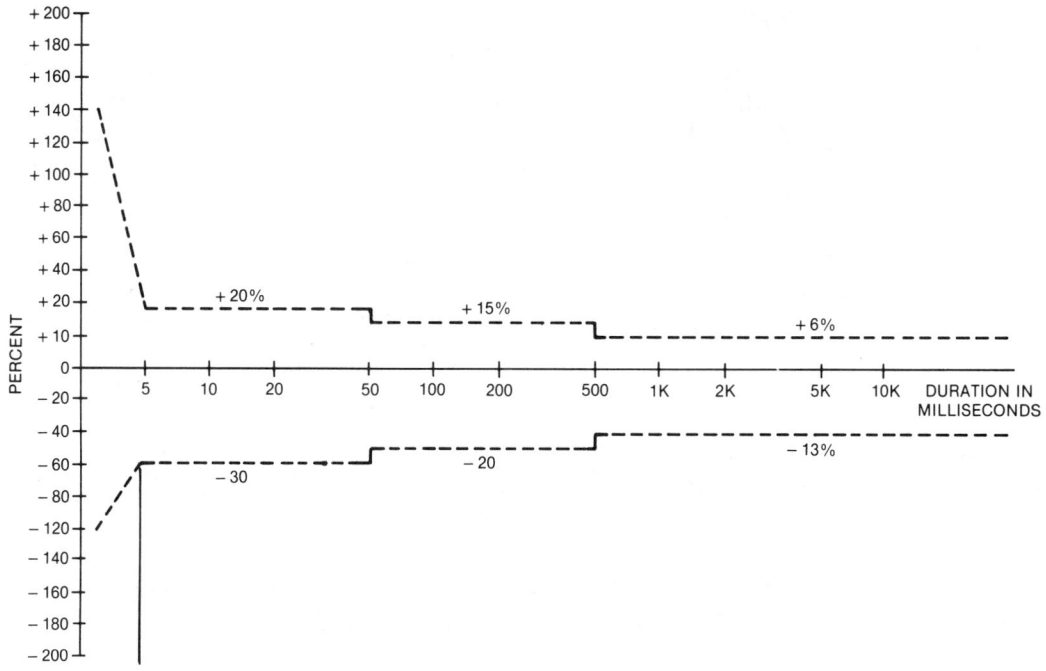

Fig. 2-6.
Standards for utility power ANSI C84.1.

that it is seldom a problem. But, with the increasing trend toward cogeneration and alternative sources of power, frequency can be a problem causing aspect of local power and should not be ignored.

Another consideration in determining power tolerance of a computer installation is its size. Office-grade computers can usually tolerate power standards of roughly +6 percent to −13 percent (ANSI C84.1). For peak performance, ADP line voltage should not fluctuate by more than +3 percent to −3 percent. The National Bureau of Standards FIPS PUB 94 states that tighter limits would not result in better system performance or reliability.

There is a wealth of information contained in these graphs. Simply stated, they show that computers have very little tolerance for voltage variations. The longer the perturbation the less tolerance they have.

Obviously, computers perform better when supplied with a steady source of "clean" power. By clean power we mean pure, unchanging sine waves at a constant rate of 60 per second. The tolerance of computers and their peripherals to line voltage and frequency changes vary from manufacturer to manufacturer and by product, even from the same company. Therefore, we must be guided by the published specifications for a particular device when looking for upper and lower limits of voltage variances over time.

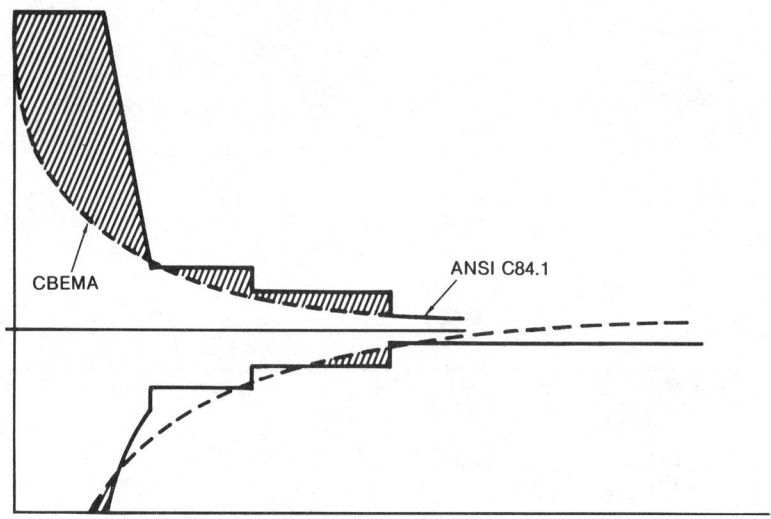

Fig. 2-7.
Utility power profile and CBEMA criteria. Shaded areas denote those areas of conflict between standards.

Deviations from a narrow envelope of the slow average line voltage for a computer cannot be tolerated. Some sources state that if the voltage exceeds 20 percent for a duration as short as 1 to 10 milliseconds, the computer will make errors. These voltage excursions even cause downtime or component failure if allowed to continue. Most computers will tolerate short events such as impulses or dropouts outside those limits. As stated before, the shorter the excursion the greater the excursion which may be tolerated.

Typical computer requirements for voltage are 120/208 plus or minus 10 percent (+10 percent to −8 percent for IBM mainframes). Utility power can be expected to vary plus or minus 5 percent. Often the voltage at the equipment will be +1 percent to −9 percent because of losses between the building service and the computer load.

Computers don't want to see dips or surges greater than 20 percent for more than 30 milliseconds. These limits are often exceeded when a heavy load comes on-line in the vicinity of the site. Huge impulses can be generated in an industrial neighborhood when large air conditioners are turned on. If the steady-state voltage is already low, these impulses could drop voltage below operating limits.

Most computers will not tolerate a dropout longer than 15 milliseconds. Outages of longer duration commonly occur from utility switching operations and lightning.

Computers like to see 60 Hz power plus or minus 1/2 Hz. Sudden heavy loads can change frequency by as much as 5 Hz. This is a rare problem, but as stated earlier, local generation can have less stable frequency than utility power. Time-related peripheral devices such as clocks and disks are most sensitive to frequency deviations. Ferroresonant power supplies are also frequency sensitive since they operate using a tuned circuit. They can generally tolerate variations of only plus or minus 1 percent.

Ride Through

When power is applied to a computer or peripheral device, large filter capacitors in each power supply are charged. As we stated in the previous chapter, load circuit elements such as capacitors and inductors draw load current without dissipating significant energy. In other words, they use line voltage and current without permanently retaining or dissipating the stored energy. These elements in load circuits are what cause a leading or lagging power factor.

During a dropout, for example, these large filter capacitors, as well as other components like RF noise filters, will dissipate some stored energy into the load. This helps the device "ride through" the event. Of course, if the event is very short, little energy is used and the overall performance of the device might not be affected. The safety margin for ride through of this type can be as long as 30 milliseconds or longer. Not all computers have this same time margin. It might also come to mind that the higher quality the power supply of the device the longer the ride through.

The flip side of this issue is protection. These circuit elements have a cushioning effect on incoming impulses or short-term overvoltage conditions. By these means, digital circuits receive some protection from very short-term line variations that might otherwise cause malfunctions or component failures.

Unfortunately, as the pressure of competition has grown, cost cutting practices have often focused on a computer's power supply. It is an easy area to cut costs since power problems can usually be blamed on the utility. The trend in computer power supplies has been to move away from transformers to switching power supplies where rectifiers are connected directly to the power line. The power-supply transformer was a low impedance source of clean power since the transformer had the ability to absorb many voltage perturbations without transferring them to the load. The elimination of it as a component means that the load now sees more of the variations coming down the line. Of course, the tradeoff is small, lighter power supplies. The typical RF noise filter in a switching power supply will also give some protection against fast rise-time impulses.

Power Quality

Con Edison states that on the 120/208 volt network system a user could expect to experience a voltage drop of 25 percent (to 90 volts for 6 cycles or 100 milliseconds) once or twice a month. They also state that once or twice a month these excursions will last 30 cycles (500 milliseconds). In addition, once or twice a month the voltage is predicted to drop 54 percent (to 55 volts for 12 cycles), and may drop to 0 volt for 12 cycles on rare occasions. If you add this up, you find that the Con Edison voltage on a 120/208 system could potentially bring down your computer a minimum of three times a month, probably six times a month, or more.

The IBM Survey

A landmark study of power was done by George Allen and Donald Segall of IBM® during 1970–1972. A total of 29 locations were monitored for a total of 3312 monitoring days. Thresholds for the data recording were set such that most computers would experience problems from the voltages being recorded. Table 2-1 shows a summary of their findings.

The numbers in Table 2-1 were not encouraging. They suggested that something undesirable was happening on the average of twice a day. The result of this must certainly be processing errors.

The Bell Telephone Survey

In May of 1977, M. Goldstein and P.D. Speranza of Bell Labs set out to assess the quality of power at Bell sites around the country. The sites were scientifically monitored for up to 24 months to determine the nature and extent of power disturbances. They also wanted to devise a way of predicting their occurrences. Their ultimate goal was to reduce or eliminate computer downtime throughout the Bell System by choosing the most appropriate and cost effective power-conditioning equipment.

A power-line monitor was used at each site (connected and set in the same way) to record sags, surges, power failures, and impulses.

When all the data had been gathered, it was found that the rates of disturbances varied widely from site to site. Often one site would be clean while another site experienced every disturbance known on a regular basis.

Table 2-1.
Results of IBM Survey

Type of Disturbance	Total Number	Average Days Between
Undervoltage	1569	2.1
Overvoltage	103	32.2
Outages	65	51.0
Switching Spikes	2831	1.2
Other Impulses	1676	2.0
Total	6244	.5

The overall data showed the probability of an incident at any given site was rare.

Overall, the study found that 56 percent of the sites experienced steady-state voltages outside the ANSI bandwidth. Frequency was between 58.7 and 60.7 Hz.

Eighty-seven percent of all disturbances recorded were sags, while 4.7 percent were power failures or outages. This means that low-voltage type conditions accounted for 92.7 percent of all events. Impulses were 7.4 percent of the total, and surges were 0.7 percent of all recorded events.

Goldstein and Speranza were surprised to find that lightning caused sags were reported more often than associated impulses. And impulses appeared no more often in lightning-prone areas than other sites. They concluded that utility lightning devices suppress impulses while producing sags seen throughout the power system.

Recent Surveys

IBM is known to have conducted two more recent surveys. Although the results of the latest have not been published, a representative of IBM gave a verbal report of it at a recent meeting of the IEEE Power Engineering Society. Reportedly, indications from those findings point to a considerable degradation over the 10 year period—this should not be particularly surprising. The growth in power generation capacity slowed considerably during the time frame while loading of existing lines has increased. Conservation measures have been implemented since the oil embargo, and planned brownouts are now common in many geographical areas.

Interaction Between a Computer and Its Source

To this point we have assumed that power problems are generated outside the computer site and fed down the line. A good portion of power disturbances are caused by the interaction of the computer and its peripherals with the power source. This can be as simple as the voltage drop caused by load current or as subtle as harmonic currents in rectifier loads.

Inrush Currents

On initial start-up, most devices draw four to six times their normal steady-state current demands. A disk drive that draws 10 amps might have an inrush demand of 40 amps for 10 seconds. A CPU (central processing unit) with a constant load of 24 kVA can present a 1500 percent transient for 100 milliseconds. It may take a drive motor 5 to 7 times its rate for full-load current to start in 3 seconds. Inrush from nearby peripherals might have a 20 to 30 percent impact on the voltage available to the CPU.

There are special sequencing techniques used to reduce this problem.

Manual turn on of devices one at a time is one method. Many facilities have automatic restart contactors that step the increased loads to ease start-up. But even with these kinds of techniques, inrush currents can cause undesirable voltage excursions.

Even after the entire computer facility is up and running, the site presents a dynamic load to the power source. Severe load transients can be created by the motors of various devices turning on and off. When an actuator motor moves across a disk to place a read/write head, heavy current is drawn. Many of these operations can be happening simultaneously. Disk spindle motors, printer drivers, mag tape drivers and capstans, and any special servo motors present a large, ever-changing current demand to the source. Each device might not be significant in and of itself, but when added to all the other elements, a dynamic load of significant proportions is at work.

The resultant voltage drop in the load is a function of the source impedance. If the source is not capable of delivering instantaneous peak current demands, voltage will sag. A long feeder length is often a cause of high source impedance.

On the other hand, motors can be a blessing to a computer facility. During short-duration surges, motors absorb energy and, like generators, return energy during short term sags. Induction motors act like generators when power is shut off by feeding energy back into the line. If, however, line voltage is restored before the magnetic flux in the motor's coils has been dissipated, there is a possibility that the line voltage might be out of phase with the self-generated voltage causing even greater inrush demands.

Transformers can create large starting transients. Inrush can be 5 to 15 times normal full-load current. Switching power supplies eliminate the need for a transformer. Rectifiers are connected directly to the line. Filter capacitors in these circuits present a short across the line while they charge. This may occur during the first half cycle and create a very large starting inrush current.

J.F. Kalbach, an engineering consultant, uses a typical example of a 400 ampere peak inrush line current where the computer's rated current is 35 amps at 208 volts. He states in his course notes for the Power Sources Conference, "Power sources must be able to supply these currents without excessive voltage drop if other units sharing the same power source are not to be disturbed."

Switching power supplies cause another serious problem, harmonic distortion. Since these devices draw large amounts of current during only a small portion of the sine wave (called conduction angle), harmonic distortion of the sine wave occurs. This line voltage distortion causes increased loading on power circuits and additional heating. This is a very simple explanation of a complex relationship that is beyond the purpose of this book. The fact that this interaction takes place and may affect other equipment is the important thing to remember.

Under certain circumstances a direct-current component may increase the current flow in the neutral conductor of a three-phase circuit—this causes unsafe heating of the conductor and may be a source of electrical noise.

Mr. Kalbach states that line voltage drop at a load is primarily due to load current flowing through the internal impedance of the power source and its conductors. He sites ten factors that determine the magnitude and duration of these interactions:

1. Amplitude-versus-time profile of varying load currents
2. Transients caused by load changes
3. Nonlinear loads
4. Harmonics in load current
5. Load power factor
6. Power source output impedance over a broad frequency range
7. Effect of DC component in the AC load current
8. Resonances between inductive and capacitive elements in circuits
9. Resonance among regulators
10. Grounding

We have not presented a discussion of each one of these items. The important conclusion that we must draw from our discussion thus far is that the computer system itself does interact with its power source to introduce unwanted voltage disturbances. Electronic devices can be a source of disrupting impulses, noise, sags, and nuisance tripping of breakers due to poorly planned load step changes.

A Step Back

So how are the 2.8 million customers that Con Edison services in New York City and Westchester County? Fine, if they read the brochure. It's a vast electrical wasteland out there. Sitting in front of a PC banging out short stories might be a far cry from an 80 thousand square foot DP facility, but the quality of power is no less an issue. No one can afford to lose data. A big system might cost 100 thousand dollars a minute to be down. But how do you put a price on the files in your word processor?

3

Inside the Building

In this chapter we will explore some of the things, right and wrong, about power once it gets inside the home or office. Most of our discussion will deal with the world of business where all kinds of motors, air-conditioning equipment, computers, and a wide variety of other devices must coexist.

This does not mean that the home is any less interesting when it comes to the variations that can occur. The screen on a PC may shrink to half its size when the iron turns on. A refrigerator motor can cause a significant problem for a PC on the same branch circuit. Since the industrial environment contains more elements in the complex scheme of using power than a home, the potential for strange things happening is somewhat greater, although equally strange things happen on every block in every neighborhood.

Two Shocking Stories

Our first story takes place many years ago at the National Trucking Institute. It seemed this poor lady was being shocked, literally, by her IBM typewriter. Every now and then she would be typing away and ZAP! This experience repeated itself often enough that, had she been like Pavlov's dog, she might have sought a new line of work.

Several times the IBM customer engineer was called in. He would go over the machine carefully looking for a problem. After all, there is only a motor and a switch in a Selectric where the shock could be coming from, not much to look for. Each time he would shrug his shoulders and walk away.

Then one fateful day, she received another jolt and called for service.

Fortunately, the regular service man was on vacation, and the replacement the company sent out was a smart young man who was undaunted in his pursuit of customer satisfaction and just a little clumsy.

While looking the machine over, he suddenly dropped a metal tool. While resting one hand on the machine, he reached down to grab the tool and ZAP! Confused and alarmed the young man looked at the floor. There, neatly placed among the linoleum tiles was the cover plate for an electrical outlet.

He turned to the typist and asked if she ever took off her shoes when she worked. "Oh, yes, every so often," she replied. Carefully, he placed one probe of his VOM (volt ohm meter) across the cover plate and the other on the frame of the typewriter. Every few minutes he observed the needle on the meter move to 90 volts AC then swing back to zero. It didn't take long for the enterprising young man to notice that the surge happened every time someone used the copier a few feet away. The building electrician stopped by, watched the meter reading, and stated emphatically, "it must be static electricity." The young man said that obviously the power ground connection to the copier was not correct.

In our second story, there was a home owner who built an addition to his kitchen. An electrician stopped by one day and wired up all the outlets. The home owner liked his new kitchen.

Sometime later his wife moved the living-room lamp and a buzzing noise could be heard in the kitchen. But what was really strange was that every time his wife turned on the garbage disposal the lamp went out. There were other weird occurrences like lights dimming and an unusual kind of vibration in the refrigerator handle.

An investigation revealed that the electrician had evidently mixed up the wires in most of the three wire outlets. This lack of consistency led to feedback voltages and other dangerous byproducts. A rewiring of the addition cleared up the strange occurrences in the kitchen.

The moral of our stories is that no matter where you are, no matter how clean the power, there are still things that can happen inside the building that affect the performance of even simple devices. Obviously, these two stories are very simple examples, and problems are often not straightforward, but one piece of equipment or wiring method can definitely affect another device.

Voltage Considerations

As power is transmitted over a distribution system, a voltage drop occurs along the way. This is compensated for when the voltage is stepped down from one distribution system to another. The transformers at a substation have taps on them to adjust the voltage to compensate for losses that might reduce the output voltage. Also, utility companies use compensators that raise the voltage or lower it as the load on the line increases or decreases. This keeps the voltage within tolerances while the loading changes throughout a day, or seasonally.

What this means is that the voltage at the service entrance of a building close to the substation can be significantly higher than that of a building at the end of the distribution line. Switched capacitors can be used on the feeder to improve the voltage by switching them on-line during peak demand times.

Small buildings with a few hundred kVA of load would be fed from a distribution transformer. Larger buildings can be fed from the primary distribution system. These buildings typically have loads of several thousand kVA. Still larger buildings or complexes might be fed directly from the transmission system. In these cases, the building owner must provide primary and secondary distribution along with their associated transformers and possibly even a substation to go with the entire system.

Voltages Defined

Nominal System Voltages are identified by the associated winding of the supply transformer of the system. If the transformer is a "Y" wound 208 transformer, we would call the available voltage 208Y/120. We talked about the mathematical relationship of these numbers in the first chapter ($208 = 120 \times 1.73$). We would designate a delta-wound transformer voltage as 240/120. The higher numbers represent the phase-to-phase voltages while the lower numbers represent the phase-to-neutral voltages (see Fig. 3-1). Both of the wye and delta windings are four-wire three-phase systems. A three-wire system would be designated by a single number like 480. This means the phase-to-phase voltage is 480 volts.

Single-phase systems are designated by one number in a two-wire system and two numbers in a three-wire system. Thus, 120 indicates a single-phase two-wire system where the voltage between the conductors is 120 volts. 120/240 means that it is a three-wire system in which the phase-to-phase voltage is 240 and the phase-to-neutral voltage is 120.

Large commercial buildings generally have 480Y/277 at the service entrance. The three-phase load of the building is connected directly to 480 volts. The fluorescent ceiling lighting is connected phase-to-neutral at 277 volts.

A smaller transformer with a rating of 480 volts—280Y/120V is used to step the voltage down for 120 volts convenience outlets and 208 volts for single- and three-phase office equipment. Also, single-phase transformers with 120/240V secondaries may also be used to provide power to lighting and small office machinery.

If a building or complex of buildings is so large that the load cannot be supplied from a single transformer, the primary distribution system must be tapped to supply the proper voltage. These primary distribution voltages

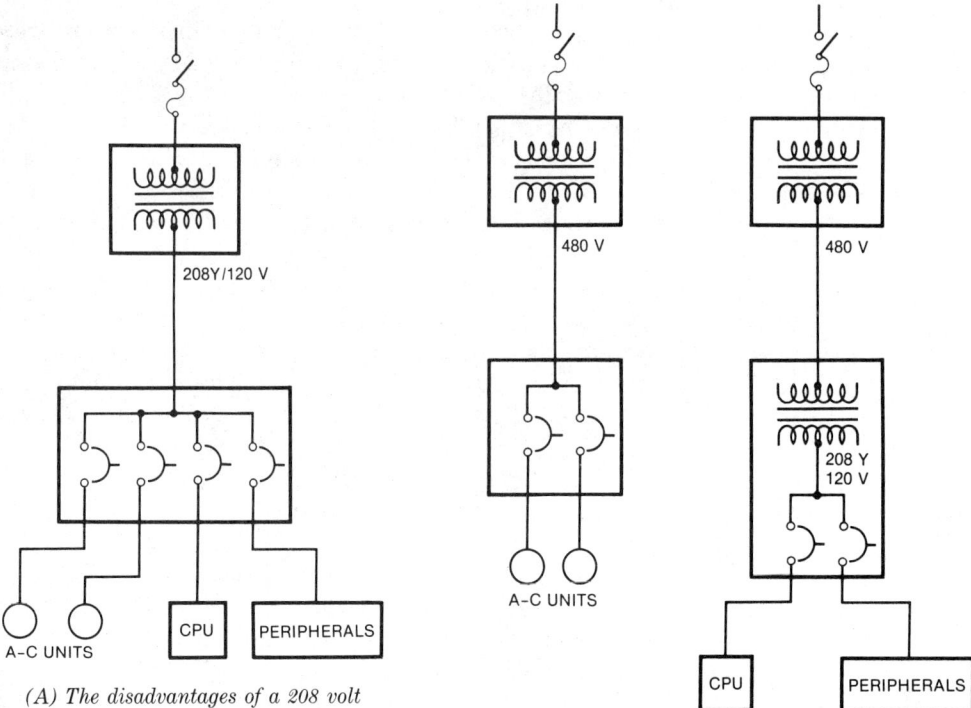

(A) The disadvantages of a 208 volt system and the opportunity for impulses generated by the air-conditioning units to interact with the computer.

(B) A dedicated 480 volt feeder that delivers power through a step-down transformer to the load.

**Fig. 3-1.
Dedicated feeders.**

may vary but 12,470Y/7200V and 13,200Y/7620V are typical. Some utilities may provide a step-down transformer to a lower voltage such as 4160Y/2400V.

Buildings Big and Small

Building distribution systems are too often selected on the basis of lowest initial investment. The best system is one that is flexible. The system must adapt to changing load conditions as time goes on. The interruption of service and cost associated with these changes must be taken into account in the initial design. If part of the system fails, what is the result on the remainder of the system? Continuity of service is another planning factor. What about changing load? Will the system respond to changes at the various load points? Overall efficiency, operating, and maintenance costs need to be taken into consideration. All these points are influenced by the type and purpose of the building.

Large Vertical Buildings (less than 12 stories)

These kinds of buildings typically house offices, hospitals, apartments, and small hotels. Reliability of supply is a major concern for the continued operation of elevators, pumps, and air-conditioning systems. Activities in large buildings depend on a continuous supply of electricity.

Tall Buildings

Tall buildings are generally located in densely populated downtown areas. Because building access is accomplished almost exclusively by elevators, a design ensuring a continuous and reliable power source is essential. Fire protection equipment as well as water supply, heating and air conditioning depend at all times on the availability of power. Air conditioning is likely to be an especially large load in tall buildings and must be accounted for. Because of long feeder lengths inside a tall building, high voltage runs may be desirable. The use of 208 volts would necessitate the installation of a substation about every 12 stories. Cost, voltage loss, and space considerations determine this limitation.

Large Horizontal Buildings

Most large horizontal buildings are shopping centers. The physical layout of the shopping center has the greatest influence on how the distribution system is laid out. There are roughly five basic layouts: strip or "L" shaped, mall, court, ring, and group or cluster of smaller buildings. This layout will suggest the most feasible and economical distribution system. The location of transformers in the shopping center will be dictated by the placement of large loads.

Groups of Small Buildings

A college campus is typical of this kind of building design. The form that power distribution takes in this setting is determined by the number and size of buildings, the spacing between them, the loading inside each individual building, and the continuity of service required. A building housing classrooms might have a lower requirement for continuous service than an administrative building full of computers.

Industrial Plants

Industrial plants usually have a wider variety of loads, varying in magnitude and characteristics, than any other building the same size. An industrial plant also experiences the addition of new loads and the relocation of loads more frequently than any other type of building. The estimation of current and future load requirements is even more critical in an industrial plant because of these factors. Each plant is an individual case that must be studied to determine the proper distribution system.

Small Commercial Buildings and Homes

There is no special engineering required to wire a house but it does take skill to do it properly. Devices like furnaces, air conditioners, and clothes dryers that need 220 volts are on their own circuits. The placement of receptacles is made with no real consideration to changing loads, and often it is difficult to determine just what outlets are wired into the same circuit.

To a large extent, the same type wiring applies to small commercial buildings. Real estate, doctors, and dentists offices may add specialized equipment like x-ray machines or computers that were never planned for in the original installation.

It would appear that the chances of interaction between devices in these settings is even greater than other buildings. While the stepping load changes are probably smaller in magnitude, the potential for malfunction is still there.

Service to the Computer

All things being equal, the lower the voltage distribution system the more expensive the equipment is that is used to distribute the power. Ohm's law tells us that at lower voltages higher currents will be generated causing wire and equipment sizes to be larger. It may cost two or three times more per foot to run 208 volt wire than 480 volt wire.

When 480 volts is supplied to a computer room, the neutral wire can be eliminated. In a 208 volt system, 120 volts is used to power some devices, so the neutral wire must be included to create a four-wire system. Using a three-wire system eliminates the cost of the fourth wire. This neutral wire can introduce undesirable noise into the EDP system. Overall, using smaller wiring, as in a high-voltage system, may offset the cost of an isolation transformer to step the voltage down. Computer power consultant, Warren Lewis, points out in the publication *Electrical Power, Grounding and Life Safety Systems for EDP Sites* that high-voltage systems have increased performance characteristics.

"Since a higher voltage system requires less current to do given work, momentary decreases (losses) in voltage that occur as a function of momentary increases in current demand by the EDP system itself result in better voltage stability to the EDP system. This marked decrease in unfavorable interaction between the power source and the EDP system is often enough to 'cure' some operational problems by itself."

When the service reaches the computer, it must be stepped down to the utilization voltage, typically 208Y/120V for larger facilities. The feeder is the building wiring that "feeds" the computer and associated peripherals from the service transformer. This might be terminated at a panel board or an isolation transformer. In a computer room, this is part of an engineered power structure that provides the proper electrical environment. For medium-size computers, the feeder may terminate at a panel board some distance away and may service other equipment along the line.

At 208 volts, for instance, feeder wire size is large and so are the associated losses. If this feeder is very long, the power source impedance, which includes the impedance of the feeder and internal impedance of the source transformer, may be large. This means the instantaneous demands for current might cause a significant loss of voltage.

The easy solution is to place an isolation transformer at the end of the feeder to be a low impedance source of power and to step down the voltage. We talk about the use of this device in a future chapter.

Usually, a major computer facility will have a dedicated feeder. However, many minicomputers have no dedicated line feeding them. It would be economically impractical to put every device on a dedicated feeder. Often, office-grade computers are on a branch circuit far away from a low impedance source of power. Also, there may be many other differing kinds of devices connected in such a way that interaction is very easy.

The electrical environment inside the building may be hostile indeed, especially the older building. Many years ago, when a building was new, it might have had an adequate power structure. As the years went by, more and more loads may have been placed on feeders and branch circuits. By now, wire size may be inadequate causing excessive heating, nuisance tripping of the breaker, and operating problems due to low voltage conditions. Circuits may have indiscriminately been added to feeders that should have been used only for EDP applications, or a new copier may have been wired into the same circuit that feeds a series of word processors.

In older urban areas, a business may expand by acquiring the adjacent building with common walls. What inevitably happens is nearby equipment might be served by feeders from two different buildings. A problem might send people scrambling to a wide variety of panel boards looking for a breaker. Now it's time to add that minicomputer. Without diligence and some expense it might never run properly.

The Culprits

In general, any large load that is constantly being switched on and off can have a significant impact on computer performance. Large step load changes cause sags, impulses, and noise. Some loads, however, can be a help to a computer. Small three-phase motors that are left on constantly can absorb surges and return energy to the line during short drops in voltage. This stabilizing action can create a friendlier environment for the computer.

Capacitors

Power factor correcting capacitors can aid in absorbing impulses. It is their switching on and off that creates substantial impulses. Power factor correction can be the source of some of the most disrupting excursions. This can be ameliorated somewhat by having soft-start resistors placed in the circuit to restrict the charging current.

Motors

There are motors in the building other than those in the computer room. Differing motor designs have different full current starting loads. Synchronous and squirrel-cage induction motors, for example, may draw current as much as seven or eight times their full load running current. This may result in excessive voltage drops in the power system. Elevators are an often cited source of in-building computer problems. Large changes in load and the associated switching on and off of the load can interact with other devices.

Air Conditioners

Air-conditioning equipment is often the single largest switching load in a building. The effects are no different than that of motors, as mentioned before. They are mentioned here separately because they are so often the source of interference with proper DP operations. It is not unusual to find the switching of AC units, even a mile away, to be the cause of large impulses in a computer facility.

Arc Equipment

Arc furnaces and arc welders have widely fluctuating loads. Arc furnaces have been known to disrupt computing even when they are outside the building, but somewhere on the same utility line. These devices not only have heavy changing current demands, but they produce unwanted harmonics in the waveform of the AC flow.

Other Culprits

Rectifiers elsewhere in the building can produce harmonics that may affect other sensitive equipment. Gaseous-discharge lamps like fluorescent and mercury lamps produce small arcs that interfere. Induction heaters like those found in many furnaces can be a source of problems.

Copiers, stamping machines, and any cycling heavy-load device can create power disturbances inside the building. Any switching of large inductive or capacitive loads causes transient impulses to be sent down the line.

Some Solutions

Voltage to the computer will vary more than voltage at the building entrance due to the voltage drop in conductors when they are loaded. Some techniques to solve this may be obvious at this point. First, computer equipment should be fed by one or more dedicated feeders (Fig. 3-1). When this is not possible, dedicated branch circuits should be used. Keep variable or switching loads off circuits that feed sensitive equipment. Especially, room air-conditioning equipment should be fed separately. Operate feeders at higher voltages to reduce current flow and voltage drop. Put the step-down transformer that provides final utilization voltage as close to the computer as possible to reduce power source impedance. Use oversized wire for feeders and branch circuits to reduce line impedance.

Providing the proper path from the building service entrance to the computer solves many problems. In the next chapter, we look at some of the worst culprits that cause the most worrisome problems for computers. These culprits are inside the building, outside the building, even in the air we breathe.

4

Lightning, Static, and Noise

Everyone knows what lightning is. Static is more properly called "Electrostatic Discharge" or EDS. Most of us have been ZAPPED by an electrostatic discharge. But what is noise?

Noise is a term used to describe repetitive high-frequency impulses that appear on the 60 cycle waveform. Consultant Warren Lewis points out that noise is a catchall phrase as is the term transient. Noise is a throwback to those days when waveform disturbances of those described in chapter 3 could be heard on a radio receiver. Obviously, electrical noise is not audible unless fed through a device capable of converting it to sound waves.

Lightning can generate noise. One listening to a radio receiver might refer to lightning as creating a "static crash." Usually, we think of static as something we pick up while walking on a thick carpet. Lightning, however, is an immense electrostatic discharge.

Needless to say, these three electrical anomalies are not only interrelated, but they create havoc with modern electronic devices.

Lightning

Protection is a key word associated with lightning. People, buildings, and computers all need protection from lightning. Since lightning is a natural phenomenon, it is hard to predict. And because of its power, it is not always easy to adequately protect against the effects of lightning. Damage to computer equipment caused by lightning can be catastrophic. Much of this damage need not take place if proper steps are taken to protect sensitive equipment. Before we take a look at those strategies later in this book, let's look at lightning itself.

There are two kinds of lightning discharges: cloud to cloud and cloud to ground. Seeing lightning is difficult since a flash, which is the proper term for the discharge, takes only about 0.5 second. A flash is broken down into strokes which last only a fraction of a millisecond. There are usually three or four strokes to each flash. These strokes are separated by a fraction of a millisecond. What appears to us to be a huge explosion of light is in reality many events taking place so fast they appear as one to us.

The beginning of a lightning strike is a faintly visible predischarge called the leader process. Opposite charges build up in the base of the cloud and the region above it. Usually, the base of the cloud is charged positively and the area above is charged negatively. Scientists speculate that a local discharge takes place. As the negative region discharges into the positive region, electrons are freed from their bonding to water particles, or even ice particles. These free electrons overshoot the positively charged region they are attracted to after neutralizing its smaller positive charge. Their trip toward the positively charged surface of the ground below is the beginning of a stroke.

Rodney Bent in his paper entitled "Lightning and the Hazards It Produces for Explosive Facilities" tells what happens next.

"The vehicle for moving the negative charge to earth is the stepped leader which moves from cloud-to-ground in rapid luminous steps about 50 m long. . . . Each leader step occurs in less than a microsecond, and the time between steps is about 50 microseconds."

A stepped leader, sometimes called a stepped ionized path, is like a ragged feeler looking for a place to discharge. This faint jagged dagger of electricity induces large amounts of positive charge below as it moves toward the earth. This buildup occurs on objects projecting above the surface (Fig. 4-1). Soon the positive charge is large enough to move toward the negatively charged stepped leader (Fig. 4-2). As these two opposites' attraction becomes stronger, an upward discharge begins. Eventually, one of these upward discharges reaches the downward moving leader and contact is made. This point is called the strike point.

When the leader reaches the ground, a huge current flows towards the earth causing the area near the ground to become very bright. This is called the return stroke, and it is the most noticeable part of lightning. According to Bent, current moves up this channel and out into the various branches at a velocity about one-tenth to one-half the speed of light. This means that the return stroke reaches the cloud in about 100 microseconds. It should be pointed out that the electrons flow earthward while the luminescence flows cloudward.

This process may be repeated several times through the same current-carrying channel, all in a fraction of a second. The *IEEE Green Book* states that the discharge current increases to a maximum in 1 to 10 microseconds, then declines over 20 to 1000 microseconds. Peak stroke current averages about 20,000 amps, but can be as high as 270,000 amps.

The point at which a lightning strike terminates is usually some tall structure of relatively good conductivity. This means that metal structures

Fig. 4-1.
The step leader overruns positive charges in the base of the cloud creating buildup of charges near the tree.

would be likely candidates for a lightning strike, but not always. Thundershowers preceding lightning dampens wooden structures, trees, masonry buildings, and concrete making them sufficiently conductive to permit the flow of charges upward. But they are insufficient conductors to allow large current flow without high resistance in the current path. This results in extreme heating and mechanical pressures.

Temperatures reaching 60,000 degrees Fahrenheit can occur after a few microseconds. This could potentially penetrate or warp thin metal, or create sparking at metal joints. Flammable material presents grave poten-

Fig. 4-2.
A positive charge on the tree begins moving toward the step leader.

tial danger since it might be ignited. Wooden structures could sustain heavy damage as structural members explode from the pressure of moisture inside being turned to steam. Bark vaporizes on trees, bricks explode, enormous blocks of concrete are demolished, even the ground is sometimes furrowed for several hundred feet. This effect of lightning is as powerful as many hundreds of pounds of TNT.

Meanwhile, the mechanical effects of lightning are no less profound. Super heating expands the air around the current channel creating a shock wave. This expanding shock wave not only is the cause of thunder, but can result in widespread damage to roof material in surrounding structures.

The attractive forces of metal caught in a lightning discharge can cause fusing of parallel conductors and squashing of hollow conductors. In addition, lightning following a conductor will apply mechanical pressure to the conductor as it goes around corners. This is very much like forcing high-pressure water through a garden hose. The lightning will exert a mechanical force, thus trying to straighten it. This bending force can be as high as 5000 pounds. Thus, sharp rectangular bends in conductors will lead to trouble.

The Electrical Effect of Lightning

What we are most concerned about in regard to computers is the ability of lightning to cause surges of a damaging or disruptive variety. There are several ways this can happen.

1. When lightning seeks a path to ground, the potential difference between two different ground reference points may be large enough to cause equipment failure or damage.
2. When a conductor has lightning-generated current traveling through it, a nearby conductor may pick up this unwanted surge through induction and carry the overvoltage to sensitive equipment.
3. Lightning could strike directly the wire or wires feeding a building.
4. What's known as a side flash might occur. This is the result of energy being coupled from one conductor to another by the flash jumping to a less resistive path. Remember, to lightning even a power line is at ground potential.
5. Conductors can act as an antenna for the effects of lightning and can feed energy into electrical systems. Buried cable is an ideal path for lightning.

According to Bent, the largest lightning voltage recorded on a transmission line was 5 million volts. It reached its peak in less than 2 microseconds. Since the strike occurred 4 miles up the line, data indicated the voltage rose on the order of 10 million volts per microsecond.

Even lightning discharges between clouds can induce impulses of several thousand volts in conductors several miles away. These high voltages can break down insulators, affect the surface of printed-circuit boards, and break down the insulation between windings in a coil.

Lightning Frequency

The probability that a given building will be struck by lightning can be calculated. Even the current carrying size of a stroke can be predicted. This information must be inferred from actual statistics. In the United States, the statistic that is used as the basis for these calculations is the number of thunderstorm days (Fig. 4-3). This is defined as the number of days on which thunder is heard at a given location.

By refining this information, scientists have calculated the lightning strike density of a given locale. These are only estimates based on a small number of observations over a short period of time.

This information, along with other factors, is used in the design of building protection systems. Some of the other factors include personnel hazards, possible production loss, possible damage and repair costs, insurance premiums, value and variety of structure, and the cost of protection.

Protection

Speak of lightning and most people think of lightning rods. A lightning rod serves the purposes of diverting lightning to ground and away from more

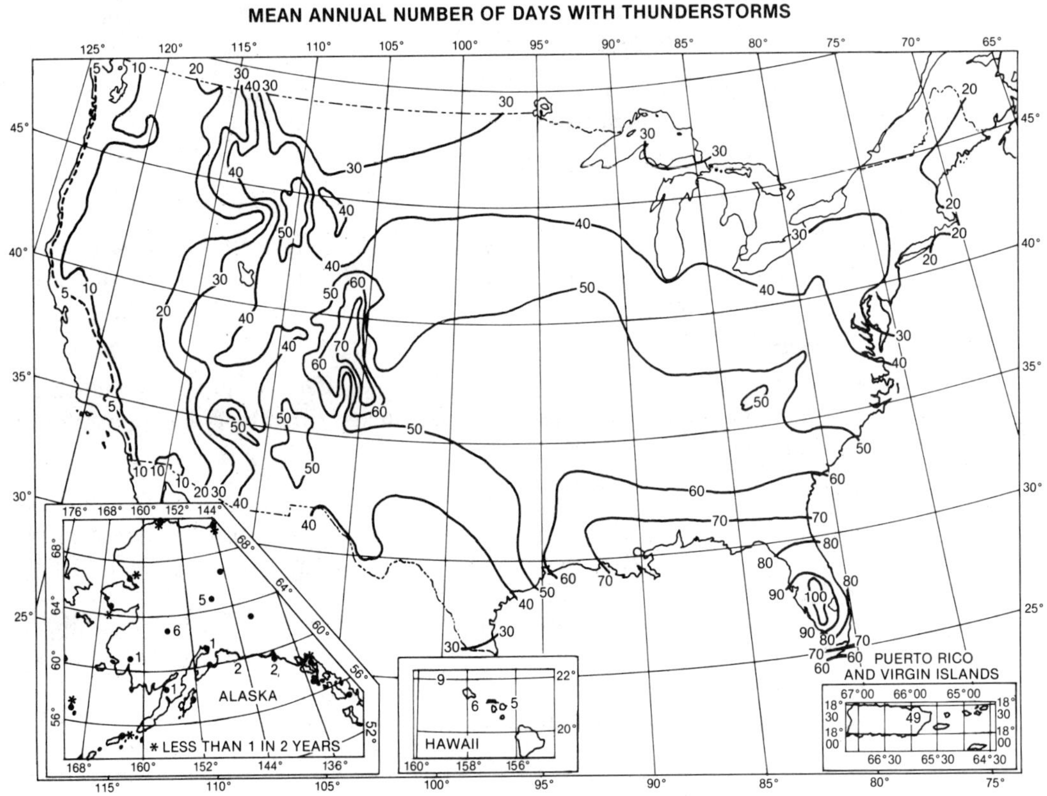

Fig. 4-3.
Annual isoceraunic map of the United States showing mean annual number of days with thunderstorms.
(Courtesy National Weather Service)

harmful discharge routes. It is a common misconception that a lightning rod has the ability to discharge clouds or prevent lightning. Its purpose is to intercept the stepped leader thereby keeping it away from the building.

There are three requirements for protection against a direct lightning strike that call for the use of a lightning rod. A conductor must be established to deliberately attract the step leader. A low impedance path to ground must be provided. Care must be taken that the impedance is so low that no other less desirable path might present itself. Also, the physical connection to the earth itself must be low in resistance.

Often lightning rods are not rods at all, but elaborate arrays. Beware of arrays! Lightning protection has many nonscientific practitioners that approach the subject as if it were magic. Terms like corona discharge and excessive ionization are tip-offs that need professional verification. Bent states that arrays do no more than conventional lightning rods, and may do less.

If care is not taken in providing a low impedance path to ground, a side flash may be the result (Fig. 4-4). Side flashing can be prevented by having parallel ground conductors. The math of electronics tells us that inductors in parallel have roughly half the inductance of a single conductor. For this reason two, and sometimes more, conductors are used.

Next, proper termination in the ground is important. Ground resistance, the location of buried cables or pipes, and the type of grounding electrodes are all important considerations.

Lightning arresters are common devices used to pass large overvoltage conditions to ground. They should be more properly called diverters instead of arresters. When the voltage on the line becomes sufficiently high, arresters become conductive and create a path to ground through a ground conductor to a driven rod or earth electrodes. When the voltage reaches zero and remains there long enough, the arrester becomes an insulator again. This process can take several cycles and will be repeated with each stroke of lightning.

In areas of high lightning activity, the utility may have a lightning arrester from each phase to ground in addition to a ground conductor at each pole.

As lightning generated energy moves toward a building through the distribution system, it is attenuated by the impedance of the path it follows. At the building service entrance, this surge must go from the primary to the secondary of the supply transformer where it is greatly attenuated. Since protective devices are incapable of absorbing even part of the energy released by a direct strike, near the secondary of the building transformer is a good place to install a surge or lightning arrester. At that point, high energy spikes can be shunted to ground before they have a chance to enter the building.

The point is to have this destructive energy arrested as far away from the computer as possible. If the overvoltage condition is allowed to reach

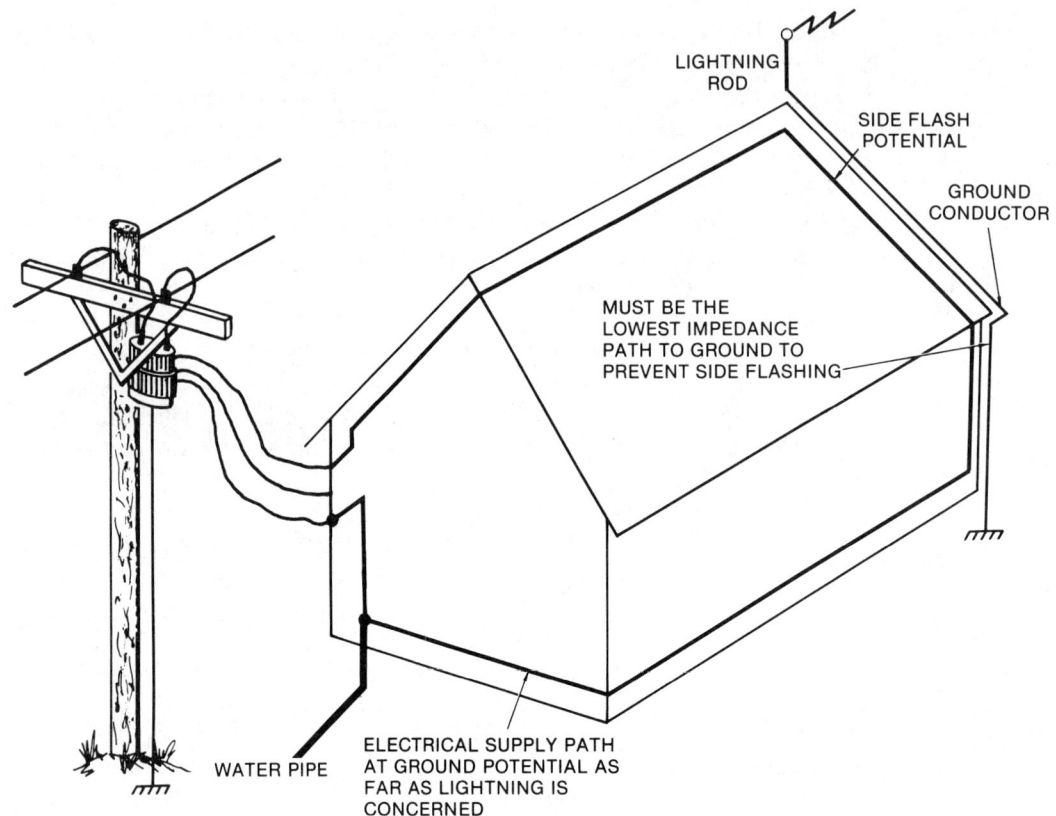

Fig. 4-4.
Lightning can side flash and injure people inside the building.

the computer room, the only ground available is the same ground used by the data processing equipment. This could result in serious damage.

There can be many other unwanted paths for surges to enter a computer's electrical environment. Communication lines, TV cable, water pipes, and duct work are paths for surges to find a computer. In particular, much machinery like air conditioners, heat exchangers, and fire extinguishing sprinklers have some exposure on the roof of a building. These can be low-impedance paths for lightning energy to be transmitted throughout the building because some electrician indiscriminately tied these paths together with those feeding sensitive equipment.

Transient Overvoltages

We are really concerned about two problems with regard to lightning. First, how do we keep lightning out of the building and most assuredly away from the computer? Second, how do we protect our equipment from the transient overvoltages or surges that will occur during a lightning storm?

We know that lightning can affect both overhead and underground power systems. If the power line is hit directly by lightning, we will see high magnitude overvoltages being fed directly to any equipment connected to it. Sparking and side flashes can have the same effect either through the current-carrying path or the ground path. Further, this current can be coupled to adjacent conductors which feed a computer.

The effects of a direct hit at or nearby a computer facility are dramatic but not our major concern. Catastrophic? Yes, but infrequent. The transient effects of lightning striking many miles away are far more frequent.

Lightning can raise the ground potential on the surface of the earth near the strike while the ground potential several miles away will remain unchanged. This condition can inject surges into a power line. Remote strikes create enormous, fast-changing electromagnetic fields that induce surges into the distribution system. Simple data links can incur lightning induced voltages of several hundred volts. The radiation of the changing field can extend over great distances and be picked up as undesirable noise by sensitive equipment.

These conditions exist during every lightning storm. The chances of a particular building being struck by lightning might be very low. But the incidences of lightning induced overvoltages is high since they might come from most anywhere on the power grid. These surges are what disturb computer equipment operations.

Lightning and its effects are yet another reason why computers live in a hostile electrical environment.

Static

Let's put ESD in perspective. As a charge discharges into a conductor, the peak voltage and current occur extremely fast—in picoseconds or nanoseconds. It is not unusual for a trace on a PC board to pick up 3 volts, or even more, from an ESD discharging through a conductor 30 centimeters away. ESD can induce logic levels causing soft errors in the operation of a computer. These extraneous bits will foul program results or create memory errors. On the other hand, hard errors are even more worrisome—this is actual hardware failure caused by ESD. ESD could have punctured the oxide of an IC gate with a 1 micron diameter hole causing system malfunction.

In an office of a dozen people, several hundred discharges of potentially damaging magnitude take place every day. Ironically, with the exception of JFETs and bipolar transistors, all semiconductor devices fail at 3 kilovolts or less, which is below our perception or feel of a static discharge.

How does a static charge form? The study of this is called "Triboelectricity." Derived from the Greek word tribo or tribos meaning the action of rubbing, triboelectricity is electricity generated through rubbing. The action of shoes rubbing against carpet creates a charge which is coupled to the body through the footwear. As humidity decreases, charges distribute with less ease around the body. Potentials tend to rise.

The two basic charged components of an atom are the proton and the electron. The proton carries a positive charge and is a permanent part of the atom in solid matter and will move when the matter moves. The electron carries a negative charge and is free to move from one atom to another as long as some energy is being expended to move it. This energy might be chemical, thermal, or mechanical.

Static electricity is generated by two unlike materials rubbed together and then separated. When the materials are in contact, electrons from the surface of one material move over and interface with the electrons of the other material. Meanwhile, their stationary counterparts, the protons, stay behind. As equilibrium is established, an attractive force builds up between the two materials. When the materials are separated, these electrons produce a negative charge on the surface and thus an electrical potential between the two surfaces is formed.

The conductivity of the material determines if this potential will equalize before the separation is complete. In good conductors, the excess electrons will return during separation. In poor conductors, the electrons will be trapped on one material causing a static charge to remain.

The *IEEE Green Book* states that static charges may build up as a result of pulverized materials passing through chutes, along conveyors, or belt drives; even gas, steam, or air passing through an opening will produce static electricity. These charges can be passed to operators who are in contact with the machinery, then discharged into sensitive electronic equipment.

Speed of separation, characteristics of the material, and area of contact all have an effect on the possible buildup of a static charge. Relative humidity has a large effect on the magnitude of ESD. Walking across a carpet in low humidity (10–20 percent) might build up a charge of over 30,000 volts. The same action at high humidity (85–90 percent) might build up a charge less than 1000 volts. Just raising an arm can generate 100 volts. Low-humidity areas may be plagued with false starts on disk drives and the like caused by the operator merely placing his or her hands on the keyboard.

The effect of this discharge energy on semiconductor devices is often junction burn-out, oxide punchthrough, or metallization burn-out. Twenty-five volts for 100 nanoseconds will destroy some memory chips and microprocessors.

The rise time of a discharge is even affected by the position a finger is in when it contacts a metal chassis. If the side of the finger touches the chassis, the rise time is considerably slower than if the tip of the finger touches. A fingernail touching the chassis is even faster, and a sharp instrument or tool touching the chassis has even a faster rise time.

Those who work with microchips on a regular basis are familiar with antistatic techniques such as wrist straps, special work surfaces, and protective packaging. Other techniques involve the use of humidifiers, ionizers, conductive floors and/or footwear, special clothing, and topical antistatic sprays.

Electrostatic discharge is yet another enemy in the electrical environment. And as the computer has moved from the controlled environment of the computer room to the office then finally to the home, the need for an understanding of ESD and its effect on computer equipment will result in enhanced performance and operator satisfaction.

Noise

There is another form of unwanted signal on power lines we have yet to talk about, commonly known as EMI (electromagnetic interference). We get some EMI from EDS, and we see its effects during a lightning display. But there is another more common source of EMI and it is often very near the computer.

When we think of high frequency noise, we often think of RFI (radio frequency interference), which is nothing more than a form of EMI. Radio and TV transmission equipment that produce strong electromagnetic fields as a result of transmission can be a strong source of interference. There are many other types of equipment that have oscillators inside. Clocks that run computers oscillate at frequencies around 8 MHz. There are many other kinds of digital mechanisms that use clocks that can be a source of EMI.

Other kinds of noise can be generated by the computer and its associated peripherals. As we mentioned earlier, switching power supplies can be a source of harmonic distortion and, therefore, a source of unwanted signals imposed on the sine wave.

Kinds of Noise

The detection and correction of all of this is complicated by the fact that noise may enter the circuit as either common-mode or normal-mode noise. Common-mode noise is an unwanted signal that appears between a phase and ground. Normal-mode, or sometimes called transverse, noise appears between phases (or phase to neutral) independent of ground (Fig. 4-5).

Common-mode noise is caused by lightning and utility switching relays. Also, it can be caused by poor grounding practices, radio transmitters, machine tools, and time clocks. This results in a single notch or spike in the sine wave. Normal-mode noise is caused by the turning on and off of heavy loads and utility power factor correction using compensating capacitors. Most impulses or transients are of the normal-mode variety as are sags and surges, dropouts or blackouts, and overvoltage and undervoltage conditions. Normal-mode impulses have a decaying oscillatory characteristic at frequencies up to and above 5 kHz. It is important to know the difference

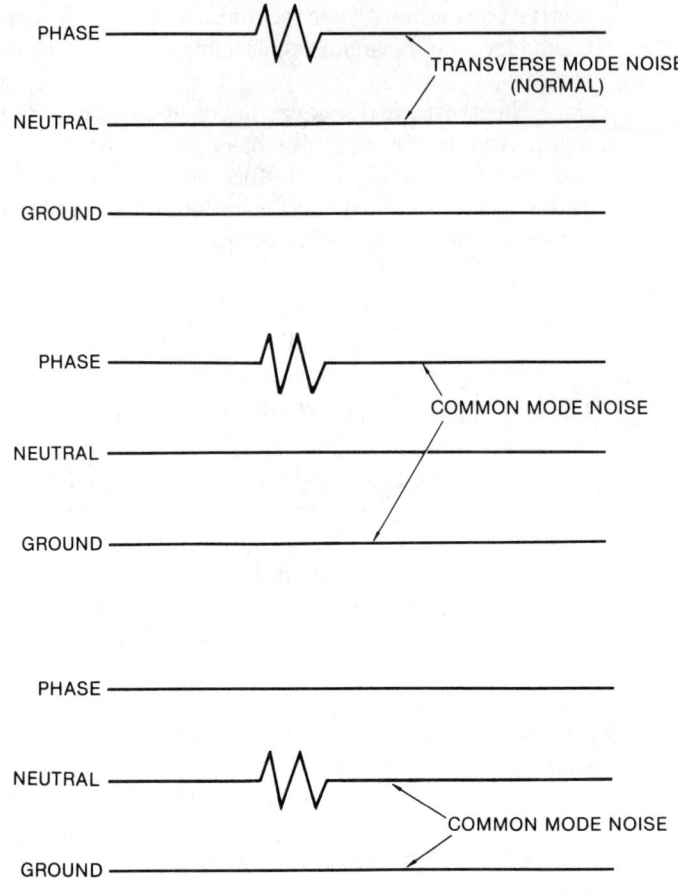

Fig. 4-5.
*Transverse- or normal-mode noise appears from line to line.
Common-mode noise appears from line to ground.*

between the two kinds of noise since their suppression entails different methods.

The use of shielded isolation transformers, proper grounding, and power conditioners will all be discussed as methods of keeping noise from interfering with computer performance.

Power Supplies

Another item that fits into the scheme of all this is the source of the direct current by which the computer operates. The computer's power supply must take whatever AC power it receives and convert it into a ripple free, well regulated source of DC.

The bottom line is cost. All computer manufacturers are capable of designing power supplies to handle the kind of hostile electrical environment we've been describing by spending enough money. They would, however, have to hire new power supply engineers since most current DC supply engineers are not competent AC power engineers.

Obviously, to protect a power supply from all the variations and noise in AC power would be very expensive. The user would not pay the difference but would go to the competition and buy a cheaper product.

How does the typical AC power fed to the computer's supply affect it? Line drops cause more current to flow producing overheating. Consequently, the life expectancy of the power supply will be reduced. Normal-mode noise can be of great enough magnitude and fast enough rise time to bypass the supply and damage PC boards and their components, including microprocessors. Common-mode noise is often not suppressed in the supply and can weaken components causing premature failure.

Furthermore, a power supply must react to a blackout in one-quarter cycle to go to backup power or an orderly shutdown process. If the power supply can't react, the end user will have to reprogram or repair the equipment as a result. Today's proliferation of computers demand a high level of performance. Faulty performance of critical computers can cause inconvenient, expensive, and even dangerous situations.

Isolation, Shielding, and Grounding

Isolation, shielding, and grounding are commonly used by experts to solve the problems of lightning, static, and noise.

A transformer, properly designed and manufactured, is an excellent isolation device. We will talk in a future chapter about the application of isolation transformers and their effects on noise attenuation. Another effective means of isolation when metallic isolation is not necessary is through the use of filters that trap or pass certain kinds of signals. Also, the use of optical isolation, by turning electrical signals into light, is an effective means of isolating subsystems electrically. Insulation, of course, is an isolation technique. But insulators can break down under extreme conditions.

Shielding conductors by wrapping them in wire mesh or sheath that is grounded is an excellent way to protect against EMI and RFI. Ribbon cables and sloppy connections are often a gateway for noise entering a system. Shielded cable can be a good defense against noise. Also, a properly grounded conductive box is another form of shielding.

One might think of metal conduit as a shield. Think again! Often there are breaks in continuity or plastic conduit used in underground applications—continuity is very important. In addition, conduit lying on or attached to other metal structures or conduit is nothing more than an antenna for interference. Although a sign above a panel board might say isolated circuit, the ceiling above may have a veritable spaghetti of conduit and electrical connections made with all sources of noise conceivable.

Proper grounding is probably the single most important consideration in the successful operation of a computer. The next chapter will deal with grounding and how it relates to noise reduction as well as safety. Needless to say, give noise a low impedance path to ground and it will stay away from other equipment. This is more often easier said than done.

5

Grounding

Ground is not always earth!

There are people who make a living just explaining what proper grounding really means. Grounding is the single most mysterious, misused, and misunderstood concept in the modern data processing environment.

To say that earth and grounding may be mutually exclusive runs cross grain to conventional wisdom. The uninformed user or electrician might think that, as long as a ground consists of a wire running to a rod driven into the earth (that we can pour electricity into like pouring water down a drain) that we have done a good job of grounding. This is wrong, dangerous, and not logical.

The basis for a lot of misunderstanding is confusion between utility power grounding, which requires an earth connection, and signal grounding between electronic devices, which does not require an earth connection. In fact, a signal reference ground does not care what its voltage is in relationship to earth ground. For generations, power engineers have been taught to provide a low-impedance path to earth ground to avoid the hazards of lightning and faults that occur when two lines come in contact with one another. Earth is a logical path for fault current in these circumstances.

Computers operate in aircraft or in space and never require an earth connection to function properly. For a variety of reasons, however, they need to be referenced to a common ground.

Another confusing dichotomy exists between safety grounding and proper EDP site grounding. The NEC (National Electrical Code), municipalities, and local inspectors all have various, sometimes different, rules that guide them in proper safety grounding. Proper computer grounding certainly can be accomplished while meeting code requirements, but usually much more attention to issues other than just safety must be given.

Safety

A little knowledge is a dangerous thing. And a lot of dangerous things have been done in the name of the NEC and grounding. But one thing is certain. Grounding in compliance with safety codes cannot be compromised.

A ground fault return path to the point where a power source neutral conductor is tied to ground is an essential safety feature. The NEC and many local codes differ on what this return path might be; it may be a conduit, a separate ground conductor, or other continuous conductive path.

This grounded neutral may be in the computer room, at the building service entrance, or outside the building. A transformer secondary with a neutral bonded to ground is considered a separately derived power source and, therefore, the point at which safety grounds must be bonded.

Should insulation break down or some other fault occur allowing a phase wire to make contact with a metal cabinet, a low impedance path to the neutral to ground bond will be a virtual short circuit. Enough current will flow causing the faulted circuit to blow a fuse or trip a breaker disconnecting it promptly (Fig. 5-1).

To eliminate the potential for shock between two cabinets, each should be tied to the same power source grounding point. This is an example of the incompatibility of computer grounding needs and the electrical code. In Fig. 5-2 we see two cabinets both properly tied to the power source. The impedance of the ground conductors (green wire grounds) is affected by their length. The longer the ground conductor the higher the impedance.

While this can be a significant problem at 60 Hz, at 10 MHz it can create special problems because the impedance of a conductor goes up as frequency is increased. High-frequency noise in one unit might appear as common-mode noise in another unit rather than being shunted through the ground conductor. Even at 60 Hz, significant touch voltage differences can appear if long ground conductor lengths are present. For these reasons, supplementary ground conductors need to be used. These additional ground conductors are not a replacement for those required by safety codes.
Note: Long ground conductors can also create dangerous touch voltage differentials between cabinets.

Shielding

While we are on the subject of high-frequency noise, we should touch on shielding for a moment. Shielding might be considered metal conduit or, more likely, a wire mesh around conductors. At 60 Hz shielding would appear to be a smart way to protect phase wires from picking up undesired signals. As we have already stated, long ground conductors, whether shielded or not, have high impedance at noise frequencies.

An ungrounded shield can act as an antenna, inducing noise into the

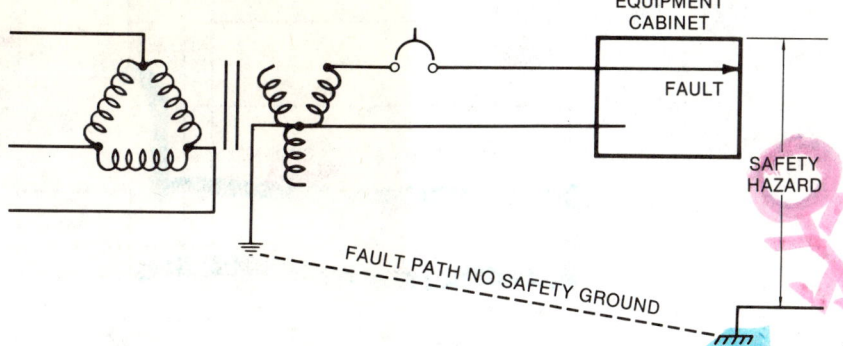

(A) A potential safety hazard exists. The fault path can be closed if someone touches the equipment.

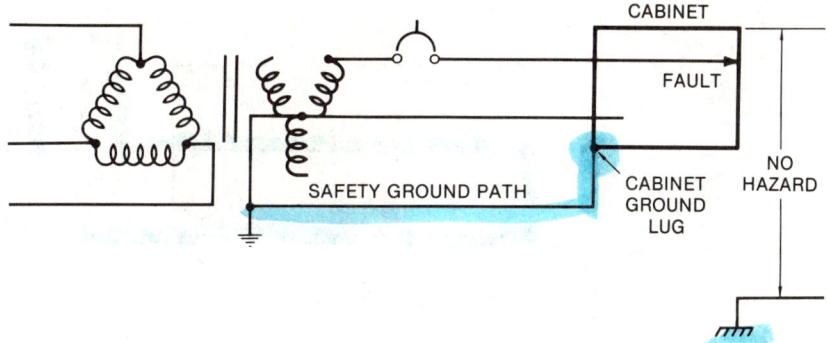

(B) No touch hazard exists, since fault current will flow through the safety ground and open the breaker immediately.

Fig. 5-1.
Examples of proper and improper grounding.

conductors. This is due to capacitance that exists between the underside of the shield and the surface of the conductor we want to protect. In other words, electrostatic noise is coupled to the shield which in turn couples it to the conductor as if many tiny capacitors were connected between the shield and the conductor.

For a variety of electronic reasons, grounding one end of the shield works better, especially at lower noise frequencies. However, as the frequency of noise goes up, the path to ground has a higher impedance than does the interlead capacitive path between the shield and the inner conductor (Fig. 5-3). The next problem with grounding a shield at only one end occurs as noise frequencies approach radio frequencies. The shield will begin to resonate at the frequencies corresponding to the shield's length and the

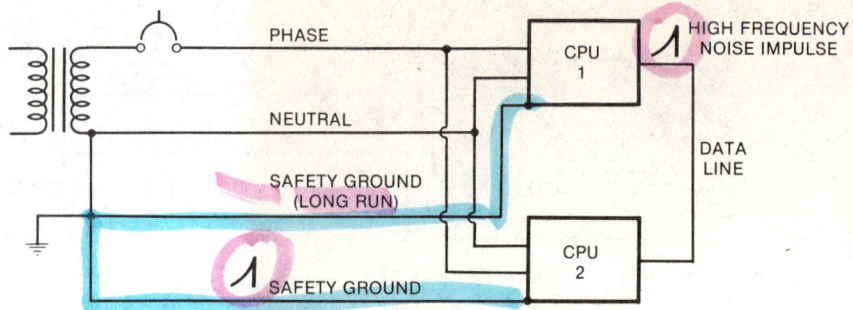

(A) The length of the long ground conductor has an impedance high enough so that high frequency noise passes from CPU1 to CPU2 via the data line.

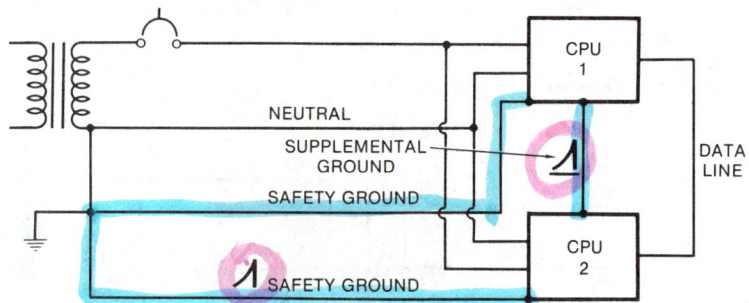

(B) A supplemental ground conductor has been added to tie the two cabinets together. This allows noise to pass to ground without corrupting data.

Fig. 5-2.
Both cabinets are properly tied to the power source.

quarter wavelength of the noise and at odd harmonics. The shield acts much like an antenna that will accept and radiate energy that is impressed on it at the resonant frequency and at its odd harmonics.

Obviously, grounding both ends of the shield help eliminate this problem. In addition, a number of grounding points along the length of the conduit, or shield, can help even more. Multiple short ground connections will be most effective at thwarting noise coupling at frequencies at 10 MHz and above.

Codes

Local wiring codes are usually based on the National Electrical Code (NFPA 70). Also, there is NFPA 75 which is the standard for the Protection of Electronic Computer/Data Processing Equipment. These codes specify wiring devices, materials, circuit protection, and methods of installation. Both

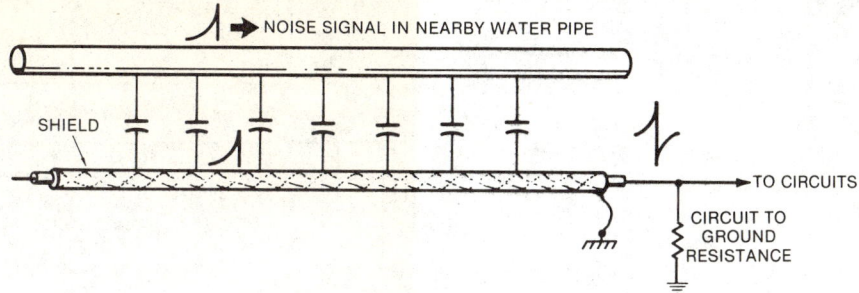

Fig. 5-3.
Noise signal has been impressed between the conductor and ground through stray capacitance.

codes are directed primarily at protecting against electrical shock, fire hazards, and other safety related concerns.

Often an interpretation of code will hinge on whether it applies to building wiring or some external power device that has been factory assembled. UL (Underwriters Laboratories) approval of a product is often used by a municipality for compliance purposes. There are other certifications from additional laboratories that can be used to meet requirements.

Grounding Myths

There are two myths about grounding that we must dispel in order to make sense out of proper grounding techniques.

As we mentioned earlier, many people believe an earth ground is like a septic tank or drain field. All we need to do to get rid of unwanted fault current or noise is to shunt it to an earth-driven rod where it will spill into the ground never to return and shock us or cause any other problems.

This is true for lightning since the earth is one of the discharge paths. For a computer, the earth has nothing to do with the electrical path of a noise source. Electricity flows in circuits, and it follows Kirchoff's laws which state that current flowing to a point equals the current flowing away from the point, and voltage generated equals voltage drops.

An earth-driven rod becomes part of a circuit, and that current flowing into it is going to come out somewhere else where there is an earth connection.

The other myth is that a computer must have an isolated ground. This is sometimes referred to as a "clean ground" as opposed to the "dirty ground" that we referred to earlier that ties the neutral to ground at the transformer (Fig. 5-4). This method violates the NEC, is extremely dangerous, and is not likely to solve noise problems.

This circuit could pass more than enough current to electrocute someone or burn insulation and equipment. If the chances of this happening seem

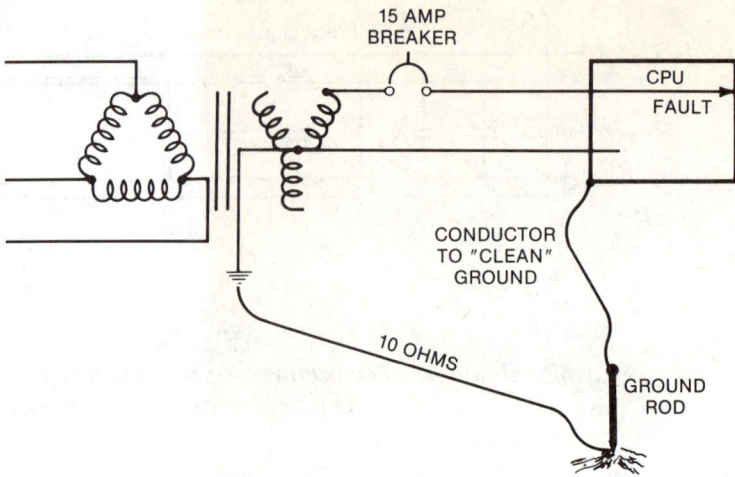

Fig. 5-4.
The two earth grounds might have a combined resistance of 10 ohms.
A 15 amp breaker needs 75 to 150 amps
to open without delay.

remote, think again! In one case recently, an electrician cut back the safety ground of a large computer installation, ran it through a building wall, and attached it to a driven rod ground. A fault occurred in a piece of power equipment that normally would have tripped a breaker immediately. Instead the equipment caught fire and the resultant heat and smoke did over 20 thousand dollars worth of damage to the facility. It might have been worse. A technician working on the equipment could easily have lost his life.

Proper Grounding Techniques

Single-point grounding is a concept that should be followed in all computer installations from micro to mainframe. The real purpose behind proper grounding is to prevent voltage differences from occurring between pieces of equipment. With each unit being referenced to a point of constant potential, no unwanted noise currents flow between them.

Multiple grounding points cause ground loops. This is a broad term meaning other circuit paths through the ground structure. These paths are a source of common-mode noise that can create a host of computer problems. When a CPU and its peripherals have different grounds, a noise voltage difference will exist between the devices, and noise current will flow through the ground system via the ground loop.

Even in very large systems where various units might be grouped together, separate grounds create unwanted ground loops. Impulses of ground current then find their way into transformer shields and coaxial cable, intercoupling noise into signal circuits. Ground loops are a frequent cause of data corruption.

For safety reasons, we want to make sure that the safety, or green wire, ground ties our system together. For noise reduction reasons, we want the green wire ground to be a low impedance path. Therefore, it is advisable to make the ground conductor as large as possible, at least as large as the other phase conductors. The electrical code will allow a much smaller wire, but in order to reference the system to as noise free a ground plane as possible, every consideration must be given to eliminate voltage differences in the ground structure.

This all sounds wonderful. But what if the computer installation is far away from the power transformer (Fig. 5-5). In that case, we might make one of two basic mistakes. We might choose to run our green wires, either tied together or not, back to the neutral to ground bond of the transformer. This would not be a low impedance path at noise frequencies because of the length of the line. Or we might have a central grounding point near the computer and not tie the grounds together, which would form a ground loop and impress common-mode noise on the line voltage. Either case is unacceptable.

So what is the answer? Placement of a separately derived power source near the computer will solve the problem. As we stated earlier, a transformer is a separately derived power source. We also stated that long feeders should be 480 volts rather than at the actual utilization voltage of the computer. This will require a step-down transformer at the computer. One of

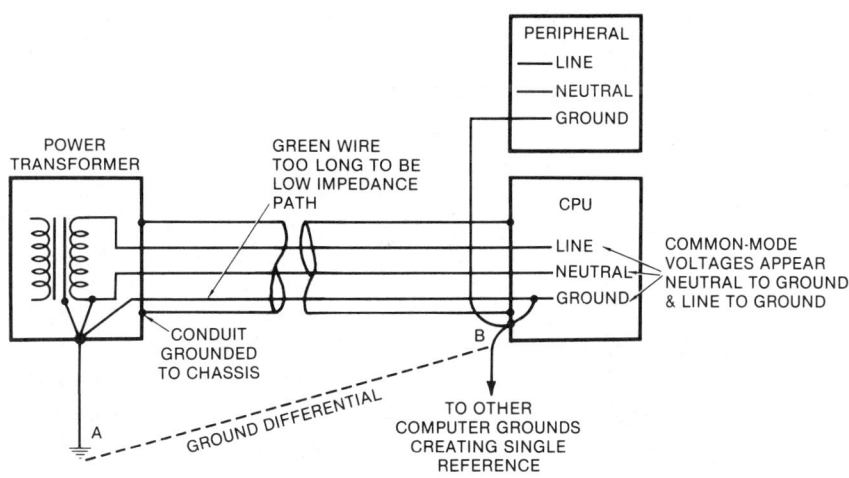

Fig. 5-5.
The ground loop formed by the different grounds, A and B, appear as common-mode voltage on all computer units.

the best ways to form single point grounding is by placement of the transformer near the computer and using the neutral to ground bonding of that transformer as a single reference.

This accomplishes two other benefits. First, it allows for a single point of entry into the computer room. Rather than feeding devices from panel boards located around a room, a single entry point allows for ground conductors to be tied together. A step-down transformer is an ideal way to terminate a dedicated feeder, have a single point of wiring entry, and form a single ground reference. Single-point entry is good practice for other feeders entering the computer area. This allows different service panels to be bonded together equalizing voltage differences between them. These other services might be for telecommunications equipment or air-conditioning units.

Also, the use of a transformer near the computer allows interconnecting leads to be shorter. As we discussed earlier, we do not want conductors to appear as resonant wavelengths at noise frequencies. If we are using a voltage equalization strap to tie units together, ideally lengths of no longer than 4.5 feet should be used. This will ensure voltage equalization at signals up to 10 MHz. Transformers inside the computer room help keep these bonding straps and ground wires short.

We will see later in this book that the transformer we use will be what is known as an isolation transformer that is specially designed to eliminate the introduction of noise into the computer environment.

For many small computers, not placed in a dedicated computer room, an isolation transformer is not practical. We will look into some grounding strategies for these computers in the next chapter.

Signal Reference Grids

A signal reference grid consists of a mesh of good conductive material on approximately 2 foot centers. This grid might be aluminum or copper wire, or copper straps bolted or soldered together. Most commonly it is the metal support structure of the computer room raised floor.

A signal reference grid has a constant potential over a wide range of frequencies. Because of its grid structure, many low-impedance paths can be found even when one or more paths are resonant at a noise frequency. Even if computer cabinets are not strapped to the grid, the capacitance between the grid and the bottom of the unit can bypass many undesirable signals.

Of course, it is desirable to bond each cabinet to the grid with short, flexible, braided, copper straps. Also, the single point ground of the system should be tied to the grid with a single short strap. This is easily done if an isolation transformer is located in the room itself. If more than one transformer must be used, the grid can be used to tie in their respective grounding conductors.

A signal reference grid is not a substitute for any safety grounding conductors required by code. The grid should be grounded for safety by a green wire enclosed in conduit just like any other safety ground, and the wire should be large enough to handle the current of the largest phase conductor in the computer room.

Transient Suppression Plates

The conduit supplying power to various devices within the computer room is subject to noise being induced by building steel or the frame of the building, which consists of all supporting members as well as the reinforcing iron embedded in concrete floors. A wide variety of equipment is grounded to building steel, and the resultant ground current from faults, loops, and other return paths can easily induce unwanted noise in computer room conduit.

A simple answer to that problem is a transient-suppression plate. This plate, about 4 feet by 4 feet, provides a bypass for this energy from building steel to the reference ground at or near the point where power enters the room.

Theory Versus Real World

We can draw diagrams and map things out according to theory. But in practice the best laid grounds can go wrong. The culprits are usually all kinds of random grounds and connections with other metal structures that contact the computer-room wiring.

Nearby computer-room wiring may include other wires in conduit, water pipes, air ducts, and a wide variety of other conductive members behind walls, under the raised floor, or in the ceiling. Hangers, clamps, and tie wires can create bonding between these culprits and computer conduits. Often, the electrician will leave one conduit lying on another with no thought as to noise induction or lightning hazards. Some of the pipes and the like may run right to the roof bringing lightning discharges into the computer room.

Obviously, its desirable to keep these other conductive elements from penetrating the computer environment.

A Few Tips

A few tips that make for good practice in designing the proper ground structure for a computer site are as follows:

1. Assure that the building steel is well bonded and the main vertical columns are well earth grounded.
2. Install a signal reference grid or raised floor if appropriate for the size of the computer.

3. Install a bonding conductor at the perimeter of the grid, bonding to each pedestal and building columns wherever possible.
4. Ground floor installations should bond the grid to the building's earth ground electrodes.
5. Bond any electrical-device box to the ground structure.
6. Bond any heating or air-conditioning equipment inside the computer room to the ground structure.
7. Bond any foreign metallic pipes, conduit, and so forth, at the point of entry into the room to the perimeter conductor.
8. Green wire grounds should be equal in size to other phase wires, and branch circuit conduit should be bonded at both ends.

When all these things are done, the room becomes like a Faraday cage or shielded room. Every effort has been made to create a friendly electrical environment for the large computer. The principles of proper grounding apply to all computers to the degree of practical application. We see in the next chapter that small computers can be made to reference a single-point ground. In the second half of this book, we see that grounding is a design philosophy of many power products.

Before we leave this topic, however, we must make a point about modern construction practices. The total cost of providing proper power and grounding for a major computer facility might only approach 10 percent of the total cost of the computer itself. Considering how economical it is to create this well engineered environment for good computer performance, only proper power and grounding make sense.

In the last few years, a trend involving purchasing or procurement has threatened to degrade computer operations everywhere. The competitive bid is a device used more and more by corporations to secure the facility that will house their computer. There is nothing wrong with a competitive bid inherently because it forces down the overall price of the computer room. The company thinks it saves money this way, and no doubt it does. The low-bidding contractor, on the other hand, must scrape and scrimp to make a profit on the job.

Scraping and scrimping do not lend themselves to providing a high-quality power and grounding structure. Many builders of computer rooms have confessed that being the low bidder has forced them to leave out many of the features of a well engineered room. If it was not specified in the quote package, it doesn't get installed.

Recently, a major corporation purchased a 7 million dollar computer system from a major manufacturer. The facility for the computer was sent out to contractors for bids in a separate package as part of a separate budget. The bid went through an electrical contractor, often not the person who knows or cares about proper computer installation, who in turn sent out for bids on the critical components of the facility.

Did the user get the best facility for the money? Probably. But he could have gotten a superior operating environment for more money. How much? Peanuts when compared to the entire project. Remember, many computer manufacturers relate 50 percent of their "no trouble found" calls to power related problems.

6

Personal Computers and Office Electronic Equipment

Let's review a little of what we have covered so far. We now know that raw utility power is not compatible with optimum computer performance. We know that there are things inside the building that can affect computer operations. Lightning, static, and noise are constant threats to our equipment. In the last chapter, we talked about the need for proper grounding to a single point of reference.

But what about micros, PCs, terminals, and minicomputers? They function in the most hostile environment of all. There is no engineered, dedicated power source to feed the computer, no signal reference grid, or no raised floor. Much of what we have discussed just cannot be economically applied to small computers.

Usually, we plug a PC into the power socket, shove it against the wall, and forget about the power. We forget about it until we loose data, "bomb" a disk, watch characters on the screen jiggle around until we get eye strain, or until we put on a telephone headset, touch our keyboard, and get knocked off our chair.

Utility Power

There is some good news about small computers and office electronic equipment. In most cases, these small devices are about as far away from utility power as possible. What this means is that influences from outside the building have a difficult time affecting them. Impulses from arc furnaces and the like might have a high magnitude at the building entrance, but by the time the impulse reaches the PC on your office desk, it may have been through two or more step-down transformers and several hundred feet of wire. The effect of all this resistance and inductance has a dampening effect on impulses. Of course, an outage is still an outage, and a sag is still a sag. But much of the transient noise and other disturbances may not reach the small computer.

Inside Your Building

Inside the building is where the real problems begin. Today, many very sophisticated computers can be plugged into a normal power receptacle and turned on. Usually these computers are placed in a corner or a closet because that was the only space left. The outlet may be on the same branch circuit as a copier or other cycling type of device. It may be on the end of a branch circuit subject to chronically low voltages. Everything we have said before about the interaction between a computer and its power source is true in the home or office.

There are two basic problems that exist in the office environment that can affect the operation of computers plugged into 120 volt outlets: Load balancing and neutral current.

In a three-phase system, current in each phase is 120 degrees apart. When we add their vectors, we find that the resultant is zero. For a well balanced three-phase system, no current should be present in the neutral conductor. Theory is one thing but reality is quite another.

It is a fairly simple matter to balance loads on paper before anyone moves furniture into an office building. Many loads are known, like building lighting, and some can be estimated with reasonable certainty. But when people start plugging in appliances of various kinds, or as the building is changed or remodeled, loads can shift dramatically. Today, many companies have gone to portable partitions that have built-in wiring. When these are added or moved, no one checks to see that the loads are balanced. Unbalanced loads create neutral current.

In a balanced load, each portion of the current adds together to form the actual current wave shape. When the loads are unbalanced, the components of current are not in phase with the line voltage. This reduces the load power factor and may interact with the power source impedance to create line voltage distortions.

As mentioned previously, computer power supplies no longer have transformers in them—typically they have switching power supplies. The power supply will only draw current during a portion of the cycle (Fig. 6-1), known as the conduction angle. A typical conduction angle would be 30 degrees. This can cause significant harmonic distortion in the load current, and can be a critical problem at sites where large numbers of terminals, PCs, or word processors are connected to a common power source. Defective power supplies can also be a source of harmonic output while the terminal itself may continue to operate.

Remember, the vector sum of three equal currents in a balanced system is zero. The third, and multiples of the third, harmonic of 60 Hz will

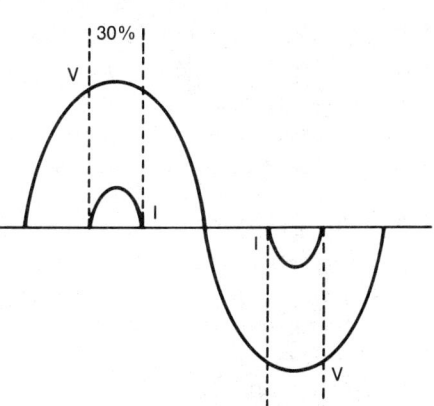

Fig. 6-1.
Switching power supply with a conduction angle of 30 degrees takes its current during the peak of the sine wave.

not be zero in a balanced system. Instead, third harmonics will add, will be their vector sum, and will appear as neutral current. At its worst, the neutral conductor might be forced to carry 1.7 times as much current as a phase conductor, which will cause excess heating. The resulting voltage drop in the neutral and the magnetic fields around the neutral conductor can be a source of noise that could be coupled into signal circuits.

Often poor performance can be traced to excessive current flowing through the neutral conductor. Even when the loads are balanced, malfunctions can occur. One obvious answer is to have separate neutral conductors for each neutral wire instead of a common wire. Another procedure that will help is to avoid daisy chaining neutrals from one outlet to another.

One would hope that the electrician would be aware of the need to balance loads and such. The only problem is that he doesn't seem to know the difference between neutral and ground. That's right, just because each outlet looks the same doesn't mean it's wired the same. Behind the faceplate of every outlet lurks a potential disaster. It might be sufficiently pleasing to plug in a lamp and turn on the light. That does not mean the thing is wired properly. (I just plugged a circuit checker into the nearest outlet in my study. It lit up indicating the receptacle was improperly grounded.)

Grounding

Usually when we set up a PC or small computer, we use half the outlets in a room and probably two extension cords. This might not be so bad if the outlets were wired properly. Even at that we might have ground loops, safety hazards, and the potential to interact with other devices.

Single-point grounding is still the best practice and can be accomplished at a very low price. The answer is power bars or power strips that allow each computer device to be plugged into its own properly wired socket. Each unit is, therefore, referenced to the same ground plane, and all the benefits we discussed in the previous chapter will accrue the small computer user.

The IG (isolated ground) receptacle is another approach which is deceptively attractive to many. These receptacles, identified by their orange colored plastic, provide at least two ground conductive paths. One ground path is not connected to the frame of the receptacle. It is routed all the way back to the power source where it is bonded to the neutral to ground connection as shown in Fig. 6-2.

A number of isolated ground schemes that use IG receptacles or insulating bushings and the like are either against code or are fraught with problems. IG receptacles do not violate code, but they act like no ground at all in many cases. This is not to say that they are not safe. If a fault were to occur surely a breaker would trip. Consider two different devices plugged into two different IG receptacles. If the power source is far away, we have no good signal reference. Instead of equalizing voltages, these long leads present a variety of high impedance paths at differing frequencies.

The other problem with IG receptacles is getting them installed right. If the simple outlet next to your desk is not grounded properly, how do you know that IG is really isolated? Any mistake in wiring IG receptacles will result in ground loops that will destroy the integrity of the system. It should be pointed out that there are applications for isolated ground engineering. They are, however, rare and specialized circumstances.

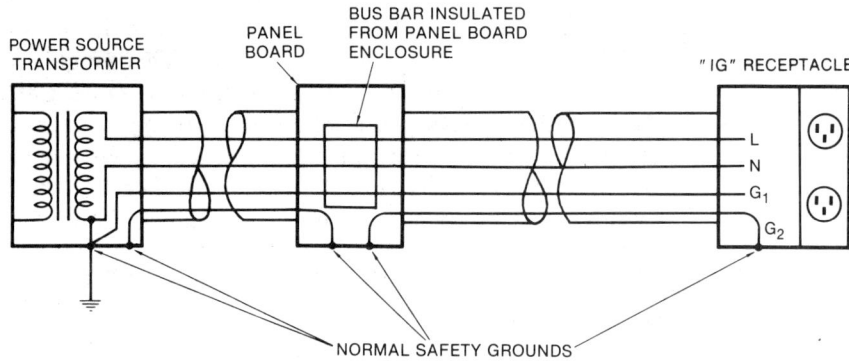

Fig. 6-2.
Isolated ground (G1) ties the face-plate ground pins all the way back to the power source without touching other devices.

Networks

We mentioned separate units plugged into different outlets. If these units are tied together by a simple RS-232 cable, ground loops can form corrupting the system. The proliferation of LANs (local area networks) in office buildings raises ground loops as a particular concern. Fig. 6-3 shows how a simple LAN might form ground loops that could potentially foul communications, create hard disk errors, or render one or more terminals useless.

The simple answer to this would be to plug all units into a common power bar. Of course, the units are usually too far away from one another for that. Another temporary solution might be to use extension cords. But that is impractical. What we are trying to do is obtain a common reference ground by taking power from the same source. We could interconnect the grounds with some new ground wire. But this solution is just as cumbersome as the others.

There are some known techniques for solving this problem. One is the use of a longitudinal coil called a balun. Placing a balun in the data signal circuit reduces common-mode ground-loop noise. The effect of a balun is to present a higher impedance in the ground-loop circuit. Other techniques that work require optical isolation, modems, fiber optics, or an isolating transformer in either the signal or the power circuit.

Telecommunications

Have you ever looked at the ground wire for a telephone system? Do you know where it goes and what it ties to? Did you know that fairly hefty

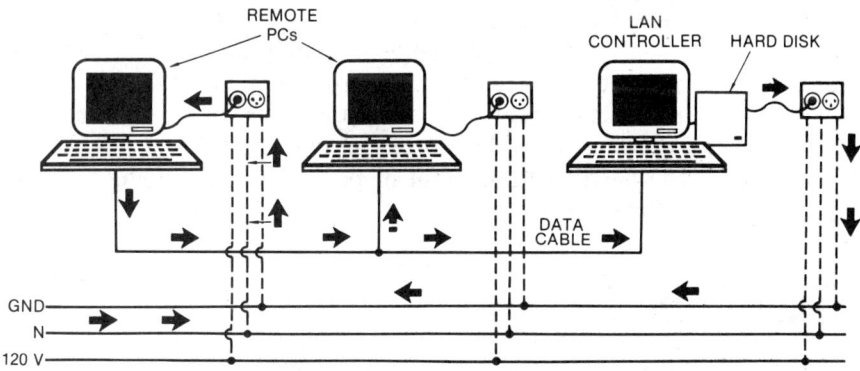

Fig. 6-3.
A simple LAN may form ground loops. The arrows show the path noise might follow.

voltage differentials (maybe only enough to tickle your ear lobe now and then) can exist between your keyboard and your telephone handset?

Consider what happens when a bulldozer cuts through the buried telephone line and the utility power at the same time. Did anyone think to properly tie the two ground systems together?

Not only is telecommunications equipment not grounded well in many cases, but little tiny wires are used for grounds and the wires are run a long way to the ground point. The incompatibility between power grounds and phone-system grounds can be a source of safety as well as operational problems. The trend is to tie more and more equipment together. All equipment must be properly grounded.

This can be as simple as bonding the frame of the computer to the ground of the phone or, in larger complexes, engineering a common ground plane for both data processing and telecommunications equipment. This common ground plane is a particular design consideration with today's wide variety of telephone companies and devices.

The Office

In an earlier chapter, we told the story of the typewriter and the copier. The office environment is full of those kinds of hazards. Recently we heard a story about a terminal that just would not operate properly. An expert was called in who discovered that if he moved the terminal away from the wall, the equipment would work fine. Soon he discovered that behind the wall was a steel member of the building structure. Sufficient ground current was flowing through the member to create a magnetic field that interfered with the function of the terminal.

Then there was the computer that malfunctioned every afternoon. It was finally found that it malfunctioned every sunny afternoon. The rays of the sun shining through the glass in one of the cabinets created the problem.

Every field-service technician has a half dozen strange and funny stories to tell. Since office, electronic equipment is just as sensitive as mainframe computers, and since the office is a very hostile and unforgiving environment, odd malfunctions can happen that might never be suspected. The need to be mindful of power and grounding is important to ensure performance.

Wiring for Data

Wiring for data is a phrase that can apply to both AC-power wiring or data-transmission wiring. It is possible to take into account the need for data in the initial plan for a building from both the standpoint of power and communication. But alas and alack, such is often not the case.

The only opportunity to do things right is when the building is being constructed. Many good things can be done when remodeling and the like. But when a building is in the process of having the wiring and electrical service installed, we have a unique opportunity to provide for a clean environment for our data.

Imagine today's office building requirements. In days gone by, we might have found one computer room with its mainframe and a couple of dozen terminals strung around the facility. Also, we might have found massive telephone trunk lines stapled to the wall and ugly holes gouged in the wall to route the wires from one office to another.

Today's environment is much different. We still have a central computer, but we can hang more terminals than ever before on the mainframe. We may have several other smaller computer networks clustered in various departments because PCs share data with minis, mainframes, and each other.

Let us not forget the phone system. Since the breakup of the phone company this area has become ever so much more complicated. And the division between voice and electronic data has continued to blur.

A new building, therefore, has a critical need for a wiring plan that takes into account voice, data, and power. To illustrate this, an engineer from a major utility was touring a power products manufacturing plant recently. It seemed the engineer was there to evaluate the feasibility of the utility entering into the computer power business in some fashion or another in order to more clearly satisfy its customers' demand for clean power.

During the plant tour, it suddenly dawned on the man that a new building might have two power services feeding it: one for the electronic/computer equipment and one for everything else. What a revolutionary idea! The utility, for little extra money, could install an additional service transformer. The building then could have a dedicated system of conduit and panelboards along with associated outlets for computer equipment alone. Lighting, air conditioning, and other office equipment could be served separately, thereby avoiding interaction between noncompatible devices.

This scheme is feasible by using today's technology with existing products. All it takes is proper planning. One of the most frequent complaints utilities hear today comes from the user whose terminals or PCs are not operating properly because they are on the same branch circuits as coffee makers, copiers, elevators, and a wide variety of devices that cause operational problems.

So why aren't more dedicated systems being installed? Recently a major commercial developer responded with a shrug when someone suggested that this be done. It's certainly not his fault. On a recent job it was observed that several major blunders had been made before the data processing manager was even consulted about the kind of considerations the computer might demand. By that time the damage had been done by the architect, consultants, contractors, and top management of the company.

Prewire for Data

It has become a widespread practice to prewire a building for telecommunications. Only recently has prewiring for data become a major consideration. It is possible to prewire a building for data no matter what kind of computer, or computers, is being installed, or what kind of phone system is going to be used. Data wiring is critical in terms of computer power. Poor data wiring can be a source of noise, ground loops, and undesirable interaction between systems. Careful planning of power, data, and voice wiring can ensure a clean electrical environment for the computer.

All too often this activity ends up being done by three or four companies: one handles the phones, one handles the mainframe, one handles the local area network, and one handles all other interconnecting systems that might be in use.

The cost of moving a computer terminal from one office to another is often 1500 dollars. It is possible to reduce this cost to only 10 percent of that by prewiring for data. This prewiring can also accommodate any future expansion that might occur. It is a well documented fact that when users become accustomed to a new system, use will double and new users will join the system.

Aldo Falossi of Cable Management Systems states in an article that appeared in the January 87 issue of *Hardcopy*, "The natural expansion of a network should be a primary planning consideration."

He goes on to say that a slow initial acceptance of a new computer system ". . . is followed by rapidly accelerated use, which then levels off to a steadier, more predictable growth."

Of course, the same thing can be said of LANs. Once one department gets a LAN and shows the benefits derived from it, soon other areas of a company will follow suit.

Cable Types

For many years, coax (coaxial cable) has been the most widely used cabling medium. Coax is immune to noise from other wiring and it can carry data at high rates over a long distance. Installation techniques are well established for coaxial cable. There is another product made very much like coax called twinaxial cable, which is essentially two coaxial cables joined together.

Coax has been the mainstay of IBM and many other large computer manufacturers. Because of its characteristics, coax was most often the choice for point-to-point or hardwired wiring schemes (Fig 6-4).

Coax has several drawbacks. The price of coax in relation to competitive alternatives has been increasing. Since coax has always been expensive to install, and other technologically advanced methods have been developed, coax has begun to give way to either inexpensive alternatives or more technologically advanced alternatives.

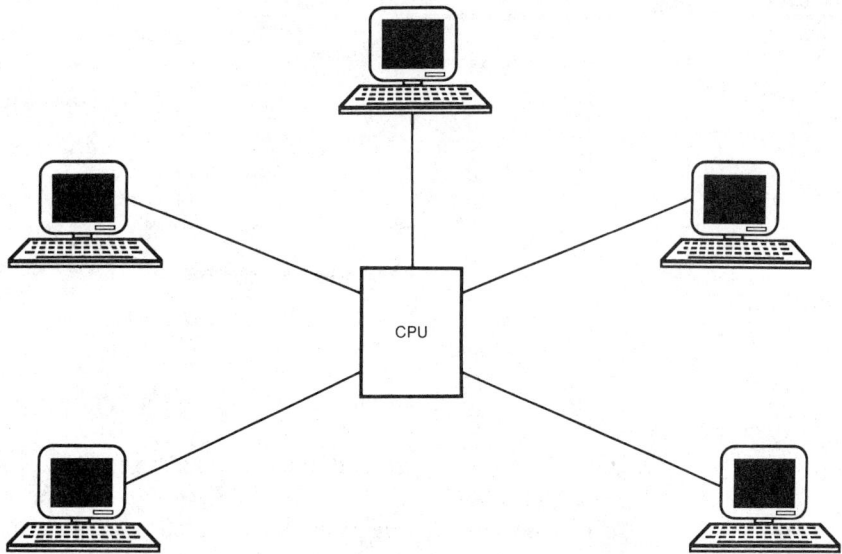

Fig. 6-4.
Point-to-point or hardwired cabling typically used coaxial or twinaxial cables.

Because of its bulkiness, coax is hard to manage and rearrange. Prewiring a building with coax for the kind of future expansion we have been talking about is expensive, cumbersome, and confusing. Keeping cables straight by means of tags (that sometimes fall off), wrestling with splicing, or rewiring existing offices with coax can give DP managers a pain in the neck as well as the pocketbook.

Fiber Optics—Fiber optics has two large advantages over coaxial cable. Since fiber-optic cable (Fig. 6-5A) is not an electrical conductor, it is immune to noise, and it won't cause ground loops. Furthermore, it is small. Most of us are aware that a bundle of fibers is considerably smaller than a bundle of copper wires. The signal carrying capacity of fiber optics is greater than coax (Fig. 6-5B), and data rates in excess of the data rates in coax can be achieved.

There are inherent problems with fiber optics. It requires special equipment to handle, splice, and test fiber-optic installations. Special units must be included in the installation to convert light signals to electrical signals. For these reasons fiber-optic-cable systems are considerably more expensive than coax systems. However, this technology is rapidly advancing and experts do not think too many more years will pass before the cost of fiber optics will approach the cost of coax. After all, silicon to make fiber is available in great abundance while copper is not.

(A) Fiber-optic-cable channel.   (B) Coaxial cable.

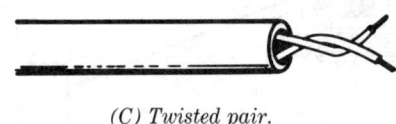

(C) Twisted pair.

Fig. 6-5.
Typical data transmission cables.

Twisted Pair—Twisted pair came to us from the telephone industry (Fig. 6-5C). It consists of pairs of wires twisted together and is available in configurations of 2 to 1200 pair counts. Twisted pair can also be obtained with shielding to give it more immunity to noise.

Twisted pair is somewhat more susceptible to noise than coax, especially the unshielded variety. Transmission rates are slower, but still within range for most DP needs.

The good news about twisted pair is that it is cheap, easy to install, and can be prewired using techniques that solve problems associated with changes, moves, and expansion. Also, twisted pair, while not having the superior data handling qualities of coax or fiber optics, can be used in more than 80 percent of all data-communications applications.

There is one more incredibly handy thing about twisted-pair wiring practices. The Bell system spent millions of dollars developing something we all probably take for granted. Yet the RJ jack and plug has made the chore of connecting computer terminals easy and inexpensive.

A cluster-cabling concept using RJ technology, 25 twisted-pair cable, and the 50-pin connector can make the whole burden of cable management easy and is a definite improvement over the point-to-point connection method (Fig. 6-6). And almost any connection can be made using conversion devices such as an RJ to RS-232 adapter.

Using various combinations of cluster cables, modular wall plates, and jacks that require no soldering, an entire building can be wired just like we wired the building for AC power earlier. We can leave some wire pairs unused for future expansion. RJ jacks come in four-, six-, and eight-wire configurations, depending on channel usage. This setup is economical, flexible, and expandable.

With the addition of punch boards, patch panels, and distribution closets, we can design an integrated voice and data system. For many years the phone company has used the distribution closet concept with success. These same advantages are appropriate for data communications. In Fig. 6-7 we see what a full system might look like.

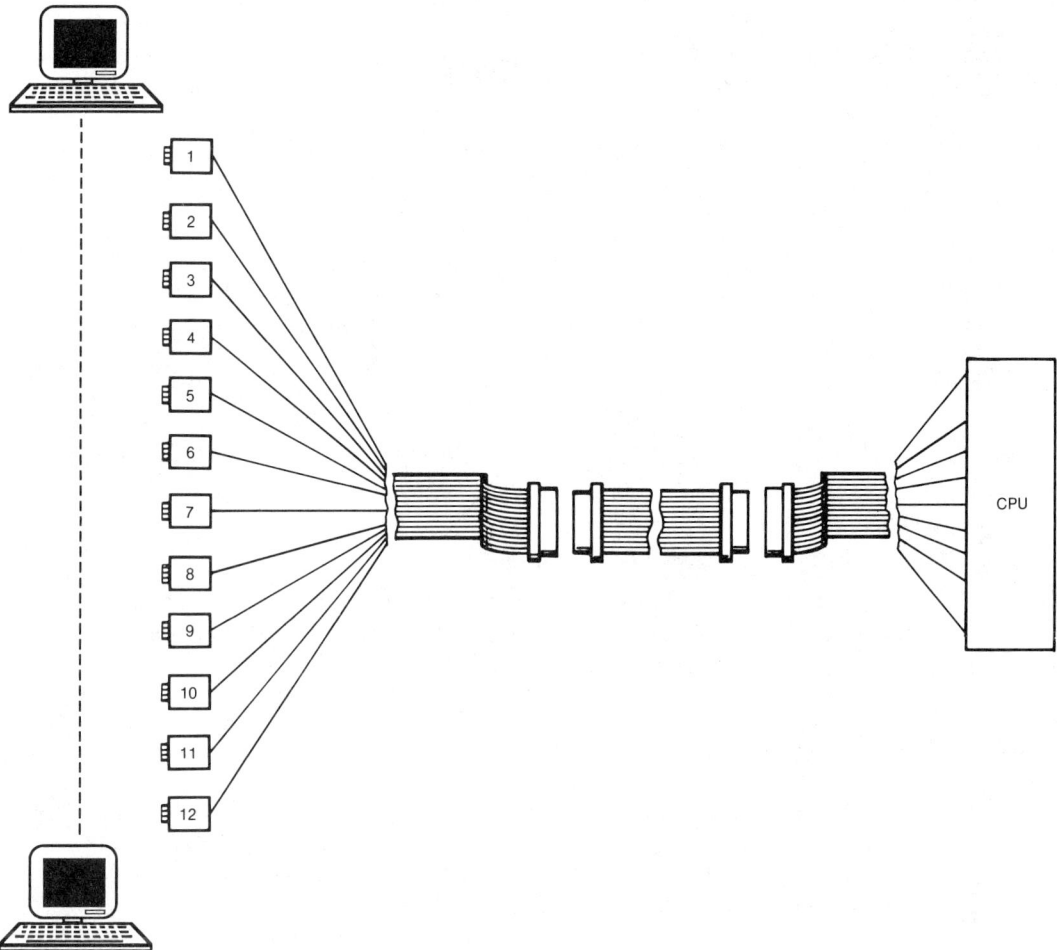

Fig. 6-6.
Cable clustering offers a 12 to 1 reduction in the number of cables used over hardwiring.

Other Considerations

Data transfer rates, cable length, and cable type are all interrelated. In some instances, a combination of twisted pair and coax might be appropriate. It has been found that twisted pair that is shielded can be used in over 95 percent of all RS-232C interfaces within 1000 feet, while unshielded wire should only be used for runs of up to 50 feet. Remember, shielded twisted pair or coax must have the shield grounded at both ends to provide the proper path for unwanted noise.

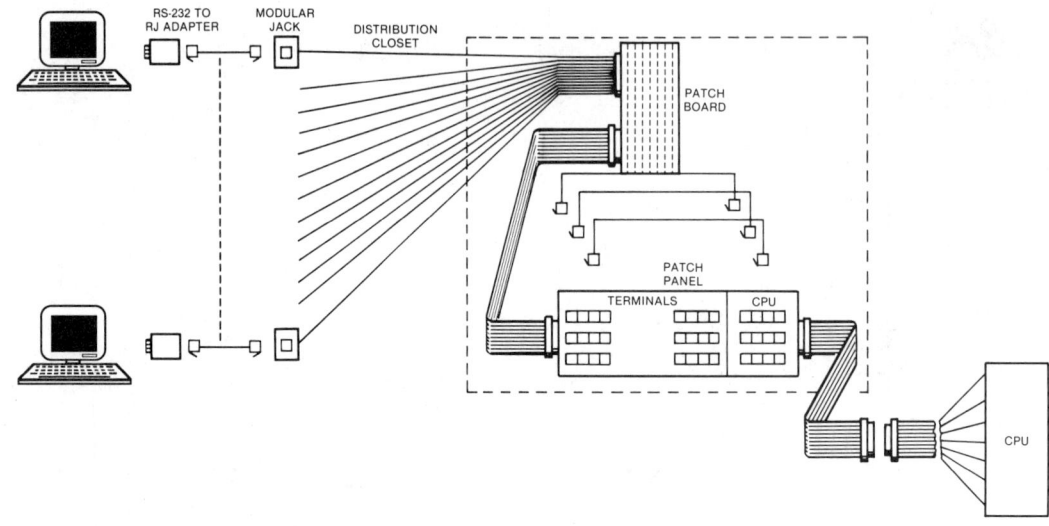

Fig. 6-7.
*The RJ system using punch boards allows prewiring of each
potential terminal location. The use of the patch panel allows for
easy changing and adding of users.*

The Smart Building

The building of the future might be prewired for computer power, voice, and data in an integrated fashion. These concepts can be stretched to suggest that tenants share computers, uninterruptible power supplies, fire protection, security systems, and video conferencing.

Certainly by using RJ connectors, patch panels, and punch boards, data and voice needs can finally be integrated in a fully flexible and expandable system. And when this is viewed with the same eye toward a building power-distribution system that maximizes the compatibility of power sources, we have a smarter building.

Make no mistake about it. IBM, Wang, DEC, and AT&T, to name a few, are moving their research and development in a direction that is combining systems of voice and data. It was no accident that IBM recently acquired Rolm, the telecommunications company. It's only a matter of time until major building tenants begin to demand a power and wiring structure that will integrate with the new products these manufacturers can provide.

7

Transient Suppression

Suddenly the jargon of power changes. We no longer refer to impulses as impulses. We call them surges or transients. To put it more clearly, we find products designed to suppress impulses that are called transient or surge suppressors. The best phrase describing these devices might be transient-overvoltage protection. Transient implies that the events themselves are transient in nature. Overvoltage implies that the event has exceeded some desirable limit either positively or negatively. And protection implies that we are preventing the event from having a damaging impact on circuit elements down line from where the protection occurs.

Transients

Transient overvoltages in power systems occur when energy originating outside the system is injected into lines that feed sensitive equipment. Also, the coupling of power-system transients into data lines is a source of damaging overvoltages. The most common causes of transients are lightning and switching.

Lightning, as we discussed earlier, has the potential of inducing voltages from line to line, through the ground, or by direct injection into a system.

Power-system-switching transients emanate from trapped energy in loads that are being turned off or from events taking place inside of the switch gear as contacts make and break. In general, transients appear whenever a sudden change takes place in a power system. The closing or opening of a switch is an abrupt change. During the actual closing of the mechanical elements in the switch the contacts may bounce. Or prestrikes can occur just before contacts close. Most simple switching transients are inherently limited to twice the peak amplitude of the steady-state voltage, but abnormal switching transients can occur that are up to three times steady-state voltages.

One of the foremost experts on this kind of phenomenon is Francois Martzloff, formerly with General Electric. He states in his paper "Origins of Transient Overvoltages" that the most frequent type of surge voltage is one with a decaying oscillation of from 5 to 500 kHz. While the waveshape of a transient or surge may have an infinite number of varieties, the IEEE in Standard 587 has put forth a guide on surge voltages in low voltage AC circuits. It is nothing more than an attempt to describe the real world and how equipment must be designed to deal with it. IEEE 587 has represented this transient as the "0.5 µs—100 kHz Ring Wave," as depicted in Fig. 7-1.

Again, this does not depict a real ring-wave transient. It is supposed to be near enough actual conditions so engineers can test to see how their equipment reacts to it. This is not all of the IEEE 587 standard, and we won't cover all of it here. What is important about this standard is how a manufacturer deals with it. Meeting this standard should be the goal of power-equipment manufacturers. If the equipment does not meet this standard, then the important question to be asked is what kind of protection does it give the computer?

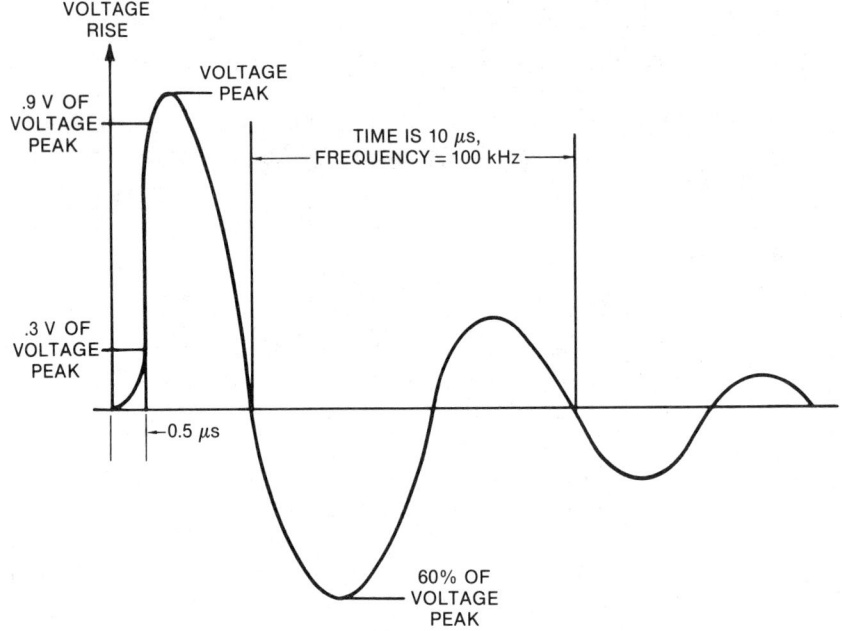

Fig. 7-1.
IEEE 587 0.5 µs—100 kHz Ring Wave.

In another paper, "The Development of a Guide On Surge Voltages In Low-Voltage AC Power Circuits," Francois Martzloff says, "Although surge voltage amplitudes and their frequency of occurrence on unprotected circuits are well known, their waveshapes and energy content are less well known." In this same paper, he confirms our contention that surge voltages can damage equipment or cause malfunction in both residential and industrial settings.

We have been talking about a transient as it might occur inside a building, on its way to our computer. But transient suppression must start outside the building. Certainly it is foolhardy to wait until lightning has penetrated the computer room before we divert, arrest, or short circuit it. IEEE 587 deals with the transient as it appears at the service entrance also (Fig. 7-2).

As we stated before, we want a transient suppressor (in this case a lightning arrester) that will handle this waveform. IEEE 587 uses voltages of up to 6 kV and up to 500 amps.

It might be tempting at some point to say, "Why should I worry about this stuff?"

Six kilovolts does sound a little high, and if all you have is a little PC tucked in the corner of the master bedroom, why worry? Well, Mr. Martzloff's research indicates that transients in a residence caused by switching appliances off and on can be 1200 volts or higher one or more times a week. Stick that in your hard disk and smoke it. Also, he sites other studies in

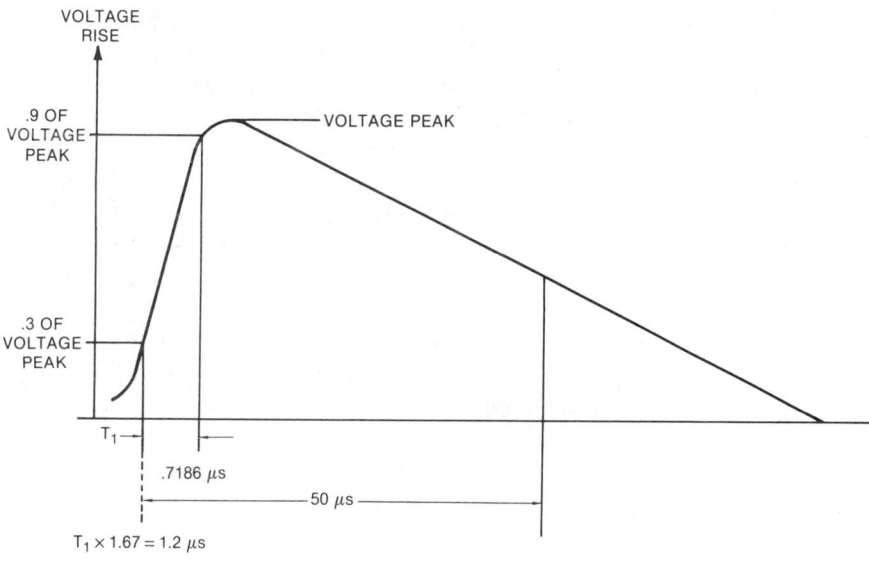

Fig. 7-2.
IEEE waveform (unidirectional) outdoor or near outdoor (service entrance).

lightning-prone areas where surges of up to 5600 volts were observed. Have you ever been typing away for an hour or so and had your disk drive suddenly fire up for no apparent reason? There is nothing more frustrating than losing several thousand words to a transient or spike.

Transient Suppressors

Various devices have been developed to protect electronic equipment from transients. The term transient suppressor is a little misleading. Actually, they either clamp, limit, or divert. They don't suppress but rather divert to ground or limit a transient to an acceptable level.

There are two basic kinds of devices that appear in transient suppressors: diverter type and restrictive type. Those devices that restrict are not particularly mystical. They simply offer a high impedance at the transient frequency or high resistance to the propagation of the transient. This is accomplished with the use of resistors or inductors in series with the circuit. But more on that later.

Diverters have properties that make them conductive under certain conditions, allowing transients to find a path to ground. Therefore, they are connected in parallel from line to ground. We are primarily interested in these diverting devices that take two basic forms: crowbars and clamps.

Crowbars

Crowbar devices are simple to understand. When an overvoltage occurs, the device changes from a high-impedance device to a low-impedance device. This low-impedance state then offers a path to ground, shunting unwanted surges away from sensitive circuits. This change in state can be inherent to the device itself. For example, spark gaps involve the breakdown of gas.

The major advantage of a crowbar device is its ability to handle large surge currents without breakdown or overheating. This means that the energy of the transient must be dissipated somewhere else in the circuit. Of course, the purpose of the device is to see that the energy is not spent inside the computer. When a gap-type device fires, it creates its own switching transient depending on the load current and characteristics of the load. It is possible for a very short duration event to trigger a longer event by firing the spark gap. However, a spark gap is a simple, low-cost device that, when used with other transient suppression methods, is a good front line of defense.

As the voltage increases across the spark gap, little conduction can take place until the breakdown voltage is reached. This voltage might be somewhere between 1500 and 3000 volts. It may take up to 10 nanoseconds for the gap to achieve conduction (Fig. 7-3). When the conduction point is reached, the gas between the conduction points breaks down and arc conduction takes place. The conduction will cease after current reaches zero and remains there long enough for the path to deionize and recover its insulating state, which may take several cycles.

The problem with this process is that while the voltage is building up, the load is left relatively unprotected. Also, because of the arc mode of conduction, this time frame varies from event to event. The typical conduction voltage can also be affected by the resting time between conduction. The physical nature of the process makes it difficult to produce consistent spark-over voltages as the voltage ratings go down. This is also a function of manufacturers' tolerances for very small gap distances. Part of these limitations can be alleviated by placing the gap in a tube filled with gas having a lower breakdown voltage than air (Fig. 7-4).

There are a number of gap-type devices. Gas-discharge tubes, carbon gaps, and rod gaps are common spark-gap devices. The utility company will have its own procedure for installing lightning arresters ahead of the building entrance. Arrester is a poor term for the device since it actually diverts the energy rather than arrests it. As a surge voltage moves toward the load, it is greatly attenuated by the transformer serving the building. The isolation of the secondary from the primary serves to dampen incoming transients. This is an ideal place to install a gap-type device. Placing an arrester on the secondary of the building service transformer effectively conditions all the power coming into the building. If arresters were placed further down the line and then only on some circuits, the computer feeder for example, surges could easily find other paths through various kinds of building metal to the computer equipment.

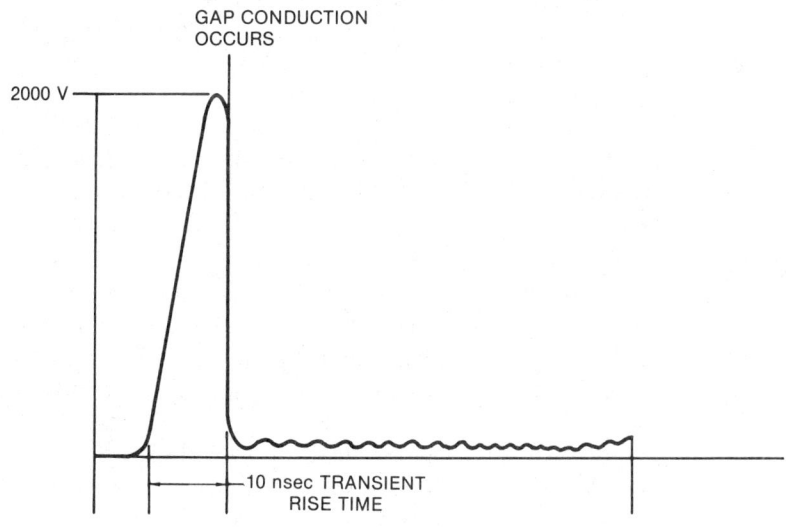

Fig. 7-3.
What a gas-filled spark-gap response might look like. Hypothetical transient triggers spark-gap conduction after 10 nanoseconds.

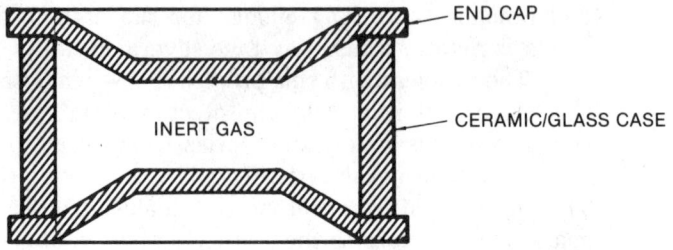

Fig. 7-4.
The gas-surge arrester, just one gap-type device, has electrical parameters that are a function of gas pressure and content, gap distance, and electrode size, content, and mass.

Some manufacturers recommend lightning arresters inside the computer room. This is the height of folly since surges of this magnitude, if diverted to ground near the computer, will travel through the computer ground. This kind of surge would be devastating to microcircuits.

Clamps

Voltage-clamping devices have a changing impedance depending on the current flowing through them or the voltage appearing across them. Clamps have a nonlinear characteristic as conditions change beyond the clamping level. We can analyze a clamp with Ohm's Law, but we must be aware that R will change with respect to the clamping device.

Unlike a spark-over-type device, the installation of a clamp will not affect the operation of the circuit at levels of steady-state voltages below the clamping level. As a transient voltage starts to rise, current flow through the device results in a voltage-clamping action. Nonlinear impedance is the result because this current rise is greater than the voltage increase. The effect of voltage clamping can be achieved with any elements that achieve this nonlinear impedance.

Avalanche Diodes—Avalanche diodes, part of the zener-diode family, were initially used as voltage regulators. Special attention to construction enhanced their voltage-clamping capabilities with regard to surge absorption. Large-diameter junctions with consideration to heat dissipation make avalanche diodes good suppressors. Typically, these devices are used in low-voltage applications, that is, 5- to 15-volt logic circuits. However, they may be stacked to achieve greater voltages and to overcome heat-dissipation problems.

Silicon-transient suppressors can be manufactured to match a wide variety of suppression characteristics (Fig. 7-5). If pulse current is plotted against clamping voltage, we find the curve to be surprisingly flat over the useful range of the device. However, since the PN junction of the diode is so thin, capacitance can be a consideration depending on the application. This can be minimized by putting diodes in series. Avalanche diodes have the property of reacting quickly to very fast rising impulses.

Varistors—Varistors function like variable resistors. As a matter of fact, that's how they got their name. Varistors include two devices that have different construction and technology. The first (silicon-carbide disks) has been in the industry for some time and has been used successfully as a transient-suppression device. Recently, another technology has produced the metal-oxide varistor.

As the story goes, the properties of silicon-carbide varistors were discovered quite by accident, and its internal process of nonlinear conduction remains the subject of speculation.

MOVs (metal-oxide varistors) have become very popular because of their wide range of application. The conductive process within an MOV takes place at the boundaries of large grains of zinc oxide grown in a delicate process and suspended in bismuth oxide. PN junctions exist effectively at the interface between these materials. (Fig. 7-6).

The basic performance characteristics of an MOV are similar to a silicon-transient suppressor. The choice between the two is largely a function of clamping voltages and energy handling capability. The MOV generally handles larger voltages and higher energy, while the silicon-transient suppressor is available at lower clamping voltages. MOVs tend to be somewhat less expensive and more flexible than silicon-transient suppressors.

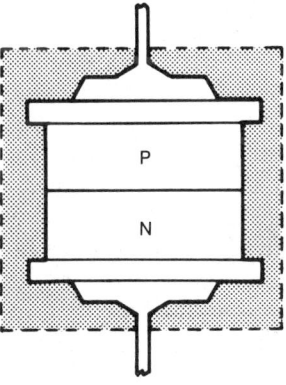

Fig. 7-5.
Silicon-transient suppressors are constructed using a large area PN junction which has been affixed between two heat sinks to protect the junction during impulse conduction.

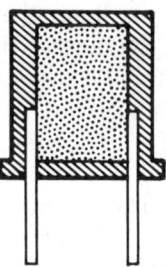

Fig 7-6.
The metal-oxide varistor is made up of zinc-oxide granules suspended in a matrix of bismuth oxide.

Failure

Gap-type devices, as stated earlier, act as a short circuit to ground and absorb little energy. Solid-state devices like MOVs do absorb energy. Because of the stress of handling this energy, MOVs eventually may fail. One heavy hit (impact of this energy) or a number of small hits might eventually cause the internal junctions to break down. Internally, the device will become a solid path for current. There are two ways of dealing with this current, and both methods involve inserting a fuse in the circuit.

Figure 7-7 shows two methods of protection using fuses. In Fig. 7-7A, we have a need to protect the equipment at all costs. We will allow the equipment to go down if the suppressor should fail. In Fig. 7-7B, we want continued operation. The device might fail by shorting and thereby tripping a breaker and interrupting power or signal transmission if it is installed on a data line. The placing of a fuse in series with the device will ensure continued operation. Also, an indicator light might be tied in with the fuse so the operator could see when to replace the protective device.

This brings up an interesting point. A popular product for today's personal computers is a transient suppressor built into a power bar or a device that plugs into an outlet ahead of the computer. Most of these devices have no way of indicating if a heavy hit has taken out the device. Usually an MOV or an avalanche diode is the protective device. And if, as we stated earlier, there are transients of up to 1200 volts pounding the thing every couple of weeks, we may have an inoperative suppressor and never know it.

These devices are as cheap as they are popular. That's the key. There might be some psychological benefit in spending a few bucks and thinking you've protected your several thousand dollar investment. If all you want is comfort, buy one and feel good about it. If you want real protection, use your new-found knowledge and shop around for something that is going to do the job and tell you when it can't.

Transient Suppression / 87

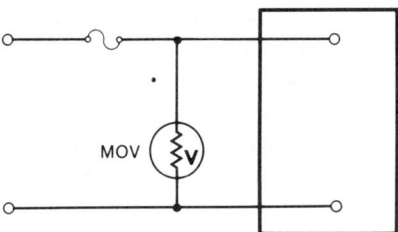

(A) Protection is always maintained because power will be interrupted when the device fails.

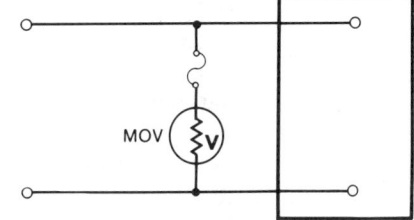

(B) Protection is sacrificed until the suppressor can be replaced.

Fig. 7-7.
Two methods of protection using fuses.

Multistage Protection

Clamps are appropriate at many places from the building service entrance to the computer itself, including data lines. Care must be taken to ensure that, since surges are being passed to ground, diversion paths do not create other problems. Also, when a device fails it may ignite and, therefore, should be properly enclosed.

Typically, a choice of one device or another need not be made for proper transient protection. The characteristics of the devices make them good companions in a well-designed system. Figure 7-8 shows how this might happen using multistage protection.

We might view this as three stages of protection. Stage one is meant to divert very high energy impulses to ground. But remember, a few nano-

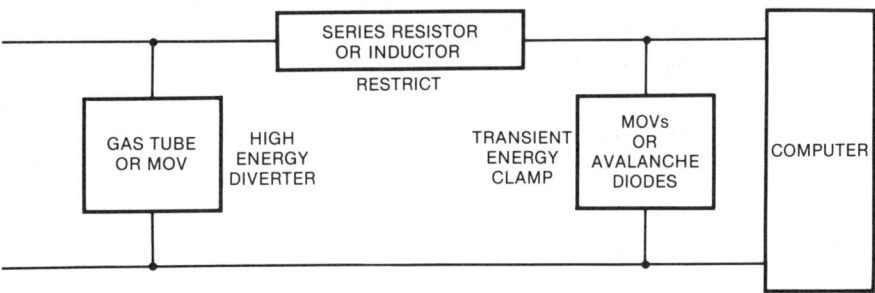

Fig. 7-8.
A typical system combines various elements to accomplish transient protection.

seconds of energy will sneak past this stage. Gas tubes will protect us from large amounts of destructive energy. But it takes a high threshold of energy to fire a gas tube and firing creates transient conditions sufficient in voltage and current to damage computer equipment.

Stage two is an inductor or resistor. A well-designed inductor will offer no significant impedance to the AC sine wave but will offer high impedance to fast rise-time transients. The faster and higher the surge is the more impedance it sees. Fifty feet or so of building wiring can have the same inductive effect. This impedance acts as a barrier to the transient, holding it up while the other suppression elements have time to react. A by-product of having this inductance in the line is its effect on noise. RFI and noise see the same impedance that a fast rise-time transient might see.

Suppressor Installation

As stated earlier, there are many appropriate locations for the installation of clamps. These include the inputs and outputs of transformers, motor-generators, UPS systems and their automatic bypass static switches, and the inputs to computer equipment. A word of caution is called for at this point. We need to take care in the placement of these devices.

Proper grounding and placement of suppressors, especially crowbar devices, cannot be overemphasized. The operation of a crowbar acts to pass large amounts of energy to ground. With this in mind let's look at Fig. 7-9. Here we have a data line entering the building. Some careful engineer has placed a multistage arrester near the building entrance and grounded it with a driven rod. The computer communications equipment is tied to a different ground.

We see there is a path through the data line, through the communication IC which is powered by a power supply that is grounded to the green-wire ground. Here we see a potential path through ground back to the arrester. The ground-lead inductance could be large enough that during arrester conduction the voltage drop across the lead inductance might be greater than the withstand capabilities of the IC.

The voltage that the IC sees is the sum of the clamping voltage of the arrester and the voltage drop across the ground-lead inductance. If the incoming transients were to be clamped by the transient suppressor at say 30 volts, the ground impedance of the device might be such that 200 volts develops across it due to current flow. The communications IC will see a potential of 200 volts between the data line and ground, and zap the IC.

The obvious solution to the problem is to tie the transient suppressor's ground point to the building service ground. This would keep the surge current far away from the computer. Since this might not be possible, practical considerations may dictate the data line entering the building at or near the computer location. If this were the case, the logical thing to do would be to bond the transient-suppressor's ground to the single-point ground plane of the computer.

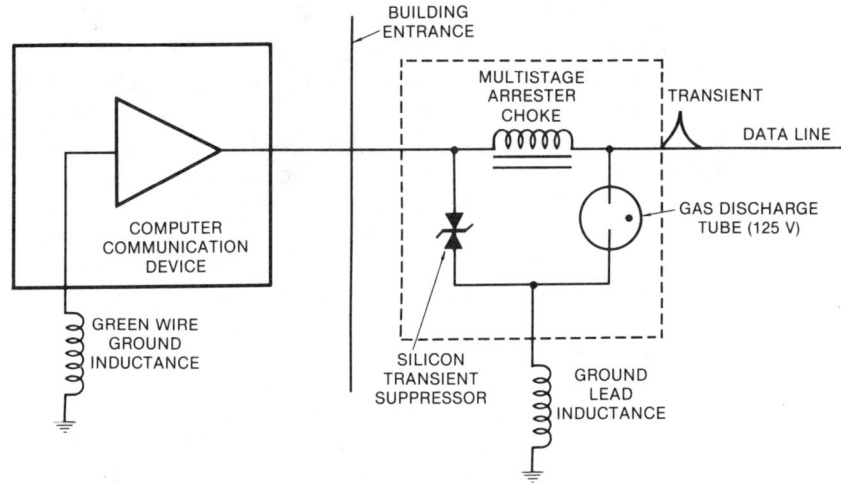

Fig. 7-9.
Surge arresters are often put on incoming data lines where they enter the building. This setup may form a hazardous ground loop that negates the use of the arrester.

With this accomplished, the voltage drop of 200 volts would be seen equally by the computer and the suppressor. This means that both the communications IC and the data line are referenced to 200 volts. Now the IC will see only the 30-volt clamping voltage on the data line.

This can be a hard concept for the human mind to accept. Our equipment doesn't care if it is referenced to a 20,000-volt ground plane. As long as this voltage is equalized between cabinets, the units will operate properly. Don't touch anything! But electrically the ground will still be a proper path in the circuit.

Strangely enough this 20,000-volt ground plane has happened very graphically during lightning storms. One technician reported being in a computer room during a lightning storm. Off and on during the storm the lights would flicker, but the computer kept running as if nothing were happening. It seemed odd to him since the computer had no on-line battery backup system, and yet the power appeared to be going off.

What was actually happening was the nearby lightning strikes were raising the building steel voltage so the lights no longer saw a potential difference between line and ground. The computer equipment was referenced to a single point and was riding up and down on the ground plane as the ground potential rose and fell with the lightning-strike current. Since the signal reference was not affected, no malfunction occurred. This is a simplified explanation of a more complex event, but it helps explain the value of proper grounding.

A well-designed transient-suppression system should take into account the kinds and magnitudes of energy to be diverted, the optimum places for diversion to take place, its effect on the ground structure, and coordination between power and communication systems. Products are available from the component level to multistage, elaborate suppression devices that address all the concerns. A knowledge of the inner workings of transient suppression will help the user and the technician toward better uptime.

8

Isolation and Distribution

We made reference in an earlier chapter to the advantages of placing a transformer near the computer. These included lower-cost feeder wiring, better voltage regulation, single-point grounding, and shorter branch-circuit lead lengths. Some other benefits are sometimes overlooked. They greatly reduce downstream fault current thereby avoiding the need to install additional current-limiting fuses to protect breakers. Three-phase delta-wye transformers provide improved power factor when they supply switching power-supply loads because they do not pass harmonic distortion upstream to the power source. They are extremely efficient devices, 95 to 98 percent, with no moving parts, and they are highly reliable. One power product manufacturer has reported no transformer failure in the field for 7 years.

In this chapter, we will look at the area of isolation and distribution. By isolation, we mean specifically isolation transformers. More specifically, we mean computer grade isolation transformers.

Also, we will look at conventional wiring distribution methods as they relate to power-distribution units. The power center is a combination of isolation and distribution. Sometimes called PDUs (power-distribution units), MPC (modular-power center), or PDS (power-distribution system), these are relatively new products that we will explore.

Isolation Transformers

When you use the term *isolation transformer*, you may find that it means different things to different people. Strictly speaking, any transformer with no direct conductive path between the primary windings and the secondary windings can be considered an isolation transformer. There is a transformer

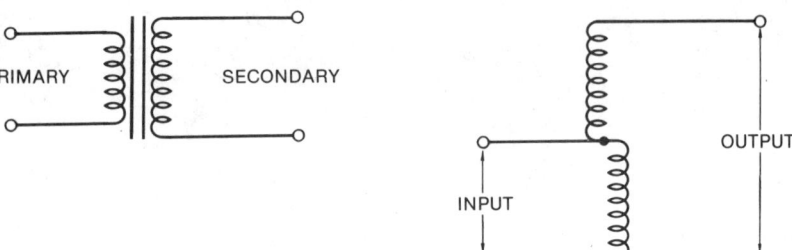

(A) Transformer with no direct conductive path.

(B) Auto transformer with continuous winding does not isolate input from output.

**Fig. 8-1.
*Isolation transformers.***

in use in the computer power industry that has a direct conductive path between its coils. It is called an auto transformer (Fig. 8-1).

For our purposes, a computer grade isolation transformer is more than just an ordinary transformer (Fig. 8-2). It is designed to allow a minimum

**Fig. 8-2.
*Isolation and suppression transformers.***
(Courtesy Emergency Power Engineering, Inc.)

of noise or transients to pass from the primary to the secondary. Even ordinary transformers attenuate common-mode noise, depending on design and construction. But isolation transformers are specifically made to attenuate noise that might interfere with computer operations.

The one thing no transformer can do is compensate for slow-moving sags or surges. And it certainly cannot compensate for total loss of power. It does have the ability to reduce high frequency common-mode noise and fast rise-time impulses.

Noise Coupling

Probably the biggest design consideration of an isolation transformer is the passage of noise from the primary to the secondary. As stated earlier, some attenuation will take place, but the very nature of the transformer itself will allow high-frequency transients and noise to move from the primary to the secondary.

To understand how this happens, we must understand the construction of the average isolation transformer. In order to achieve good electromagnetic coupling, we must place the primary and secondary coils physically close to one another. This is generally done jelly roll style with the secondary wound around the core, then insulating material is layered next to it. Next comes the primary winding, again in jelly roll fashion. This construction method provides for the close magnetic proximity we need for maximum energy transfer.

This closeness is what causes the problem. At power frequencies we have achieved good isolation. But at radio frequencies we have made a crude sort of capacitor. We have created a capacitive coupling between the faces of the nested windings. It is this feature that allows common-mode noise to pass from primary to secondary (Fig. 8-3). And as the frequency of the noise goes up, the passage of noise is easier, since capacitive reactance between the windings decreases as frequency increases.

In addition, conversion of common-mode noise into normal-mode noise may occur. Certain isolation transformers, because of poor design and construction, have a particular problem in this area. How does this happen?

The capacitive reactance between windings and along the coupling path is not equally distributed. In fact, there may be many differences the common-mode signal encounters as it travels from the terminal of the transformer toward the core. Also, since it takes time, albeit a very small amount of time, for the signal to travel from the terminal to the center of the primary winding, the signal does not appear instantaneously across the entire length of the winding. Remember, we have a common-mode pulse moving along each line toward the center of the primary winding. When it arrives, theoretically the signals will cancel each other out. Because of the discontinuities in the windings and the time differences, a flux current is produced in the primary that is proportional to the difference of the two signals. This dif-

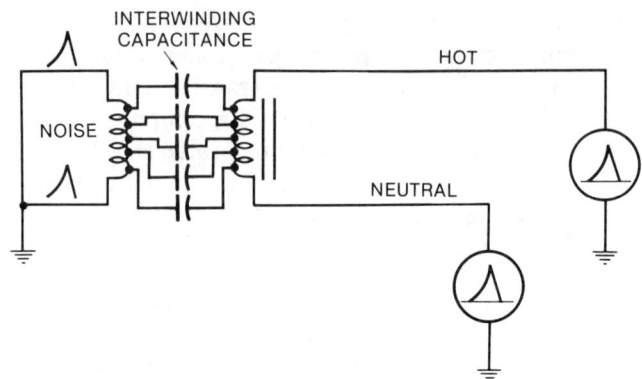

Fig. 8-3.
Common-mode noise pulses are coupled to the secondary by unequally distributed interwinding capacitance.

ference is induced into the secondary winding and appears as normal-mode voltage on the transformer's output (Fig. 8-4).

Normal-mode noise uses this same capacitive path to travel from the input to the output of the transformer. The ability of the normal-mode signal to couple to the secondary has to do with the frequency-response curve of the transformer. As the frequency goes up, the electrical characteristics of transformer material change somewhat, and the response curve might show high noise attenuation at some frequencies and low noise attenuation at others. The core material of a transformer might change the rise time of a transient as it tries to pass through the capacitive path from primary to secondary. Because of this, the impulse waveform is likely to be distorted by the process, but the magnitude of the noise itself may still be as strong (Fig. 8-5).

In summary, we can see that the propensity of a transformer to pass either common- or normal-mode noise is dependent on the frequency of the noise and the design characteristics of the transformer. Since the coupling

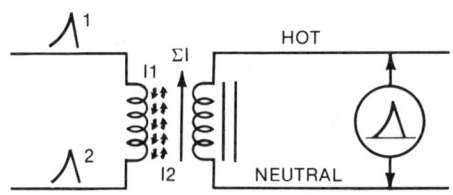

Fig. 8-4.
The differences of unequal currents I1 and I2 become a current in the secondary, creating normal-mode noise.

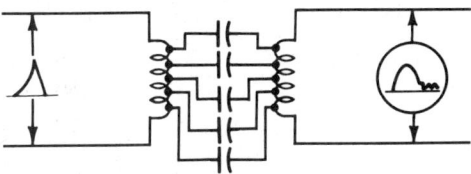

Fig. 8-5.
Normal-mode noise passes through the transformer. The impulse waveshape has been distorted, but the magnitude has been relatively unaffected.

of the noise is capacitive, reactance goes down as frequency goes up. Also, we have shown how the load might receive both common- and normal-mode noise as a result of a common-mode noise impulse.

Computer Grade Isolation Transformers

A significant step in reducing these noise-coupling problems can be made through the use of an electrostatic shield. Sometimes referred to as a Faraday shield, this is generally a layer of copper foil that is wrapped, just like another layer of jelly in our jelly roll, in a single turn. Care is taken to see that one end of the shield is insulated from the other so a shorted turn does not develop in the transformer.

As seen in Fig. 8-6, the electrostatic shield has been inserted between primary and secondary windings. Since this is a solid-copper shield with no holes, it is a very affective coupling path to ground. We might point out that it is possible to couple noise from the secondary to the primary. The shield is effective in shunting noise to ground no matter which direction it comes from. On the primary side, the shield completes a noise current path so the noise can circulate to its point of origin without traveling through the secondary or the load.

Capacitors in series have the property of reducing capacitive reactance rather than increasing it. Therefore, the inclusion of an electrostatic shield reduces interwinding capacitance and the associated coupling of noise. The good news is that this can be even further reduced by putting in another shield. Double-shielded isolation transformers are almost a standard in the computer power industry. Triple-shielded transformers are specified from time to time also.

There are products on the market that use various forms of box shielding and other techniques to further reduce stray capacitance. Manufacturers of these "super-isolation" transformers make claims of common-mode noise attenuation of from 120 to 150 dB. While there may be certain products that might perform to those specifications, there are also several manufacturers that advertise 140 dB noise attenuation for simple double-shielded isolation transformers.

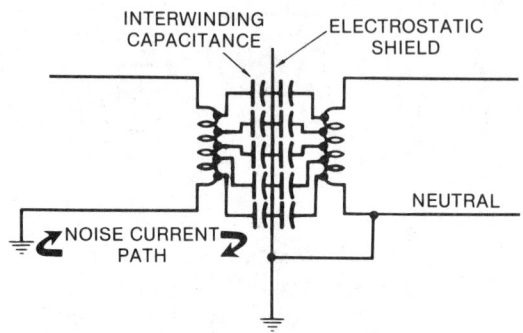

Fig. 8-6.
The electrostatic shield can give an attenuation ratio of up to 1000 to 1 or −60 dB.

Now, 140 dB is a ratio exceeding 10,000,000 to 1. This claim means, if taken at face value, that if the primary was hit with a 10 million-volt spike that only 1 volt would appear across the secondary.

At 10 million volts, the physics of electricity and its effect on conductors is a bit exotic. A 10 million-volt spike sees a transformer in a different light, so to speak, as would a 1000-volt spike. The other thing to consider is that impulses of this magnitude find many other paths into a computer room. To obtain this kind of attenuation throughout the site we have a lot of other shielding to do. Of course, the manufacturer has said nothing about rise time, frequency, or duration. Where does this 140 dB come from and how does it work? What test will verify this claim? Does it conform to IEEE standards? The answers to these questions are essential in determining the legitimacy of outlandish claims.

Back to the real world. Significant improvement of normal-mode noise can be realized by putting capacitors of the correct value between hot and neutral on the secondary of the transformer. At noise-signal frequencies, the impedance through these capacitors would be much lower than the path through the load (Fig. 8-7).

The exact size of these capacitors will be determined by the frequency of noise present at a given site. There are many variables that may come into account in determining the value of the capacitors. These capacitors often will be within the transformer's enclosure. Carefully plan the lead length and mounting of the transformer, especially as the frequency approaches radio frequencies.

Notice in Fig. 8-7 how the shield, neutral, and transformer core are all bonded together.

Isolation transformers are an integral part of any power distribution scheme. They are available in either single or three phase. If there is a standard transformer, it is the three phase with 208Y/120V output. Typical

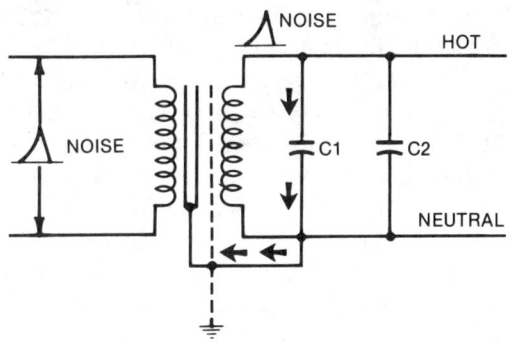

Fig. 8-7.
Addition of capacitors C1 and C2 provide a low-impedance path for normal-mode noise.

input voltages are 600, 480, 240, and 208 line to line for 15 kVA and larger. Typically single-phase input voltages are 120, 208, 240, 277, 480, and 600 in sizes from 500 VA to 10 kVA.

Distribution

Let us assume that we are in a typical computer facility. Upon inspection we see that careful consideration has been given to bringing power to the room. We have a dedicated 480 volt feeder that terminates at a 208Y/120V double shielded isolation transformer. The transformer is just behind the wall, and on the wall we see one or more gray boxes which we recognize immediately as a panel box full of branch circuit breakers.

Conventional Wiring

From the wall-mounted circuit breakers, we notice that rigid conduit carries the circuit wires from the breaker to the device. We lift up a few of the raised floor panels and see the rigid conduit that looks like a water pipe which if not fastened down will tend to vibrate when current passes through it. This happens because of the expanding and contracting magnetic fields around the wires inside the conduit.

Local codes determine the method of fastening conduit to the floor. Usually a unistrut channel is affixed to the concrete subfloor. In Fig. 8-8, we see that on top of this sturdy channel that the conduit has been mechanically fastened to the channel using steel clamps.

This situation presents several problems not the least of which is moving equipment. In many major data centers, just keeping track of the equipment and where it is moved to is a full time job for one person. What happens to the conduit when equipment is moved? It is usually cut off and new conduit is installed. It doesn't take too long before the subfloor of many computer rooms is a maze of discarded conduit even though the electrical code prohibits the existence of abandoned wiring. Although the cost associated with this kind of construction is substantial, moving or adding conventional computer wiring is more expensive.

Another problem is that, as we see in Fig. 8-8, each conduit is electrically connected to every other one. Remember that this conduit is part of the ground structure for our computer. Any noise in any conduit will be transferred to the others. For example, if someone were to plug a vacuum cleaner into the wall outlet we might experience a computer problem.

You may have already figured out the other problem. Conduits touching may be the source of undesirable ground loops. Since each conduit is electrically connected, we have created an infinite number of potential current paths. As we discussed in the chapter on grounding, this can create severe disturbances.

An interesting point about conventional wiring, it is engineered and installed by noncomputer people. To them, wiring is considered part of the building and is dictated by the electrical code; they give no thought beyond code as to proper grounding or trouble free operation.

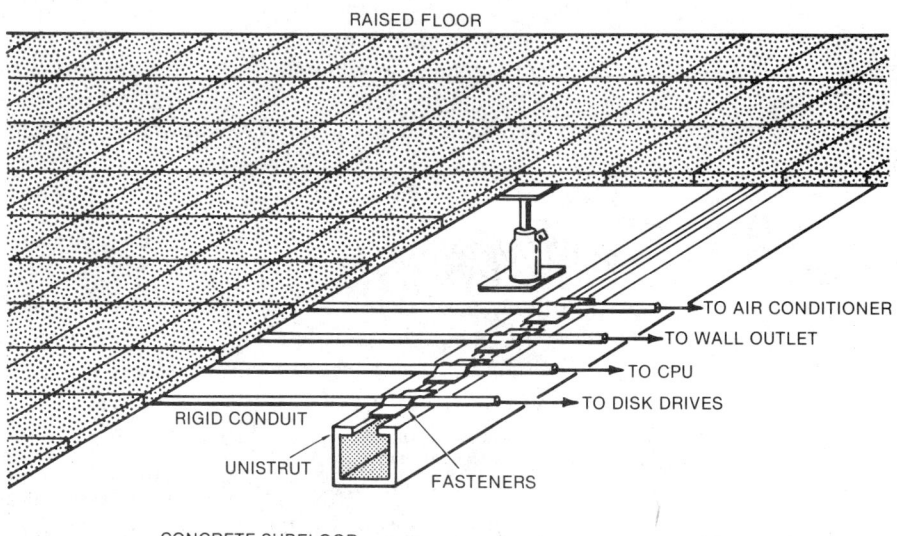

Fig. 8-8.
Conventional wiring method of fastening all circuit conduits to metal unistrut channels.

The PDU (Power Distribution Unit)

Not too many years ago there lived a bright young man by the name of Warren Lewis who worked for a large computer company. As the story goes, he was in charge of a particular installation where changes in equipment and equipment placement were made often, too often for Warren. To make a long story short, he invented the first power distribution unit to avoid the time, effort, and cost associated with frequent moves. In doing so, he came up with a better way to install a computer.

Today, there are PDUs that perform the function of distribution only. But most PDUs are built with both isolation and distribution. The isolation transformer, the kind we described earlier, is placed in a mobile frame with leveling jacks and casters because it is so heavy. This also allows the unit to be moved easily and to rest on a sturdy base.

PDUs are built to look like other pieces of computer equipment. Some models are built into computer-style cabinets, so the PDU is virtually indistinguishable from other computer peripherals. The NEC allows properly packaged transformers to be placed right inside the computer room, not behind the wall or in the basement. Since we may now place the unit very near the devices it powers, this enhances the value of the transformer and improves the grounding structure by providing short lead lengths.

Instead of bringing power into a large main breaker on the wall, we can now bring the feeder into what is known as a junction box, or J-Box. Wall space, any space, is valuable in a computer room. A junction box allows us to bring the feeder in under the raised floor. We can buy the J-Box with connectors on it and plug the PDU into the J-Box which may be mounted under the floor just about anywhere.

This gives us an opportunity to run a full size green wire ground back to the building service grounding point. This dedicated ground should be tied to the conduit at both ends, and the conduit carrying the dedicated feeder and ground should not be allowed to touch any other conduit on its way to the building service. Now, we can roll the power center into place and plug it into the J-Box.

Instead of installing a panel board on the wall and running metal conduit to the various devices in the room, we will put the main circuit breaker in the PDU. Also, we will put all the output circuit breakers in the cabinet and label each circuit. Clear identification of each device associated with each circuit is a benefit we may not get with conventional wiring.

Finally, to facilitate installation and future moves, let us use flexible conduit carrying the lines from our PDU to peripheral devices. While we are at it let's put a copper shield around it to shunt to ground any unwanted noise and to protect data and power lines from interfering with one another. Then let's put an insulating coating of plastic around the conduit. This will prevent unwanted electrical signals from being directly injected from other touching metal and will also prevent troublesome ground loops from developing.

We have now given our conduit flexibility, shielding against radiated noise, and insulation from other metal found in the room. This basic power center is a complete, portable, friendly, electrical environment for the computer.

Features and Benefits—A word of caution is appropriate here. Think back for a moment to our discussion in another chapter about the bidding process might not always ensure the best environment for the computer. This same principle applies to PDUs. In the early days when the modular power center was a new concept, it was sold to the DP manager as the proper way to install and protect the computer. Today, there is often no selling involved. In fact, the DP manager may have nothing to say about the PDU that will be purchased.

The PDU has become a commodity and the lowest bidder gets the order. In many cases, the PDU that is provided is the absolute minimum that is required to meet the bid specification and sometimes not even that good. This is not to place blame. The bidding process forces everyone involved to pursue their own self interest and to put price above quality. It is the user who ultimately suffers.

I once had the DP manager of one of the largest computer users in the country tell me that PDUs were PDUs—one was no different from another. Many DP professionals view the PDU as nothing more than what an electrician would have put on or behind the wall. Only now it is in a box called a power center or something.

There are PDUs that may have design flaws like bundling transformer cables from the primary with those of the secondary or using a skinny little wire to tie the transformer core to the ground bus. Although, they may not fully protect the computer, PDUs do an admirable job of replacing conventional wiring. Warren Lewis's idea was to provide the kind of electrical environment that a computer must have to operate without power and grounding problems.

PDUs are available for small computers as well as large mainframes. A minicomputer that is not inside a computer room may have been installed in a closet because that was the only place left. This is a much more hostile environment than a computer room. A PDU in this case makes all the sense in the world. And the cost of a PDU is small in comparison to the computer it protects.

PDUs have a wide range of features and options. Some have provisions for a remote emergency power off button mounted near the exit of the computer room. Often this feature is combined with sensors for temperature and/or humidity which can shut off power if safety parameters are exceeded. Most have a status panel that displays readings like input and output voltage, output current, kVA, percent load, ground current, and input and output phase indicators. A variety of audible alarms will sound for conditions like output over/under voltage, phase loss, and transformer over temperature.

Other features might report on such items as ground integrity, phase rotation, and ground fault interrupt.

The philosophy behind the power system was to provide an electrical structure for the computer designed by computer engineers, as opposed to building wiring which is designed by engineers whose area of expertise is totally different. And the final benefit to purchasing a power system is that the first time we move our computer facility we recover the entire cost of the PDU. It is designed to move with us. Yes, we must install a new feeder at the new location, but the cost will be a small fraction of duplicating the entire power structure with new conventional wiring.

There are some other financial benefits we accrue. A PDU may be depreciated over the life of the computer. Conventional wiring must be depreciated over the life of the building. PDUs can even be leased. For some kinds of equipment there is a strong resale market, too.

But that's not all. The elements of isolation transformers and power distribution are only a part of a new generation of equipment that go one step further—power conditioners.

9

Voltage Regulation

This chapter might have been called power conditioners. Technically, so could the last chapter and the chapter before that. Anything that performs a corrective or preventative role might be termed conditioning. Certainly an isolation transformer conditions power, so do transient suppressors.

Voltage regulators also condition power, and often these devices are advertised as power conditioners. For our purposes, this term is far too broad; since, in one sense or another, everything we are mentioning in the last half of this book conditions power. Therefore, the term regulator more accurately defines the products discussed here.

Filters

But before we leave the thought of conditioning power, let us mention something that may be found in many devices. Filters, as we may remember from basic electronics, are a combination of capacitive and inductive elements connected in such a way that certain signals may or may not pass through them. Low-pass filters are the most common type filters found in power equipment. This differs from ripple filters and the like found in power supplies. Low-pass filters are tuned to pass 60-cycle power and its harmonics, thus forming a nice smooth sine wave. However, noise and high-frequency impulses will be attenuated.

It is not our intention to discuss the theory and operation of filters, although the author does recommend a complete reading of the subject, since the behavior of electricity at different frequencies underlies much of the structure of this book. We do want to point out that many users and consultants will specify filtering on the input, output, or both of many power devices.

A well engineered scheme of input and output filtering in a power center or regulator can probably be justified. Since the engineers of such devices have no idea of the vagaries of each computer site, they try to build a device that will provide a friendly electrical environment for the computer no matter where it is installed.

The key phrase here is well engineered. Power products are subject to the same market pressures as cosmetics. Hanging filters, bells, and whistles on a power line conditioner is similar to shampooing with beer, eggs, or honey. The use of filters may be an intelligent choice or an expensive mistake.

Filters that are not well engineered can cause ground loops, line voltage distortion, or interaction with filtering elements of other devices. On the other hand, proper use of filters and baluns can prevent common-mode noise, ground-loop current problems, protect against noise, and operate efficiently when input and output impedances are matched.

Line-Voltage Regulators

Line-voltage regulators are the solution to the problem of sags and surges. Each computer has, to some degree, the ability to tolerate changes in the line voltage. When the voltage drops long enough below the threshold of the circuit elements inside the computer, and this stored energy has been expended, the computer will shut down. Most computer power supplies have some voltage regulation built into them, but they are designed to handle small changes. Since many of the latest generation of computers will shut themselves down when they sense these variations in voltage, a line-voltage regulator should be used to keep the voltage within the computer's operating range by electronically or mechanically adjusting to fluctuations.

Variable-Ratio Transformer

The motor operated variable-ratio auto transformer is shown in Fig. 9-1. This device has several varieties which either move a wiper arm or change taps by motor power. Changes in voltage are measured against a standard by the voltage sensor. A deviation causes the motor to move to a new position on the transformer thereby compensating for the change in voltage. Altering the transformation ratio keeps the voltage within the computer's tolerance. Some auto-transformer regulators use buck-boost windings to adjust to voltage changes.

The biggest disadvantage to this method is obvious. The response time of a motor-driven regulator is on the order of 10 cycles, an eternity for any computer. Another obvious flaw is the auto transformer provides no isolation unless another transformer were to be placed somewhere else in the circuit. If we are talking about a motor-driven tap changer, spikes or transients would be generated as the connection from one winding to another was

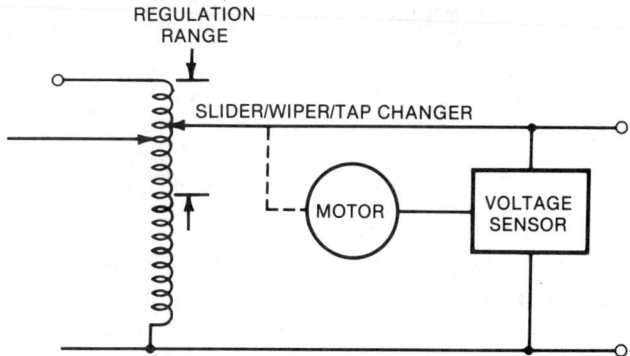

Fig. 9-1.
Motor-operated variable-ratio auto transformer.

broken and remade. A wiping or slider action would use brushes to make contacts which would cause heating and reduce the maximum current rating of the unit.

Variable-Induction Regulators

Induction regulators are constructed like a three-phase motor, but the rotor does not rotate as in a motor. Usually, a motor-operated worm gear moves it. This movement allows the relationship between the rotor and the stator to change causing phase shifts to occur. Voltage regulation results from this changing angle thereby adding or subtracting from the line voltage (Fig. 9-2).

Variable induction regulators are suitable for stabilizing voltage in circuits of hundreds of kilowatts. For computer loads, however, variable-

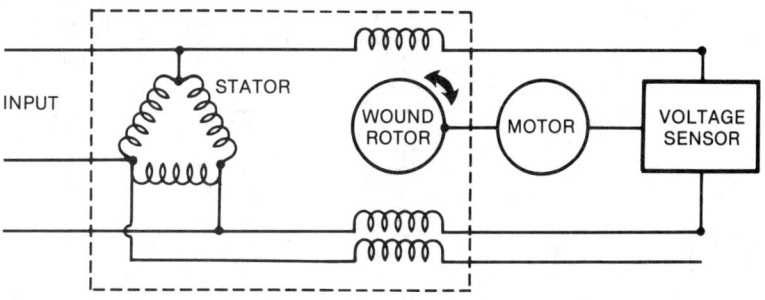

Fig. 9-2.
Variable-induction regulator holds output voltage constant by changing the angle between the rotor and stator.

induction regulators are sluggish. A change can take tens of cycles. In addition, there is virtually no attenuation of impulses between input and output.

Saturable Reactors

Saturable reactors use a feedback circuit to sense the output voltage that produces a dc output that corresponds to the change in voltage. The dc circuit uses a coil positioned around a reactor core so that the magnetic saturation of the core changes in response to the change in dc. The reactor core links this dc coil with an input and output coil. The voltage in the output coil is a function of the degree of magnetic saturation. This action acts like a valve that increases or decreases the output voltage in response to the dc achieving a stable output.

Saturable reactors have a slow response to input changes. The beauty of their operation is they require no moving parts. Again, there is no attenuation between input and output.

Magnetic Coupling Controlled Regulators

These devices (Fig. 9-3) use a direct current-control winding to adjust the saturation in part of a special core structure. The ac flux paths of buck and boost windings are controlled by this action. The buck and boost windings act to raise or lower output voltage in response to a sensing circuit. The regulator sensing circuit is solid state and the voltage changes are smooth. The response time, however, is slow—3 to 6 cycles or longer.

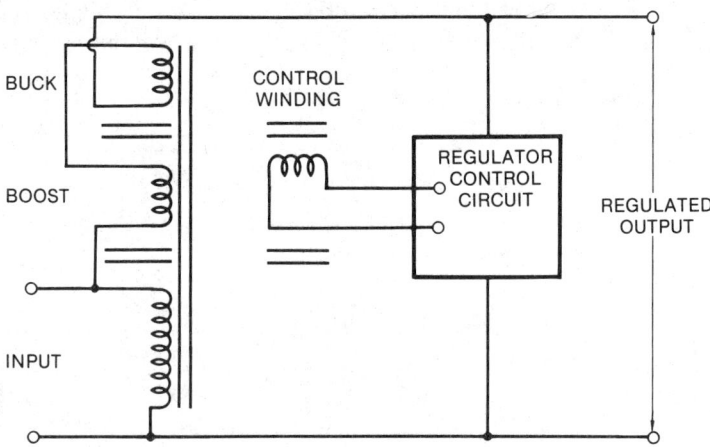

Fig. 9-3.
Magnetic coupling controlled regulator uses controlled buck and boost to regulate voltage.

Isolation Regulators

We do not often see the first few kinds of regulators we have mentioned in the computer environment. The lack of isolation and noise attenuation, slow response, and somewhat outmoded technology of these devices has driven them from the computer environment. By combining the characteristics of a computer grade isolation transformer and overcoming the problem areas, we have the most common regulators in use today. The ferroresonant transformer and the electronic-tap switcher are the two most common and versatile voltage regulators in use. We shall look at both in depth.

Again, the literature does not agree as to what to call devices. Terms like line conditioners, isolator/regulators, and voltage regulators get jumbled up and their definitions can often depend on who you are talking to or what a particular sales brochure might say. The distinguishing characteristic of isolator/regulators is that the output windings are separated from the input windings. The regulation technology is radically different between ferroresonant and tap switching.

Ferroresonant Transformers

A ferroresonant transformer is basically a single-phase device. It is sometimes called a CVT (constant-voltage transformer). Three-phase transformation is accomplished by making the proper connections of three single phase windings to form delta/wye or the desired configuration.

Ferroresonant transformers produce a constant voltage output for a fluctuating input voltage. This can happen because of the way the transformer operates as opposed to the way a simple power transformer operates. Normally, the current in a transformer primary produces flux lines which cut through the secondary inducing a voltage in it.

If we operate a transformer at high enough primary current, the core will become saturated with flux lines. Theoretically, an increase in primary current when the core is saturated will produce no increase in secondary voltage. In this sense then, a transformer driven to saturation is a voltage regulator. Operating a standard power transformer in saturation is impractical since primary saturation currents are so close to short circuit levels.

The ferroresonant transformer is designed to be operated in saturation. If we look at Fig. 9-4, we see that an air gap exists between the primary and secondary windings. This is a key element in determining the regulation characteristic of the transformer. The other element that determines regulation is the value of the capacitor across the secondary.

The air gap gives the center core high reluctance as the current flow starts at low levels. This means that the flux is primarily through the outer core. As the current flow increases, secondary voltage is determined by the turns ratio. As the flux lines increase, the current in the secondary increases, causing the reactance of the secondary winding to increase. When the re-

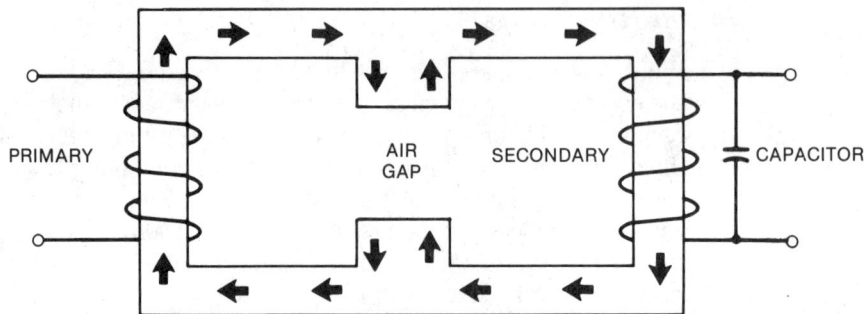

Fig. 9-4.
A simple drawing of the flux paths of a ferroresonant transformer.

actance of the secondary winding rises to become equal to the reactance of the capacitor, the secondary and capacitor become resonant. This causes the reluctance of the center core to drop and the transformer to go into saturation. Subsequent increases in the primary current have a small influence on the secondary voltage.

To compensate for this small change in voltage, another winding can be added (Fig. 9-5). If we place the winding in series opposing the secondary, we can correct the minor variations in voltage.

This ferroresonant-transformer design has been around nearly 40 years as a regulator for controlling voltage to electric lighting and other loads which were not particularly bothered by harmonic distortion. The output of the transformer shown in Fig. 9-5 is a square wave and will not work for computer power requirements. To correct this phenomenon, we add yet another winding.

Fig. 9-6 shows the addition of a neutralizing winding linked to the primary winding by flux leakage so a small amount of line voltage appears across it. Notice also that it is linked to the secondary by flux coupling. This

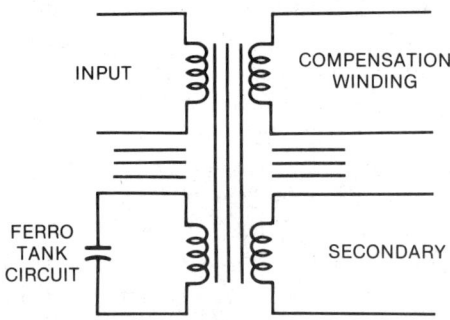

Fig. 9-5.
Ferroresonant transformer with compensating winding to offset voltage variations.

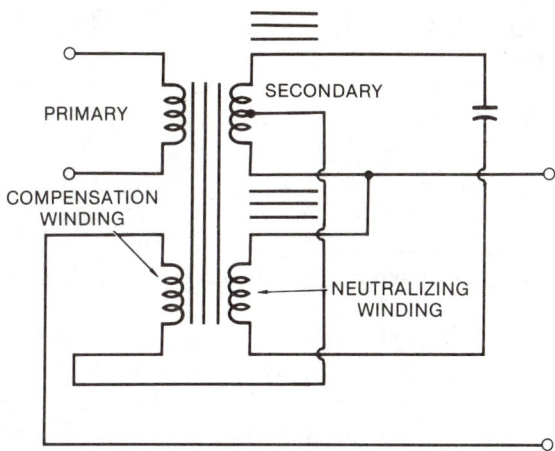

Fig. 9-6.
Adding a neutralizing winding plus additional filtering will produce a sinusoidal output.

arrangement effectively feeds back harmonics against those present in the secondary thereby cancelling one another out. Adding an output filter provides a sine wave with little distortion that is acceptable to sensitive electronic equipment.

A ferroresonant transformer has the unique ability to reduce normal-mode noise. Since the secondary winding is driven to saturation, increases in the primary-winding current flow will not affect the secondary voltage level. Therefore, noise impulses appearing at the input are effectively clipped as a result of the saturation of the secondary.

On the other hand, a ferroresonant transformer has virtually no ability to attenuate common-mode noise. Shielding can be added around the primary and compensation windings to reduce the coupling of common-mode noise.

The ferroresonant transformer has three major shortcomings which need to be explored. If we look carefully we will see these three problems are a logical derivation of the design of the device itself. Going out of resonance, excessive weight, and reduced operating efficiency are the three problems and they are all related to one another. The size of the device will be a deciding factor in just how big these shortcomings are.

First, we look at the tendency of a ferroresonant transformer to go out of resonance. Remember, we said that we drive the secondary into saturation when we achieve resonance between the secondary winding and the capacitor. Actually, this capacitor is a series of small capacitors all connected so their collective capacitive reactances will equal the reactance of the winding at resonance. This forms a tank circuit in which the entire current requirement of the load must circulate. If the load demands more than 125 to 150 percent of the full rated load of the transformer, the tank circuit will go out of resonance. When this happens, the core demagnetizes and the voltage output collapses.

How would the load demand more than 100 percent of full rated load? Inrush current is usually the culprit. When drive motors start up or on initial start-up of most equipment, current demands can be many times the current for a normal running load. Even when we are careful to select a device with sufficient capacity, the inrush of two drives starting can be enough to foil the ferroresonant transformer. There are certain systems that when fed from a properly sized ferroresonant transformer simply will not start up.

This leads to the second problem with ferroresonant-transformer technology, excessive weight. The only way to ensure that the ferroresonant transformer doesn't suddenly go out of resonance and collapse its output voltage is to size the unit against this possibility. It may be necessary to oversize a ferroresonant transformer by as much as 30 percent to avoid this. The alternative is for the manufacturer to do it. Design engineers, knowing of the potential problem, often build in more capacity than the nameplate rating.

The ferroresonant-transformer technology relies on core saturation and multiple windings. It is essentially a single-phase device. Making it a three-phase device is simple but not compact. The size of core and windings all lumped together to form a single three-phase transformer is a bulky package. When you couple these considerations with those sizing issues we just mentioned, you get one large, heavy unit. A ferroresonant transformer will outweigh a standard isolation transformer by five times or more—the size difference is substantial also. One more thing. All that extra iron and wire adds up to additional cost.

This, then, leads to our next problem. Since the ferroresonant-transformer device is always in saturation, it is ready to deliver full load when called upon. If the load is light, the operating efficiency is low. This large, constantly circulating current is still generating heat and using power far in excess of what the load needs. Typically, a ferroresonant transformer is designed to run at no less than 80 percent of full load. At 80 percent it will run at between 85 and 90 percent efficiency. At moderate and light loads efficiency drops dramatically, possibly to 65 percent in some cases. If we run at 80 percent and have a sudden demand for current, we may exceed the ferroresonant transformer's overload capacity. Our argument has come full circle.

Overload protection can be a problem with ferroresonant transformers, since no load, full load, and short circuits vary the current flow so little that a fuse or circuit breaker may not operate selectively enough to see the difference. Ferroresonant transformers can also generate excessive heat and noise. They are also very sensitive to frequency variations because they use a tuned circuit. While this might not be a problem when using utility power, it can be a major problem when using on-site generated power because on-site generators have much less frequency stability than utility power.

Under 10 kVA, many of these problems are small enough not to be key operational issues. Obviously, as size goes up, the magnitude of these issues increases. At 100 kVA, noise, heat, weight, efficiency, and overload conditions need scrutiny.

The good news is that ferroresonant transformers are simple. There are no moving parts to fail. There are a lack of solid-state components that may fail. And there are no adjustments to be made. A ferroresonant transformer or CVT has the ability to regulate over a wide range of input voltages, and the device itself has a high degree of reliability. Under moderate load conditions, efficiency aside, there may be enough energy stored in the core to sustain the output for up to one-half cycle of ride through should the utility power fail. A three-phase ferroresonant transformer might still operate under moderate load almost indefinitely if one phase were to lose power. This, to one degree or another, is true of any three-phase transformer, but because of the tremendous quantity of iron in a ferroresonant transformer the effect is more dramatic.

It should be pointed out that the manufacturers of ferroresonant devices are well aware of these advantages and disadvantages. Each manufacturer, in its own way, has designed enhancements to the basic unit to overcome many of these shortcomings. Let the buyer beware. Some manufacturers build ferroresonant devices and call them something else. It is always wise to ask what technology is being used in spite of the fancy name attached to it.

Tap-Switching Regulators

It hasn't been that long ago that solid-state switching devices were made that could handle high enough voltages and current flows to be useful in power products like the Micropower II shown in Fig. 9-7. When they became available, design engineers were ready for them. Now they had an easy way to overcome the mechanical shackles of the past. The result was the tap-switching regulator.

The silicon-controlled rectifier is not only the key element in the tap-switching regulator, but it is widely used in all sorts of other power devices. This was not the case until recently when large SCRs were developed (triacs are sometimes used in smaller units). This enables switching quickly from one tap to another with little or no disturbance in the waveform from the switching.

The heart of the tap-switching regulator is a computer grade isolation transformer. This is one of the things that makes it such an attractive unit. Because of the transformer design, it has low internal impedance, meaning it can deliver extremely high current demands instantaneously. It is not

Fig. 9-7.
The Micropower II is a 3 to 10 kVA tap-switching regulator. Its back panel can be configured for power distribution. It is a complete portable, friendly electrical environment for the small computer.
(Courtesy Computer Power Systems)

unusual for a transformer of this design to withstand a 1000 percent overload for a very short time. What this means is that inrush currents will have no effect in most cases.

Another advantage is very high efficiency. Efficiencies of up to 96 to 98 percent are common. This is true from about 25 percent to full load. In other words, a tap-switching regulator starts with all the advantages of a high grade isolation transformer.

The first tap switchers were designed to switch when the voltage sine wave crossed the zero-voltage point. This is called the zero-crossing point. There is another zero crossing in the flow of electricity. It is the zero-current-crossing point. Switching taps at the zero-voltage-crossing point seemed like the logical design alternative. Early units were built so that as the regulator changed it changed at the zero-crossing point.

The problem with this approach was that computer loads do not usually present a unity power factor to the power source. This is due to inductive and capacitive reactance within the computer circuits. Because of this, the current waveform may lead or lag the voltage waveform. Switching at the zero-voltage crossing ignores the fact that substantial current may be flowing during the switching process. This puts stress on the SCRs and can cause switching transients. These spikes due to phase difference between voltage and current were one of the principal arguments against the tap switcher.

Today, most designs have gone to switching at the zero-current-crossing point. Switching at zero-current crossing eliminates much of the worry over switching impulses. It is done by placing a current doughnut around the line. The other advantage to this method is that no current is flowing through the SCRs when the switching takes place. Therefore, no undue stress is placed on the SCRs during the transfer.

There are three basic designs for tap switchers. Fig. 9-8 shows an earlier version. In this design, the output voltage was measured and a feedback circuit switched from one SCR to another as needs required. This design in many respects is ideal. It looks at the same voltage the load sees which enables it to make adjustments that more accurately reflect the requirements of the load.

Putting the SCRs on the primary side isolates the load from any switching transients that might occur. Also, since the primary side is the high-voltage side in most computer-room transformers, the stress on the SCR is considerably lower. Typically, this would be a 480 primary with a 208 secondary. Ohm's law tells us that much less current will flow in the primary than in the secondary. This means that primary switching will be easier on solid-state components.

The big disadvantage to this design is similar to the disadvantage we saw in the magnetic-coupled buck-boost regulator. Because of response time in the feedback circuit, tap changes are slower than other designs.

Figure 9-9 overcomes this time lag by moving the taps to the secondary side. This gives us the advantage of fast response time and accurate voltage

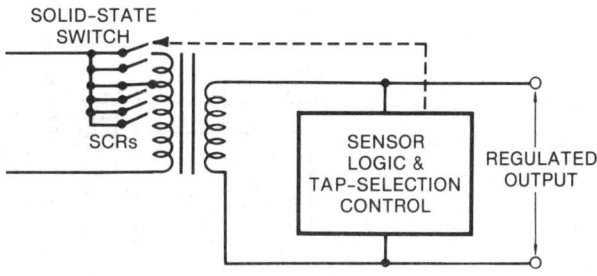

Fig. 9-8.
One of the earliest versions of a tap switcher with SCRs on the primary side and switching logic on the secondary side.

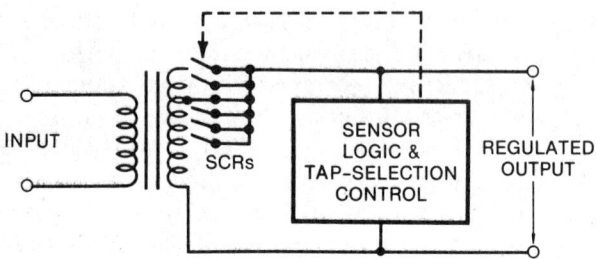

Fig. 9-9.
Secondary side tap switching.

adjustments. The disadvantages are that any switching transients have no transformer to buffer them from the load. And, the full-load current is now flowing through the solid-state device.

This brings us to Fig. 9-10. In this design we regulate the input voltage to the primary winding of the transformer. Here we have the advantage of buffering from tap-switching transients. We are on the high-voltage side of the transformer so current flow is relatively lower through the SCRs. And fast switching can be accomplished because of the relationship of the logic-control circuit. The disadvantage is that regulation to the load is not as exact as in the design shown in Fig. 9-9.

Which design is best, primary switching or secondary switching? It's the kind of thing engineers and super-techs might debate. For larger kVA sizes, the limits of the technology seem to dictate primary switching due to the current handling capability of SCRs. At lower sizing requirements, this is no longer a big concern.

One argument that seems to continue is one over the issue of response time. Depending on which salesperson you hear, faster is said to be better. But more thoughtful people know that faster can defeat the whole purpose behind the regulator itself.

What we are referring to is the claim that one regulator can switch in

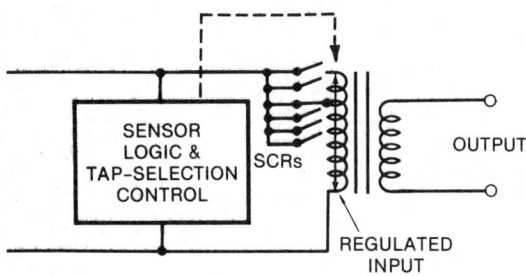

Fig. 9-10.
Tap switching with regulated input.

as little as one-half cycle. This line of thinking goes on to conclude that the fastest switcher is the better switcher. But is it really? Inside the power supply of the computer is a small regulator. As a surge starts to occur, it will try to adjust the voltage down. At the same time, our very fast tap switcher is changing to a tap to lower the voltage. The result from a momentary surge might be an even longer sag caused by interaction between the regulator and the power supply. It might not stop there. The power supply might then compensate in the other direction while the regulator reacts to the return of the voltage to normal. This seesaw kind of interaction is termed tap dancing and it is detrimental to optimum computer operation.

A reasonable approach to switching is to extend the sensing period to one full cycle then switch in the following cycle. This will avoid tap dancing and avoid making too many unnecessary adjustments.

Tap-switching regulators do have disadvantages. SCRs are vulnerable to breakdown when subjected to large surge currents. It is possible to observe switching noise, although this can be greatly reduced using zero-current crossing. And the voltage adjustments are in steps rather than in smooth continuous changes.

There are many approaches to voltage regulation. Ferroresonant transformers and tap switchers are two of the most popular answers to the regulation problem. While a ferroresonant transformer, under just the right conditions, may ride through a very short term (less than one-half cycle) blackout, a tap switcher cannot. In the next chapter, we will look at technologies that can weather even blackouts. The interesting thing about all these varied approaches is that each unique product has inherent advantages and disadvantages. This places a burden on the buyer, DP manager, field engineer, or other decision-maker to be knowledgeable about the technology behind each approach.

10

M-G Sets, RUPS, and UPS

The study of rotary and static backup power products could easily be a complete book in itself. Not only is the debate over which technology is preferable long and detailed, but the comparison of manufacturers' products within each classification brings out imperatives that a buyer must be aware of. Our purpose in this chapter is to give the reader enough of an understanding of these products to separate jargon and hype from reality and technical advantages.

M-G Sets

M-G (motor-generator) sets, sometimes called motor alternators, are yet another kind of power-conditioning device. They are inherently capable of isolating computer loads from variations of input power. As the name motor-generator implies, this device uses a motor to turn a generator. This arrangement has several immediate advantages.

Since the utility power is used by a motor to provide torque to an independent power source, the generated power can be regulated independent of line voltage changes that may occur at the motor's input. The rotational mass of the spinning generator provides inertia that can be a source of stored energy during momentary sags or outages. This prevents drastic changes, up or down, in the input voltage from affecting the output. Finally, the windings of the motor are electrically separated from the windings of the generator. This acts to isolate the input from the output giving the device the common-mode-attenuation characteristics of an isolation transformer (Fig. 10-1).

The main advantage of rotating-power technology is the ability to ride through momentary outages. During a sag or total loss of power, the gen-

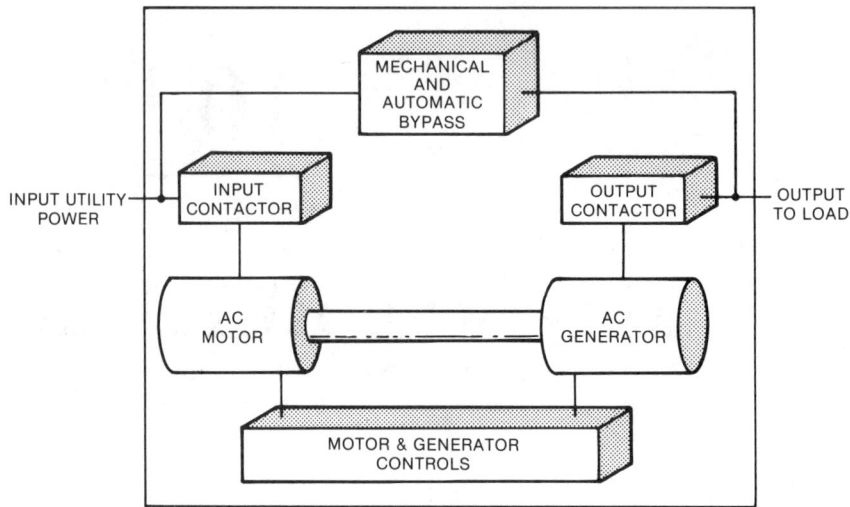

Fig. 10-1.
In this M-G set, utility power drives the ac motor which in turn drives the generator.

erator will continue to provide power to the load for a period of up to 500 milliseconds. This rotational inertia can be increased through the use of a flywheel. With this additional spinning mass, ride through can last many seconds.

Nothing comes free, however. This additional ride-through capability using a flywheel is achieved by adding weight, size, and cost to the system. Also, efficiency and bearing life must be sacrificed. Increased air friction because of the flywheel causes decreased efficiency. The flywheel takes more input power during start-up and a larger motor to restore RPM lost during an outage. According to an update written for the *IEEE Orange* book, Dick Bowyer states that it takes a mass of steel approximately 6 inches thick and 4 feet in diameter to maintain a 30 kVA load with less than 1 cycle frequency change for 0.5 second.

Induction Motors

There are three basic motors that may drive an AC generator: the induction motor, the synchronous motor, and the DC motor. DC motors are used in conjunction with a battery backup system called RUPS. Like many of the product approaches we have talked about in earlier chapters, induction and synchronous motors have advantages and disadvantages.

The single biggest advantage of an induction motor is cost. Among the alternatives, induction motors can deliver the most horsepower for the dollar. Another advantage of the induction motor is its good starting torque.

This means it has the ability to start under full-load conditions or to restart after a momentary outage.

The induction motor has a big disadvantage. The rotor of an induction motor turns slightly slower than the rotating field produced by the power source. If the motor and generator are connected end to end by their shafts (1 to 1 ratio), the unit will be unable to produce 60 Hz power from a 60 Hz source. Another way of stating this is to say that the output RPM is less than that of a synchronous motor because of what is called slip. This means that a motor rated for 1800 RPM would produce on the order of 1790 RPM with a slip of 0.4 to 0.7 percent.

The shaft speed and frequency of the output power decrease as the load increases. A low slip type induction motor will reduce generator-output frequency by about 0.3 Hz. Dynamic load changes might mean variations of from 1750 to 1780 RPM and frequency shifts from 58.3 to 59.4 Hz. Most computer manufacturers specify frequency to be within plus or minus 0.5 Hz. The answer to this problem might be to oversize the induction motor enough, possibly three to four times, to reduce the effects of changing load requirements. Obviously, this introduces cost, weight, heat, and other inefficiencies.

Synchronous Motors

Synchronous motors with a 1 to 1 coupling to its associated generator lock on to the 60 Hz frequency and the result is no degradation of output frequency. This means that load demand and input voltage will not affect the shaft speed and output frequency up to the pull-out torque. Synchronous motors typically have better efficiency than induction motors. In addition, synchronous motors have a power factor of unity as opposed to the 80 to 90 percent of an induction motor. This built-in power factor correction capability has been a selling point of this technology.

The one large disadvantage associated with synchronous motors is they have a very weak starting torque. Usually, a small auxiliary motor must be used to help start the synchronous motor. Sometimes called pony motors, they are mounted piggy-back style and coupled by belts or pulleys to larger motors.

Overall Considerations

Some manufacturers have overcome these difficulties by using a motor that literally converts from an induction motor to a synchronous motor as the frequency moves above 59.5 Hz. Other manufacturers have combined the motor and generator stators into one stator. Still others have designed synchronous motors with starting-pole-face windings which provide starting torque.

The motor seems to be the most controversial item in an M-G set, but nearly as important is the electronic control. As smarter chips have been made available, the design of the electronic heart of the unit has become more and more a competitive factor.

The MTBF (mean time between failure) of a motor-generator has been demonstrated to be very long. The bearings are the most vulnerable to failure, but their replacement can be planned (approximately once every 7 to 10 years). Today, with more and more electronics being packed into all equipment, the MTBF of a motor-generator also relates to the complicated control circuitry as well as the actual moving parts. More about MTBF later.

RUPS

RUPS (rotary uninterruptible power system) is the term used to describe an M-G set using a battery backup system (Fig. 10-2). This is a standard type M-G set with the addition of a DC motor that can run off a battery bank if power should fail. While utility power is normal, the DC motor acts as a generator that charges the batteries. When utility power fails, the control circuits of the unit operate the DC motor from battery power. The result is a continuous flow of power to the load. The rotary UPS can be housed in a cabinet as shown in Fig. 10-3.

There are alternatives to this design, but this design and others that will be described gives a potential buyer an advantage. Most power failures are momentary, less than a few hundred milliseconds. The rotating inertia of an M-G set can provide enough ride through to survive those kinds of

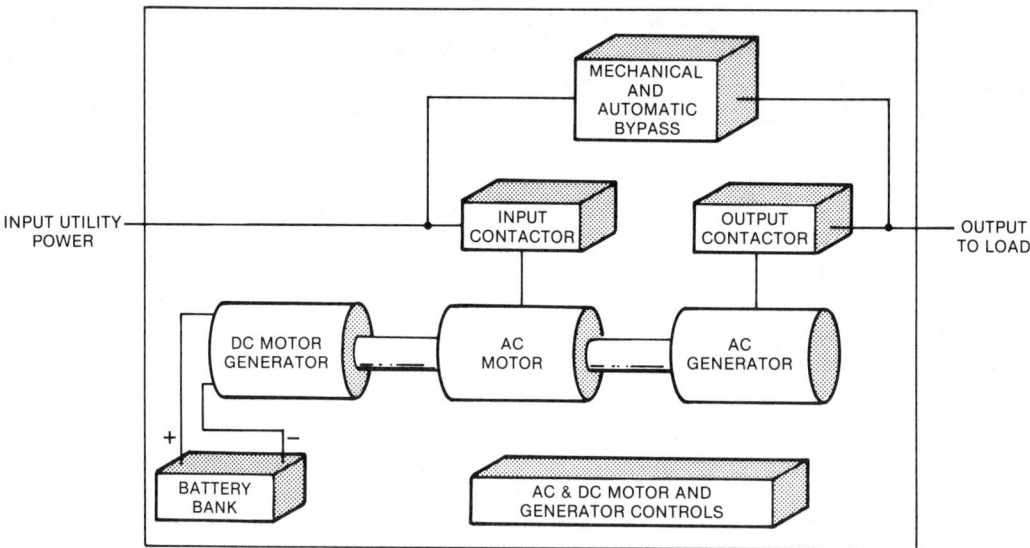

Fig. 10-2.
Rotary UPS—RUPS

Fig. 10-3.
This attractive cabinet houses the ultrapower series rotary UPS.
(Courtesy Atlas Energy Systems of Irvine, CA)

events. If the customer can afford only that much protection, he or she may buy the M-G set and wait until more funds are available to buy the additional motor and/or batteries thereby creating a RUPS. This modular, add on, approach has been used by several manufacturers as an attractive way to build toward the future. It can be less painful but does result in more capital outlay in the long run. Alternatives to the DC motor/generator approach include the use of a rectifier charger to convert incoming utility power to DC. This DC is used by a motor to turn a generator and by batteries as a charging source (Fig. 10-4). Although less expensive than the first design, it has the disadvantage of the constant running DC motor and the subsequent brush wear and maintenance. However, modern silicon rectifiers are more efficient than DC motors for charging batteries.

Yet another approach is to substitute a solid-state-AC inverter for the DC motor in Fig. 10-4. The arrangement is depicted in Fig. 10-5. A variation of this is to make the inverter on line all the time (Fig. 10-6).

Finally, there are setups using internal combustion engines to either drive the M-G set through a clutch, or an engine generator which supplies supplemental power in the event of a failure. Both designs use the ride-through time generated by a flywheel to start and engage the action of the engine.

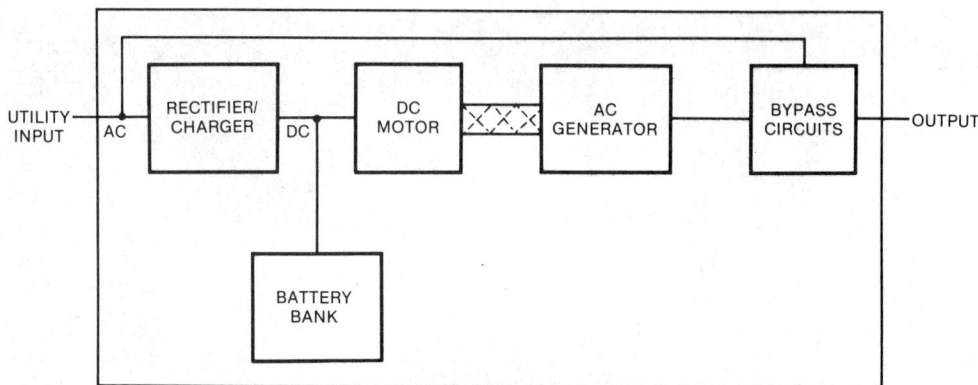

Fig. 10-4.
Battery/dc motor/ac generator.

All UPS systems have one form or another of a bypass switch. There are three reasons to have a bypass switch. The first is to supply power to the load while maintenance or repair is performed on the unit. The second is to connect the load to utility power in case of a failure in the UPS. And the third is to provide a nondamaging path for fault currents to flow. Large currents can be a source of damage to UPS products. It is desirable to pass this current requirement upstream rather than to risk passing it through the UPS.

Before we leave the subject of rotating technology, we must point out

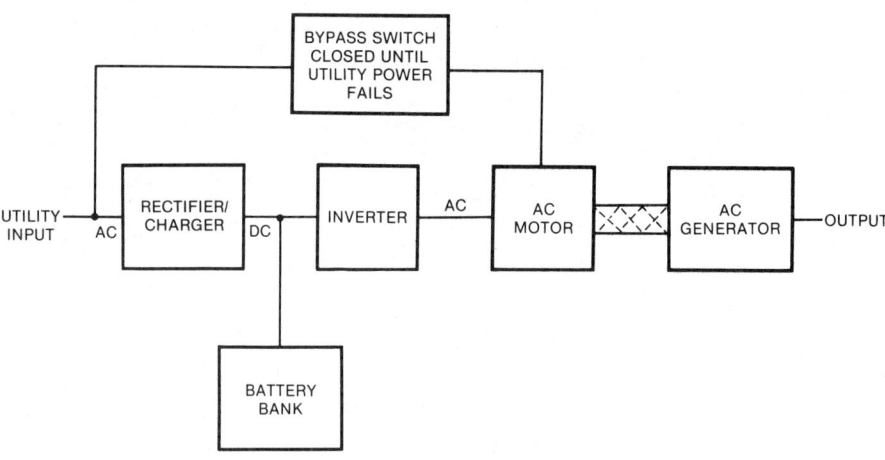

Fig. 10-5.
Off-line inverter/mg system.

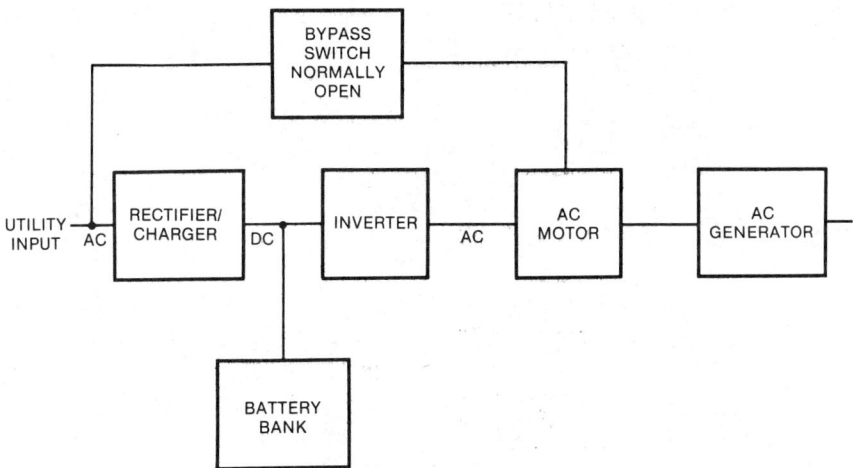

Fig. 10-6.
On-line inverter/M-G system—bypass switch is normally open.

that over the years many large computers have required 415 Hz power. Although there is a trend away from this, use of the 415 Hz M-G set and 415 Hz RUPS helped establish it as a credible product among a large population of DP professionals.

UPS

More correctly termed static UPS (uninterruptible power systems), they have no moving parts and are the most widely used form of backup power for computers. In recent years, advances in solid-state technology have improved the performance of UPS and reduced their price. Today, there are UPS available from a few hundred watts to systems of thousands of kilowatts. Static UPS manufacturers can boast of something RUPS manufacturers can't, they have brought the UPS into the computer room. For the first time, electronic and battery technology will let the static UPS fit in a cabinet small enough to fit in a computer room instead of a basement or equipment room.

UPS Building Blocks

Figure 10-7 shows the basic building blocks of a static UPS. We can see that power from the AC source is converted to DC by the rectifier/battery charger. This DC feeds both the inverter and the battery bank. If the source power should ever fail, power from the batteries is instantaneously available to drive the inverter. The inverter converts the DC back into AC for the load. The static-transfer-bypass switch transfers the load to the bypass power source when the current demand exceeds the ability of the UPS to deliver. The manual bypass is used for maintenance and repair.

Notice that the bypass power source may not be the main power source. Sometimes it is more desirable to have a redundant feeder feeding the bypass line. Usually the reason is that the main input-voltage level is 480 volts. Often the output is the computer utilization voltage of 208 volts. Obviously, the voltage of the bypass must also be at the utilization voltage.

Rectifier/Charger—The first building block is the rectifier/charger. This device must be able to provide peak current demands to the inverter and full charge to the batteries at the same time. This means that it must be able to handle overloads of up to 150 percent for short periods. After an outage when the batteries are low, the rectifier/charger must be able to supply 100 percent power to the load plus another 15 to 25 percent power to charge the batteries. The quality of power charging the batteries is important, since improper charging can shorten battery life.

The time it takes to charge batteries is typically from 8 to 10 times the discharge time. Therefore, if an outage lasted 1 hour, it would take 8 to 10 hours to fully recharge the batteries.

When an outage has taken place, it is necessary to protect the rectifier/charger from these huge inrush currents. Most well designed UPSs allow for a soft-start or walk-in period of about 15 seconds. Current limiting is applied so that no more than 20 to 25 percent current flows initially. This is allowed to step up to 100 percent over the soft-start period.

Current limiting is an important factor during a sag in voltage. The

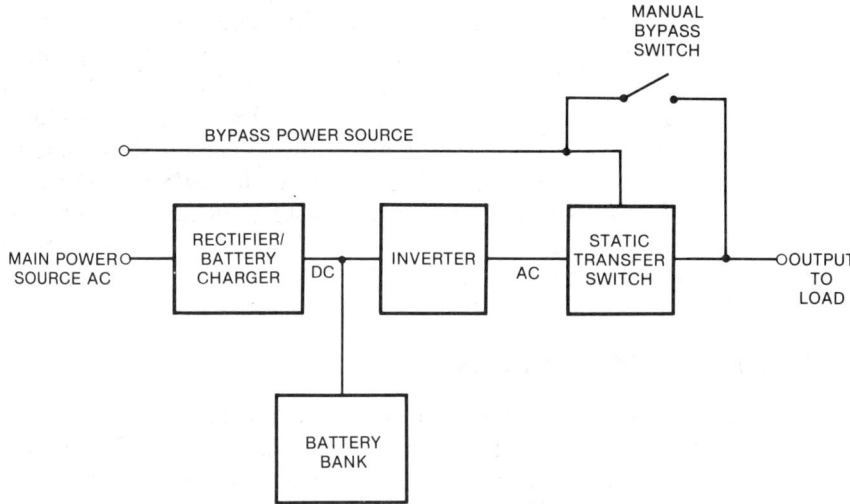

Fig. 10-7. Basic building blocks of a UPS.

UPS will maintain output voltage while input voltage goes down, causing increased current flow. It is necessary to limit this current flow to approximately 125 percent of normal input current. When the voltage falls below −15 percent, the unit will go to battery power.

Inverter—The inverter is perhaps the most controversial area of the UPS. There are several different approaches that have been used by various manufacturers. Which design a customer might select bears directly on the quality of power the UPS will deliver. Each vendor has a story to tell as to why one design is better than the other. A look at Fig. 10-7 shows us that if the inverter fails we must go to the bypass. The job of the inverter is to change DC voltage from the rectifier/charger to pulsating DC which, when filtered, becomes AC. It is the most important section of the total unit.

There are three basic methods of converting DC to AC in UPS inverter designs: the ferroresonant inverter, the pulse-width modulation inverter, and the step-wave inverter.

The ferroresonant inverter UPS (Fig. 10-8) has all the inherent problems and advantages of the ferroresonant regulator that was discussed in an earlier chapter. It is considerably more bulky than other designs, adds more losses to the system, and does not behave well under overload conditions.

The pulse-width modulation inverter (Fig. 10-9) produces a series of variable-width pulses that can be easily adjusted and filtered into high-quality AC. The advantages of pulse-width modulation inverter are its small filter component size and, when coupled with microprocessor control logic, it can respond to changes in the load. It has high efficiency and compact construction. These features make the pulse-width modulation inverter a popular design for "in room" models (Fig. 10-10 and 10-11) which sit next

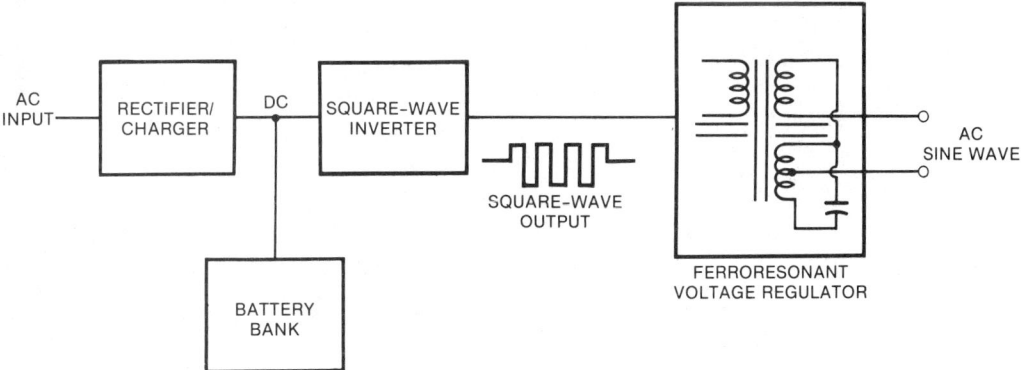

Fig. 10-8.
The ferroresonant inverter uses a ferroresonant-voltage regulator to convert square-wave voltage to sinusoidal voltage.

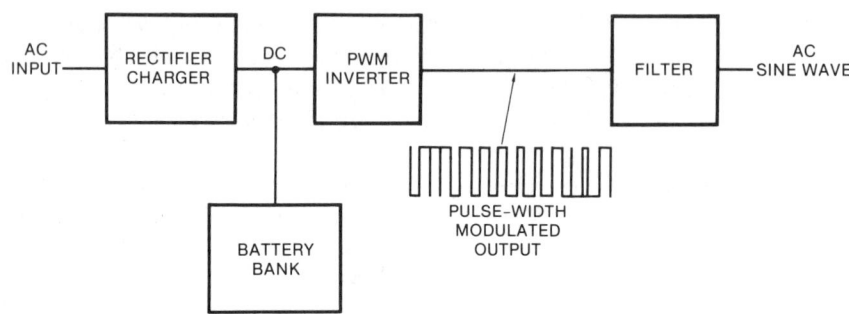

Fig. 10-9.
The PWM inverter provides a series of variable-width pulses which are shaped by a filter.

to the computer rather than in an equipment room or basement such as the UPS unit shown in Fig. 10-12.

The step-wave inverter has been the choice of the larger manufacturers of UPS for many years. A semi-sine wave output, however, allows output filters to be smaller with lower losses. There are two basic designs of step-wave inverters: 6 step inverter and 12 step inverter. It would appear that

Fig. 10-10.
The AP100.
(Courtesy Emerson Computer Power)

Fig. 10-11.
The AP300.
(Courtesy Emerson Computer Power)

the 12-step wave would be more desirable. Obviously, a wave with 12 small steps (Fig. 10-13) is easier to filter to a smooth sine wave than one with 6 large steps. The problem is that the inverter that produces these 12 steps might contain as many as 48 SCRs as opposed to only 12 SCRs for the 6 step method. The six-step design requires bigger and more expensive filter components. However, this filter has the advantage of being tuned to the same odd harmonics that are produced by the computer's own switching power supply. The output harmonic content of both the 6- and 12-step designs is comparable. The six-step design has the advantage of a simpler layout with a lower component count that theoretically makes the product more reliable. Suppressing load-generated harmonics is a bonus of the six-step design.

On-Line Versus Standby

There are many hybrids, combinations, and variations of the three inverter designs we have discussed. Another kind of product we have not discussed is called the standby power system. Designs are similar to those of UPS

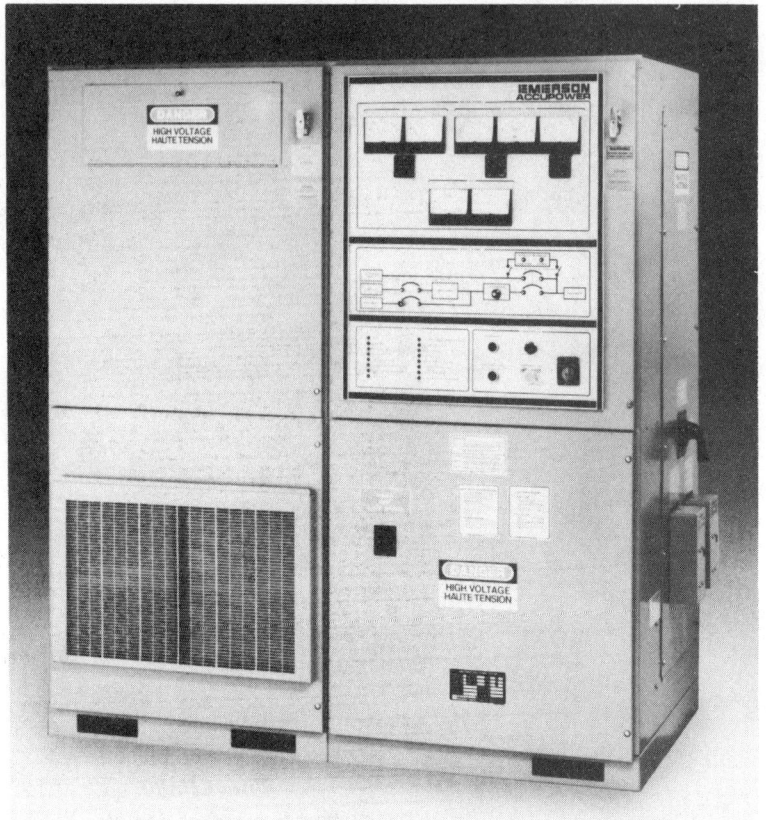

Fig. 10-12.
Large sizes of UPS come in industrial grade cabinets and are designed to be installed in equipment rooms or basements.
(Courtesy Emerson Electric Industrial Controls Division)

products. The single biggest difference is that the computer is operated from raw utility power until an outage is detected, then batteries are switched into the circuit to supply power to the load. While off-line or standby systems are cheaper due to the smaller size of the charger, the less sophisticated inverter, and the elimination of an elaborate bypass circuit, a transient of significant size can be the by-product of its switching.

Under normal operation, the power is fed from the raw utility line. This means that there is no power conditioning being performed. Transfer time from the utility feed to the batteries may be from 2 to 48 milliseconds. Some computers may see this as an outage. If there are problems with the inverter, they will not be detected until there is an outage because the inverter is only in operation at that time. Because a smaller trickle charger is used, recharge time may be significantly longer.

On-line systems are much more expensive than off-line systems. How-

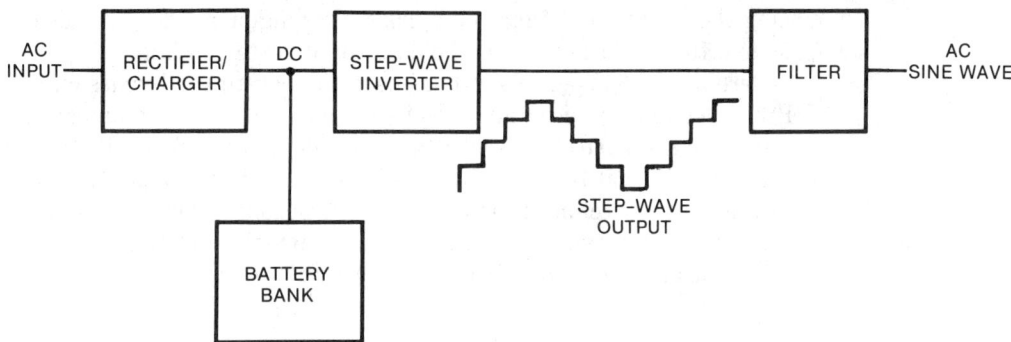

Fig. 10-13.
Step-wave inverters produce a semi-sine wave output which is then filtered.

ever, they are the system of choice for most installations because they provide continuously conditioned power to the critical load. On-line UPS provides isolation from both voltage and frequency variations. There is no switching transient generated when power is switched to the batteries. Battery recharge time is generally faster. The use of an on-line inverter and static-transfer switch ensure power is always delivered to the load.

When 100 percent of the load is suddenly switched to the inverter in an off-line system, thermal stress of components can be a threat to reliable operation. This is not a concern in an on-line system because the load is continuously being served by the inverter.

You may have noticed we use terms like normally, generally, could, and maybe. As with all of the equipment we have discussed in this book, each design has advantages and disadvantages. Engineers are continually coming up with methods of compensating for a weakness at the expense of some other operational consideration.

Transfer Switches

Switching from the inverter to raw utility power may occur for several reasons. A fault somewhere in the load circuit could damage the UPS unless the load is transferred to a bypass. This allows sufficient current to flow to clear the fault by blowing a fuse or tripping a breaker. An internal failure of some kind will also cause the load to be transferred to the bypass line. Even very heavy load current demands in excess of what the inverter can safely deliver will be transferred momentarily to the bypass.

The topic of fault clearing generates controversy among UPS manufacturers. Each design transfers the load a little differently. And each design brings the load back on line differently. Some poor designs are constantly bouncing the load to and from the bypass. One ingenious design pulses the bypass line to clear a fault while holding the inverter on line.

There are two types of switches used to operate the bypass circuit of a UPS: electromechanical and electronic or static. Electromechanical-transfer switches sense changes and operate relays. Transfer-switching time is on the order of 50 to 100 milliseconds. Electrostatic- or static-transfer switches have a switching time of 3 to 4 milliseconds. These switches are in addition to the mechanical make-before-break maintenance bypass switches that are included in nearly every UPS.

Redundancy

It is not unusual to find that a given site has a fixed cost for downtime. An airline, for instance, may have calculated that when their computerized-reservation system goes down, they start losing revenue. This could be because impatient customers go to other airlines. The cost of downtime is a very real problem in most data centers. Costs exceeding 50,000 to 100,000 dollars per hour are not unheard of. For this reason, many companies choose a redundant system.

We can define redundancy as one or more UPS modules than necessary to hold up the load during an outage. This costs much more than a simple single-module system. But the cost of downtime is so great that many companies need redundancy to protect themselves.

The advantages of redundancy start with the fact that if one module became inoperative, the other module would be of sufficient size to supply power to the load. Another important feature of redundancy is sharing. Since the modules are connected in parallel, the power requirement is shared by both modules. This reduces the possibility of overloads and prolongs the life of the equipment (Fig. 10-14).

In situations where uptime is critical, the UPS is in turn backed up by one or more engine generators. Battery time is used to fire up the generators and bring them to full speed. Then automatic circuits switch the load to the generators. Huge data centers might have many tens of thousands of gallons of fuel stored on site to carry the system through a prolonged blackout.

It should be noted that in some very large installations the multimodule approach is the only way to build a UPS large enough to carry the load. By putting units in parallel, the size of a UPS can be thousands of kVA.

The cost of downtime can usually be used to justify the purchase of a quality UPS system. But, as we have stated in earlier chapters, this consideration is often ignored in favor of price. There are UPS manufacturers that build the cheapest product that will meet the minimum requirements of most bid specifications. Since the UPS must always provide quality power to the load, it would seem that a quality product backed by a company that will stand behind it makes sense.

A DP manager recently disclosed that when his data center lost power

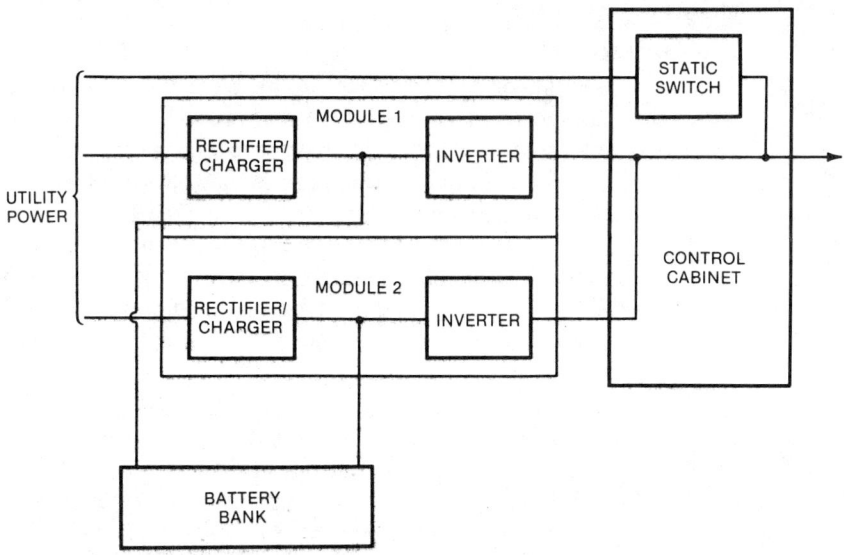

Fig. 10-14.
A redundant system using two UPS modules.

it took him 8 hours to fully restore the system. This is an incredible length of time considering this was a small data center that served a nationwide network of offices and manufacturing facilities. This data center is obviously an ideal candidate for a UPS.

With the introduction of smaller, more powerful computers, recovery time is more and more important. Many new computer systems will begin a programmed cycle down if power goes off. They are designed to recover (theoretically) to the exact program instruction point that was executed when the power went off. This is a great idea, but circumstances might dictate that recovery time could be on the order of 30 minutes to 3 hours depending on the memory and programming load. The ideal solution is the installation of a UPS.

Batteries

A battery is really a group of single cells connected either in series or parallel. Batteries come in two basic types in the UPS environment: lead acid and sealed maintenance free.

The lead acid type battery must be inspected and cared for. Like a car battery, it must be filled with water and it must be vented so dangerous gas that is emitted during charging does not accumulate. Sealed maintenance-free batteries are sealed and are maintenance free. But, like so much in life, maintenance comes free only at the expense of life expectancy. Sealed-type batteries have one-fourth to one-half of the useful life of a lead-acid battery.

The sheer physical size of the batteries and the racks they come in plus the footprint of the UPS itself are significant considerations. Safety, operating temperatures, and even earthquakes are important considerations in planning, installing, and maintaining a large UPS.

Small in-room designs use sealed batteries, come in attractive cabinets, and are on casters for mobility. Venting is not a problem and they will fit inside a normal freight elevator. It is not unusual to see a large UPS being hoisted high overhead and placed inside an unfinished building. In an existing site, walls and windows may have to be removed to accommodate a UPS.

MTBF and MTTR

As we mentioned before, MTBF stands for *mean time between failures*. MTTR stands for *mean time to repair*. Any system, rotary or static, that backs up a computer system must be extremely reliable in order to justify the expense of purchasing and installing one. These two acronyms relate mathematically to Mil-STD 217B. This standard developed by the military is the basis for evaluating the reliability of certain equipment. Originally, it was to be applied to individual components like resistors and capacitors. Later the mathematics was applied to model reliability for assemblies and then entire working units.

Although statistics don't lie, there are many ways of interpreting and rearranging the facts. The battle among manufacturers to show the highest reliability rages on. Most static UPS manufacturers boast of MTBFs of 100,000 hours or much longer. Most RUPS manufacturers claim reliability in excess of 500,000 hours. Some literature claims that static UPSs have almost twice the MTBF of rotary UPSs and can be repaired in one-third the time. Still other literature claims rotary products have four to five times the MTBF. Of course, each says theirs is the easiest to repair.

So what are we supposed to believe? When evaluating one system against another, it may be impossible to answer the MTBF, MTTR challenge by looking at literature and listening to company employees. There are a few things that we might look for that will give us a warm and fuzzy feeling about the MTBF figures we are being shown. First, we might ask to look at the backup data and talk to some other users if historical data is used. A visual inspection of the equipment will tell much about its ease of repair. Ask about component counts, number of circuit boards, and the like. Even factory inspections might be called for to determine quality control procedures, final testing, manufacturing techniques, and calibration. The point is that a good, clean, simple design that is assembled from high quality components which is laid out well and tested thoroughly will perform reliably.

But all equipment fails. Issues like field service, spare parts, and ease of repair are critical to uptime. This is not to say that MTBF and MTTR figures are not relevant, they are. But it makes no sense to buy a product with a little higher published MTBF when the firm has no field service in the area. All the issues must be evaluated to determine maximum satisfaction at any given site.

Personal preference is often a consideration. Many DP managers have a preference for static technology over rotary, or vice versa. No amount of literature or data will change their mind. One method has tradeoffs over the other. For example, static UPSs tend to be slightly less efficient, while rotary UPSs are more noisy. Rotary technology is viewed by many as outdated, obsolete, and too mechanical. Static UPSs can take up more floor space. The list goes on, but things like esthetics and image can be considerations in the decision-making process, legitimate or not.

One thing is clear. The trend has been away from moving parts and toward solid-state devices. Rotary manufacturers have built more sophisticated control devices using printed-circuit boards, thyristors, SCRs, and microprocessors, further blurring the reliability and repair distinctions between the two approaches. And to stay competitive, rotary manufacturers are trying to follow the shrinking size of the computer and its power requirements, which is something static UPS manufacturers have already accomplished.

With the smaller power requirements of mini and personal computers, UPS manufacturers have responded with smaller products that are more esthetically matched to the appropriate environment. Today, the purchase of a UPS to support a PC is often a requirement for ensured performance at a fraction of the total cost of the system. We have waited until Chapter 12 to discuss the technology that is used in the most critical environments. Even the PCs are being used to support worldwide networks of users on a 24 hour basis. Certainly, the threat of power outages is a concern for every user from the major data center to the home or office.

11

Batteries for UPS Systems

In the last chapter we touched on the subject of batteries as an integral part of a working UPS system. But batteries are an important subject in and of themselves. In this chapter we will look deeper into the subject.

The role of batteries in today's power equipment does not vary. Battery power would seem to be a fairly straightforward subject. But wait! What happens when you order a UPS and you must install the battery yourself? Suppose you are an in-house site engineer. Is battery maintenance suddenly part of your job? What do you mean you just found out the batteries were in a separate room? You say the DP manager wants three hours of battery power? How do we get that?

Suddenly batteries become a little more important when people start asking a lot of questions.

Let's start at the beginning. A battery is an electrochemical device that converts stored chemical energy into electrical energy. The basic unit of a battery is called a *cell*. The cell is made up of plates and electrolyte. It is the chemical reaction of the plates with the electrolyte that causes the flow of electrons within the cell.

From the cell we graduate to the *jar*. The jar is the actual container of the cell. As many as six cells may be found in one jar. What we call a battery in layman's terms is really a number of cells packaged together. Most curious children (even adults) have dismantled a spent flashlight battery to see what was inside. The square battery we normally associate with transistor radios is a 9-volt battery made up of six 1 1/2-volt cells.

Other devices that require more power might use four AA batteries. This would yield 6 volts. But since the cell size is larger, more capacity is available. Each different device has differing design considerations. The combination of cell size, voltage required, and cell life are all taken into account in deciding which battery is appropriate.

Sizing batteries for UPS is not much different. All the same considerations come into play. This leads us to the next term in battery language, string. A string is a single chain of battery cells or jars which produce a single flow of current. Multiple strings are then connected in parallel. A string is normally expressed in terms of cells rather than jars. A typical number of cells per string to support a mainframe computer might be 171 to 181. The number of cells per jar remains the same throughout the string, so calculating the number of jars is simple. It is important to know the number of jars so that plans can be made to house batteries and their racks.

Battery Types

Uninterruptible power systems are designed to operate from almost any kind of battery. Of course, the battery voltage and current configurations must conform to the UPS specifications. There are five basic types of batteries we might find used in the typical computer facility. First, there are nickel-cadmium, alkaline, and lead calcium gel cell batteries. Then come three varieties of wet cell, lead-acid batteries: lead antimony, lead calcium, and Plante', or pure lead. There are two other considerations that are important other than the physical properties of each type of battery: manufacturer's warranty and expected life.

Lead Acid

In UPS applications we see that the batteries spend most of their life floating. That is the rectifier charger maintains the battery charge while the batteries sit or float on the DC bus waiting for an outage to occur. It is this floating characteristic that makes lead-acid batteries so often the choice for UPS applications. Add to that their relatively low cost and excellent reliability and it's easy to see why their use is widespread.

Lead-acid batteries use sponge-like lead plates as electrodes and sulfuric acid as the solution for the electrolyte. As the cells discharge, the chemical reaction taking place produces lead sulfate at the plates and water in the electrolyte. When charged, the opposite reaction occurs. The amount of charge can be determined by measuring the specific gravity or electrolyte concentration, which increases during charge and decreases during discharge.

Ventilation and Temperature—Lead-acid batteries produce hydrogen gas while they are being charged. This is why a battery room will have large fans venting room air to the outside to prevent the buildup of gas in the room. Both the size of the room and the number of batteries must be taken into account when providing for ventilation. A rule of thumb is from one to four air exchanges per hour for safety and the comfort of on-site personnel.

You might wonder what happens during an outage. Obviously, the fans won't work and thus no ventilation will take place. Lead-acid batteries only give off gas when they charge, so when they discharge this is not a problem.

We know that battery operation results from chemical interactions with each cell. This process is greatly affected by the outside temperature. The room temperature where the batteries are located play an important part in terms of life and performance. It is for this reason that battery rooms are kept at approximately 77 degrees Fahrenheit; 72 to 80 degrees Fahrenheit are acceptable.

Factors like keeping batteries away from direct sunlight, intercell temperature differentials, and spacing of jars are all design considerations for a proper battery facility.

Three Kinds of Batteries in Use

The most popular lead-acid batteries available are lead antimony, lead calcium, and lead Plante', or pure lead.

Lead calcium is the choice of most designers since it offers the best trade cost versus reliability of the three varieties. A typical warranty for lead calcium would be 20 years and the life expectancy would range from 20 to 25 years. Compared to lead antimony, lead calcium generates less hydrogen gas and maintenance is less frequent.

Lead antimony, on the other hand is better suited for applications where they are cycled (charged and discharged) more often. In an environment where the power frequently goes out and the batteries must be discharged and charged as a result, lead antimony might be found in use. Warranties for these batteries run from 15 to 20 years and life expectancy can be as high as 22 years.

Plante' batteries are pure lead and contain no impurities such as calcium in their structure. Because of this, cost will be two to three times that of lead antimony and lead calcium. Plante' batteries are durable whether used in a frequently cycling environment or when floating for long periods of time. They tolerate high operating temperatures and require less maintenance. Plante' batteries come with a 20 to 25 year warranty, but unlike lead calcium and lead antimony, they will still have nearly all of their capacity left at the end of the warranty period.

We must note that lead-acid batteries are now available in sealed maintenance free versions for stationary applications. Typically, warranties are for 5 to 10 years on these batteries. Notice the battery specification we have shown in Table 11-1. Logic might lead us to suspect that if we can draw 1000 watts for 5 minutes we should only get 500 watts for 10 minutes. Obviously this is not the case. Discharge time as a function of load is not a linear relationship. Figure 11-1 shows the battery curve of a typical UPS.

Table 11-1.
Typical Sealed Maintenance-Free Battery Specifications

Voltage	Final Volts per Cell	Watts/Battery at 77°F	
		Time	Watts
12	1.75	5 min.	1000
12	1.75	10 min.	700
12	1.75	15 min.	547
12	1.75	20 min.	450
12	1.75	30 min.	348
12	1.75	60 min.	215
12	1.75	90 min.	157
12	1.75	2 hrs.	125
12	1.75	4 hrs.	71
12	1.75	8 hrs.	40
12	1.75	20 hrs.	19

Nickel Cadmium

NICAD (nickel cadmium) batteries are three times more expensive than lead calcium batteries. It takes 92 NICAD cells to equal 60 cells of lead calcium. So why would anyone use them? For a given capacity, they are

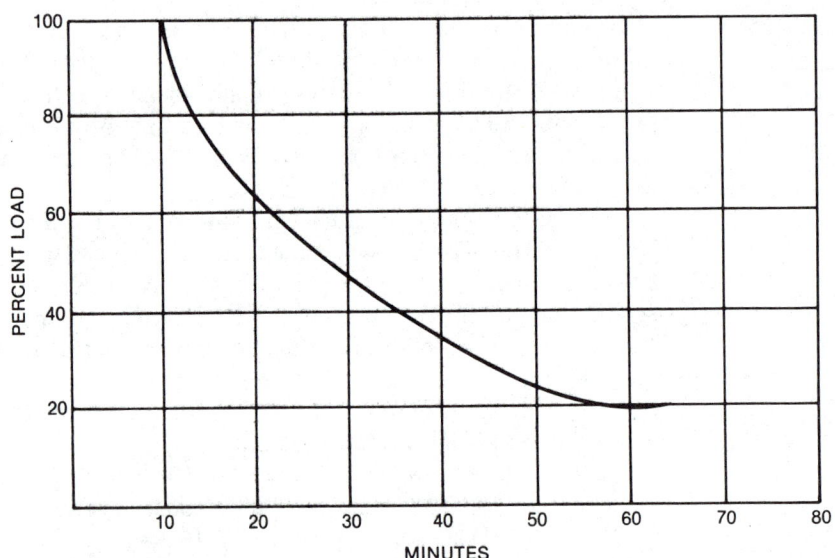

Fig. 11-1.
Battery time versus percent load.

considerably smaller in size and weight. They tolerate temperature change well and their life expectancy is 25 years.

Gel Cells

Lead calcium gel cells, instead of having a liquid electrolyte, have a semi-solid, gelled electrolyte. Even if the battery case becomes cracked, they will not leak. The other considerable advantage this unit has is the battery is sealed. This means that virtually no gas is ever vented. This makes gel cells suitable for use in unventilated areas.

Gel cells have made possible a new generation of UPS products that can be used in the home, inside the computer room, or wherever the special requirements of wet cells are impractical. But like everything else we have discussed in this book, there are tradeoffs. Gel cells have a useful life of only about 5 years, and the warranty is usually only 2 years.

Outages

During an outage the battery discharges. The customer purchases a UPS with a finite battery time for the load. A customer may want a battery time of only long enough for diesel generators to fire and come up to speed, thus providing power for the load, or the customer may want up to an hour of pure battery power. In either case, we must know the end voltage of the

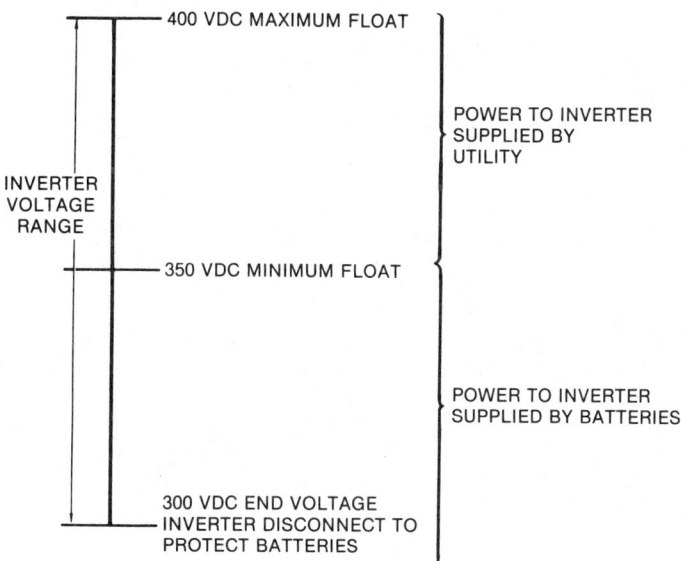

Fig. 11-2.
Typical voltage range usable by a UPS inverter.

battery bank. The end voltage is the lowest point cell voltage can safely go before damage to the batteries will occur. When the end voltage is reached, the inverter should be designed to automatically disconnect from the batteries to allow time to turn on auxiliary power, do an orderly shut down of the computer, or for the power to be restored. Figure 11-2 shows the inverter voltage range, or that range of voltage that is usable by the inverter.

When the power does return, recharging of the battery takes place. At this point the batteries will want to absorb any current they can in order to restore their charge. In effect, they act much like a dead short across the DC bus. This action must be limited by some current-limiting device within the UPS, so power will be restored to the load. It is for this reason that power equipment servicing the UPS must be sized for 25 percent of the load. After discharge, the load will demand 100 percent and the remaining 25 percent will be channeled to recharge the batteries. Recharge time will typically be eight to ten times the discharge time.

12

PC Power

Voodoo is a word that conjures up the mystical, the evil, and the magical. Voodoo is a word that seems appropriate when we talk about the technology of power problem solving as it is applied in the world of PCs (personal computers), terminals, point-of-sale terminals, work stations, and the like. We've all seen what has happened in recent years in the PC marketplace. It's a free-for-all. Companies spring up, grow, then fold so fast we often have a hard time keeping track of them.

The PC accessory marketplace, in many cases, is even more of a whirlwind—here today and gone tomorrow. There is nothing more overwhelming than the mastery of all the disk drives, printers, spoolers, modems, cards, boards, and so forth. The ads claim faster, better, cheaper, and truly compatible.

Hidden amongst all the glitter and hoopla are the PC power products. Often classed in with tapes, disks, and paper, we find all kinds of off-the-wall claims, colors, and functions. There are basically three kinds of devices: UPS or standby power, voltage regulators, and surge suppressors. In this area, voodoo has never been a more descriptive term. Why voodoo? Because the manufacturers are now dealing with the public where a little knowledge is a dangerous thing. Specifications are no longer as important as packaging. Substance gives way to style. Margins start getting small. Every added resistor can mean the difference between profit and perish.

UPS

The single largest market for PC power products is for UPS products. Everyone dreads losing power during a critical job. Most people would like to have the time to save data and shut down their system. A UPS then will

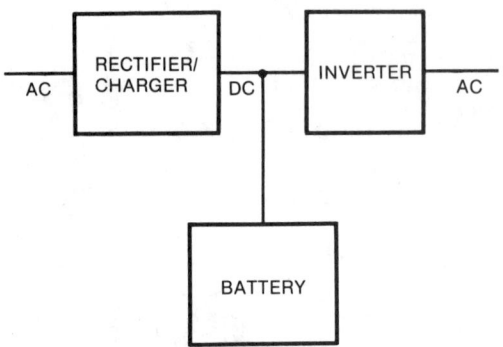

Fig. 12-1.
Block diagram of a true UPS.

solve our PC power problems, won't it? But we immediately run into a problem. Here we must be careful because UPS does not always mean UPS, or does it? This discussion is a sword that cuts both ways. So follow closely.

A block diagram of a true UPS is shown in Fig. 12-1. We call it a true UPS because power is always being conditioned by the action of the AC to DC to AC conversion that takes place. A block diagram of an SPS (standby power system) is shown in Fig. 12-2. What is the difference? Obviously, the big difference between the two is that the load is using raw utility power until an outage occurs with the SPS, then a transfer must take place to provide power to the inverter from the battery.

In a previous chapter, we stated that this transfer time was too long for a large computer to tolerate. We also listed other negative effects of this

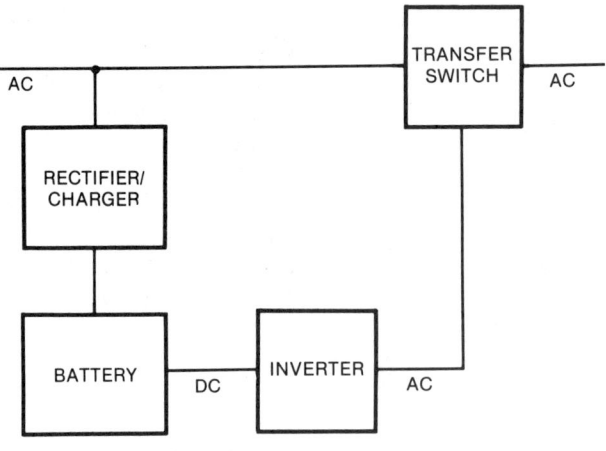

Fig. 12-2.
Block diagram of an SPS (standby power system).

design. But we are now in the world of the PC and the rules are just a bit different.

Let's look at cost for a moment. If we had an IBM XT with a few peripherals and expansion boards, we might determine that a 300-watt UPS would be an excellent choice. So we step out on a lovely Saturday morning to find our product, safe in the knowledge that once we have our computer plugged into it all our power problems will be over. We find a nice looking 300-watt unit for about 500 dollars. But wait, this is an SPS. That's funny. The manufacturer is calling it a UPS. Do we want to settle for that?

Our search brings us to another store where we find a true 300-watt UPS. The price, 1000 dollars. What? We could buy a clone for that kind of money!

Obviously, the difference between these two designs is important to PC users in more ways than one. True UPS designs might be great for a computer room or next to a minicomputer. But the additional size, noise generation, heat and inefficiencies, and cost make them undesirable for most PC environments. No busy executive wants a heavy, noisy piece of equipment sitting in his or her office.

Transfer Time

In order to make the choice between an SPS and a UPS, we need to know if the SPS will switch fast enough. In chapter 2, we made the statement that most computers do not like to see dropouts of longer than 15 milliseconds. On the other hand, most personal computers will ride through a power failure of from 20 to 40 milliseconds with no problem.

There is one glaring exception to this. From the time the IBM XT was introduced to the middle of 1985, power supplies made in Mexico by Zenith were used. These units were totally intolerant of power-line disturbances. According to Winn Rosch in his article entitled "Backup Power" in the September 86 issue of *PC Magazine*, all PCs used a special lead from the power supply to monitor the electrical supply. If the supply exceeded certain normal limits, a signal would be sent and the PC would shut itself down.

As we stated in chapter 2, when power fails the capacitive elements within the power supply will return energy to circuits. In a PC, this ride through can be from 30 to 45 milliseconds. Because of this, Rosch says the power good signal remains valid for 10 to 15 milliseconds after line voltage fails.

The XT with the Zenith power supply eliminates the power good signal almost immediately. This means that no switching time can be tolerated by these machines. Rosch advises that replacement of the supply may be far less expensive than buying a UPS.

Tests have shown that nearly all SPS products will switch within 17 milliseconds, most within 10 milliseconds. This means that in most cases an SPS will be sufficient for backup power. This must be the reason why those manufacturers advertise their units under the heading of UPS. In a sense, they are able to justify their claim. For this reason, most UPSs made for PCs are in reality SPSs.

Making Waves

So on that fine Saturday morning we decide to purchase a UPS that has a transfer time of from 4 to 10 milliseconds. We feel proud of ourselves and are just about to start to the checkout stand with our money when something catches our eye. Way down in the fine print of the specs on this unit it says the output waveform is rectangular. Rectangular? That must be voodoo, mumbo jumbo for square wave (Fig. 12-1).

We get a little curious so we ask the store manager for a look at the brochure on the product. On the back we see something like Fig. 12-3B. This claims to be a photo of the actual waveform. What they haven't told us is that the oscilloscope was not connected to a computer at the time but to a light bulb or some other purely resistive load.

If the photo was of the square waveform delivering full power to a load with a switching power supply, we might see something like Fig. 12-3A. Square waves are rich in harmonics. Some UPSs deliver up to 36 percent of total harmonic distortion. This can appear as noise to your PC. Remember, a switching power supply generates odd harmonics and we don't need any more.

Also, at a given voltage level, there is more energy in a square wave than in a sine wave. This extra energy will heat up the computer's power supply. This overheating will reduce the life of components.

Why would anyone design a UPS with a square wave output? It's cheaper to build. Remember, we have to use voodoo to survive in this market. As a matter of fact, we see any number of waveforms from square wave to stepped square wave to sawtooth to pulse wave modulated forms. But some UPS manufacturers do specify the output as sine wave. But what does it take to convert a step wave, or whatever, to a sine wave with only about 5 percent total harmonic distortion? Money. The extra filtering components that smooth out the wave cost money. Many of the computers on the market today demand a clean sine wave to operate properly.

Does this mean square wave products don't work? No. It means they have drawbacks. Some small computers will have problems digesting a square wave. Many will not. The point here is, all things being equal, the manufacturer that has gone to the trouble to produce a sine wave with a minimum of harmonic distortion has a superior product.

Synchronicity

Imagine that you are a power supply. It is a hot summer day and you have been working hard all morning. In order to replenish yourself, you guzzle a large frosty glass of ice water—or in power supply terms, electricity.

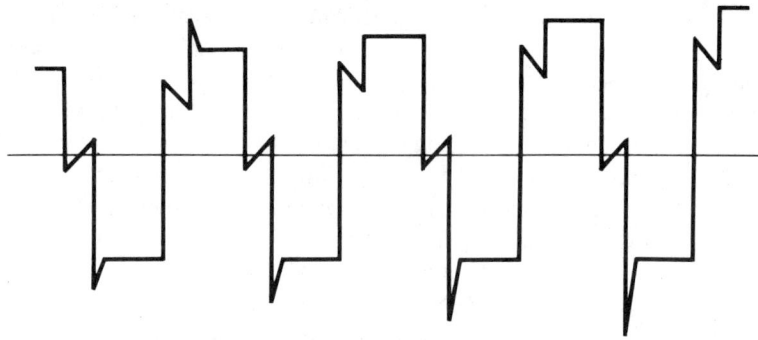

(A) What rectangular wave output looks like connected to a switching power supply.

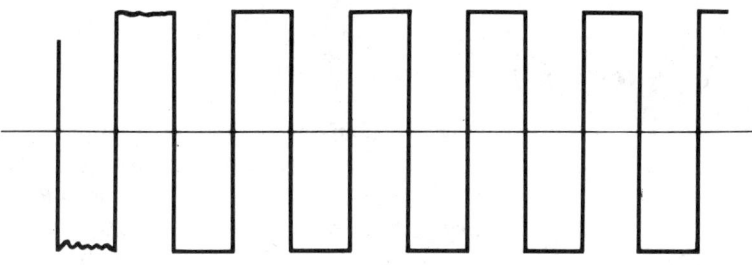

(B) What might appear on a brochure.

Fig. 12-3.
Rectangular waveforms.

Glug, glug, glug the water slides down gulp after gulp. Then suddenly your friend, the UPS, comes along and tips up the glass. A huge amount of water fills your mouth. You choke and, as your cheeks nearly burst trying to hold it all, you spew water all over. To top it all you belch.

You no sooner have recovered from that nasty trick, than UPS comes along and pulls the glass from your lips just as you gulp. But wait! You gulp air. How embarrassing. This makes you hiccup.

To a power supply, this action translates into too much energy or not enough energy. Of course, a hiccup is much worse than a belch. A belch, or too much energy being fed to the power supply, becomes heat. Heat stresses components and reduces useful life. We might not see the effects of this immediately.

A hiccup is an outage. We certainly will experience that. Our system will crash.

All this is swell, but what is our analogy really talking about? Synchronization. In order to provide a steady uninterrupted source of power, a UPS must be in synchronization with the line when it switches. Phase shifts caused by unsynchronized switching will produce the effects just discussed.

An unsynchronized switch from one sine wave to another can result in enough time delay to cause the system to see the total switching time to be much longer than the computer can tolerate. This effect is even more dramatic when seen in a square-wave inverter. Phase shifts can cause outages for as long as one cycle, an eternity for the computer.

A well designed UPS will have a circuit that constantly monitors line voltage and synchronizes the inverter to it. This provides for smooth switching transitions. If this is a part of the product spec, it will be on the specs. If the equipment does not have this feature, it's literature may be mute on the subject. Large UPS equipment has this taken care of as a matter of course. But remember, not every PC UPS manufacturer has been in the bigger UPS market. Therefore, voodoo and not good design can easily become their priority.

A Battery of Questions

The store manager has answered almost all of our questions. We have now narrowed our selection down to two alternatives. But we notice one is heavier and bigger than the other. We start asking questions again. The store manager is very patient with us.

Yes, both have true sine wave outputs. Yes, they both have line sync circuits. Yes, they both switch within 10 milliseconds. But, why is one so much larger than the other? Battery size. Battery size? But both advertise 15 to 20 minutes of battery time at their full rated load.

If we look at the chapter on batteries, the answer to this puzzle might jump out at us. The answer is to be found in a term called "End Voltage." End voltage was the lowest remaining voltage left in each cell before damage was done by discharging too much of each cell's capacity.

One manufacturer advertises their 1200 watt unit weighs 65 pounds. Another advertises their 1500 watt unit weighs 178 lbs. The first manufacturer says they have a three-year battery that will support the load for 6 minutes. The second states they use a 5-year battery that will give 15 to 20 minutes at full load.

Does that make the second UPS a dinosaur or a boat anchor? Or does this really mean the first manufacturer is practicing voodoo. Consider this. The smaller UPS is part of a family that has a 200-watt UPS that has a 20-minute full-load battery. That's funny. As their equipment gets larger, their batteries get smaller. It's the old style versus substance game again.

Manufacturer one is trying to fool us by stressing batteries, using shorter lives, and by shortening the battery time. Manufacturer two has a consistent story. They are saying from 200 watts to 1500 watts their units have 5-year batteries that will support the load for 15 to 20 minutes, and the batteries have an end voltage rating that won't destroy the cells prematurely. And, in all probability, both are using batteries that are comparable and possibly from the same company.

Backup Power Systems

These types of UPS products are most of the time SPS products. Both terms fall into the general category of backup power since that is really what they provide. These products provide power to the load when utility power fails. This is an important point to remember. If we have a critical need for backup power, we need a UPS.

Now, we have had our tongues firmly placed in our cheeks through part of the discussion. Cutting through the voodoo of PC power products is important in order to understand what we can get to fill a particular need. Some of the points we have made should be balanced with the needs of a given circumstance.

For example, in some cases size and weight can legitimately be sacrificed for battery life time. A true on-line UPS is a much more powerful product because it truly conditions power and has no switching time. But it is bigger and noisier, and it does introduce inefficiencies. And finally, a well engineered SPS might do fine even if it does produce a square wave. We need to understand the differences between square-wave output and sine-wave output to make intelligent buying decisions.

Conditioning

Many UPS products for PCs have in-line filters for noise as well as surge protectors. This means that, even though the batteries are not always on line, filters and noise suppressors (typically MOVs) are there to stop dirty power from affecting the load. Or are they? Let's look at some specs first.

One system's specs say they provide 80 joules of transient suppression. A joule is the amount of energy equal to the work done when 1 amp of current is passed through 1 ohm of resistance for 1 second. Yet another manufacturer claims that it provides 100 joules and has RFI filtering from 100 kHz to 80 MHz of -25 dB.

Clearly, the second unit provides more protection. But let's look closer. Remember that transient suppression is generally designed to work on fast rise-time spikes. What about slower moving disturbances? And what about RFI below 100 kHz?

What these manufacturers have really done is to provide protection rather than conditioning. Protection is great. But many common data threatening power problems come from things like low frequency RFI and slow moving sags. Here a point must be made that might disturb many. If you want power conditioning for your PC, don't buy an SPS.

A true UPS will condition power, providing clean power to the load.

An SPS with an in-line filter will protect the load, but it won't really condition the power. What we really need to provide a clean electrical environment for our computer, if we can afford a true UPS, is a power conditioner.

Power Conditioners

Power conditioners or line conditioners for PCs operate much the same way as the ferroresonant or tap-switching technologies that we mentioned in an earlier chapter. But again we run into the same claims of 120 dB noise attenuation and all the other things we discussed earlier. Rejection of common- and transverse-mode noise specs run from 30 dB to 120 dB. Frequency specs are in the 1 kHz to 10 MHz range. All of these products have a transformer—some with no shield and some with triple shields.

The power conditioner in Fig. 12-4 is economical and yet provides a friendly electrical environment for the PC and its peripherals. It will not regulate voltage—thereby it will not hold the voltage up during a sag.

Pound for pound all the points we made in our previous chapter on power conditioners applies here with a few exceptions. Regulation windows are often smaller. Regulation output ranges are often larger. The overall quality of the isolation transformer is not as good. Correction times may be slower. All these design considerations are determined by cost. Does this necessarily degrade the product so much that it's no good for a PC? The answer is no. Even a relatively cheap power conditioner that advertises only 30 dB of common-mode noise rejection can be a very effective product if it has good secondary transient suppression and noise filtering and reasonable response to voltage sags.

This is a size range where the ferroresonant device finally comes into its own. Because of size, most of the arguments we used against it in previous chapters have now shrunk to insignificance. For PC applications there are a wide variety of ferroresonant devices and tap-switching products available.

The product that solves power problems is a line conditioner, and the price of a good one for your PC may be only 30 percent of the price of a

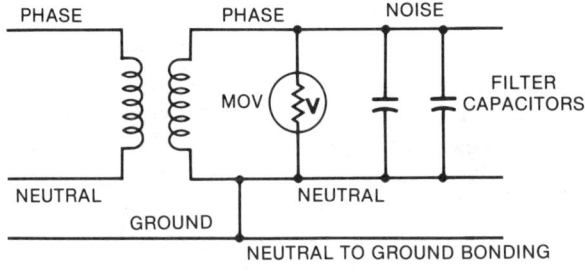

Fig. 12-4.
Power conditioner for PC.

true UPS. Providing good conditioned power to your PC is far more important in most cases than backup power. Since this device will save your hard disk, a good power conditioner is the next investment every PC owner should make. An SPS can be added later to round out the power protection picture if the up-front cost of a UPS is prohibitive.

Surge Protectors

Surge protectors are those things that we plug into the wall that have several outlets on them for our PC and peripherals. They range in cost from 5 to 150 dollars. The high quality ones have fuses, MOVs of high rating, and a wide variety of other safety and convenience features.

Many people have said, "Why would I pay 150 dollars when I can get one for 5 dollars?"

The retail marketplace is full of devices that are practically useless. How soon we forget that our primary concern is for the protection of our investment in equipment and our data, so why would we consider scrimping in this area.

A simple surge protector might be the only kind of protection we can afford. There are three critical specifications that we must look at when we make our selection: power dissipation in watts, energy dissipation in joules, and clamping voltage in volts.

A typical high quality surge protector might be rated at 1 to 2 million watts power dissipation, 100 to 200 joules, and a clamping voltage of from 140 to 200 volts. This means that the unit has 1 to 2 million watts of power absorption capability for 100 to 200 microseconds in clamping power surges and voltage spikes. Clamping response time is largely dependent on the characteristics of the MOV used and can be less than a few nanoseconds.

We must remember that our objective is to protect our investment, not to save money. We can save money by comparing features and sacrificing convenience. But sacrificing power ratings is no savings. Just because the device is a bright color and comes in a cute package doesn't mean it can protect anything. No doubt there are many cheap surge protectors still plugged into the wall that long since gave their life the first time the refrigerator cycled on. Meanwhile, the user has a false sense of security about the 20 dollar investment he or she made to protect the computer.

13

Conclusion

I met with a DP professional one day from a company that was supposed to be the largest computer user in the country. He stated, without equivocation, that one power center was just like another (similar to vodka and aspirin I suppose). His company had purchased hundreds of cheap PDUs that might just as well have been wired into the building by an unscrupulous electrician. A cheap design with poor construction practices might be worse than building wiring.

It occurred to me that this gentleman might be like so many data processing people, lacking in an understanding of the true environment that his computers must perform in. Hopefully, the reader is armed with enough of an understanding to deal with power and the products likely to be encountered.

At this point it might seem like a good idea to draw up a chart comparing one device against another. We could summarize which products protect against blackouts and which products protect against brownouts. We might even compare the relative cost of one against the other. This approach might seem to have the benefit of neatly tying it all up on one page.

There are a couple of reasons why we will resist this temptation. First, it is obvious that an isolation transformer will not protect against loss of power like a UPS or RUPS does. It is equally obvious that a PDU is far less expensive than an on-line UPS. To compare one against the other in this way is to assume that all are the same, some bigger than others.

This kind of thinking can be misleading. The decision whether to use one device or another is much more complicated than deciding which will do what and for what price. Each device has its own benefits that lend to an application in one set of circumstances or another.

The choice between a power conditioner and a UPS, for instance, has to do with the electrical environment—what kind of building the computer is in, how large it is. Is the power product going into a new site, an existing site? Will we have to alter the structure or remodel existing conditions? Factors like the remaining capacity of the building service, floor space requirements, and voltages available are all things that must be taken into careful consideration. Price, downtime costs, and future computer expansion are important. Motivation is another key consideration. Is it more important to maintain power or to protect the equipment from damaging spikes? The point is that each site with its own unique set of circumstances lends itself to one or two alternatives.

The Representative

Most manufacturers of this kind of equipment sell their products through what are called manufacturers' representatives. These are independent businesspeople who have contracts to represent one or more product lines. They may carry a wide variety of products relating to the computer and its environment.

The representative's job is to assist the user in evaluating the alternatives relative to any given set of circumstances. And, since the representative sees more computer facilities than does any given DP manager or even the factory itself, the representative is in a unique position to suggest which alternative is in the best interest of the end user. On any given job the representative might interface with the DP manager, the architect, the building engineer, one or more contractors including the electrical contractor, and the manufacturer. The representative may interface with other representatives who are providing fire protection equipment, security systems, and other key elements of a project.

A good manufacturers' representative can be a valuable person to those who must deal with power but cannot become experts in the field themselves and to those data processing professionals who don't want to hear about power and say, "Just make it work."

In recent years, field service organizations have become a source of important revenue to the computer industry. Most field service organizations have one or two in-house experts in the area of power. However, many local FEs (field engineers) and IPRs (installation planning reps) for major computer manufacturers and third party maintenance companies have found that establishing a relationship with a manufacturer's representative who carries power products can be helpful. Having professionals to turn to can relieve a tremendous burden and solve long standing problems that may have strained relationships between the service organization and key customers. Often an aggravating problem can be solved by a power professional quickly and inexpensively. Many service people have found that calling in a power representative early can help stop little power or grounding problems that bedevil certain sites.

The Environment

Much has been made of the power environment in this book. But the computer does not just exist in a power environment. Many years ago computer manufacturers realized that if certain undesirable events took place in the computer's environment, it would be advantageous to shut off power to the computer and save it from damage. Soon power centers were outfitted with building interface alarms that could detect things like fire, underfloor water, and overtemperature in the computer room.

With the advent of the microprocessor, this environmental monitoring has become increasingly sophisticated. Today, it is possible to purchase a computer, either built into a power center or standing by itself, that can monitor events occurring even blocks away where such things as emergency generators might be located.

Extensive monitoring is allowing some of the largest computer users to plan several unstaffed computer centers. Normally, a major data center would have someone watching it 24 hours a day. It has now become possible to run a computer facility "dark" and monitor it from a remote location, across town or across the country.

And they are monitoring almost everything: chilled water flow, air handlers, UPS status, under floor water, and diesel generator head pressure to name a few. Environmental monitoring has become an essential element of most major data centers.

Power and More

It might be easier now to see why comparing a power center against a UPS is so futile. Every product has so many options and can do so much more than its name implies that they defy simple comparison. An elaborate PDU with built-in monitoring like the CPS series 4000 power center shown in Fig. 13-1 might cost nearly as much as an RUPS. The development of products is in response to the needs of the marketplace. Combination products have been developed that do a number of critical tasks. The series 4000 in Fig. 13-1 is a power center, with or without regulation, that has a complete environmental monitor built into the front door of the unit. It can monitor over 100 points both internal and external to the unit itself.

Nor is this trend strictly related to power equipment. Some of the other important elements in a computer's environment include fire suppression systems, security systems, computer room air conditioning, raised flooring, lighting—all interrelated elements in a well designed facility.

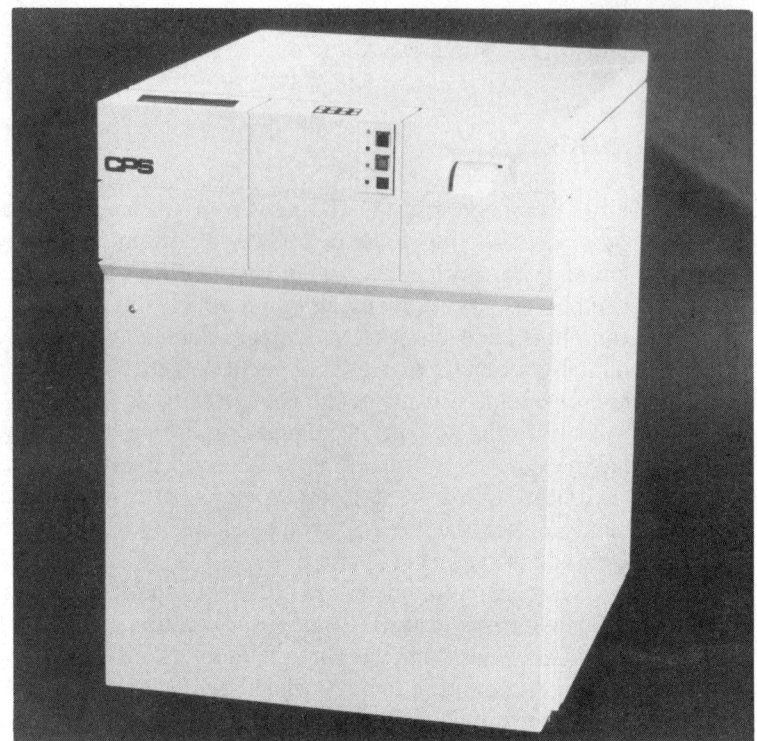

Fig. 13-1.
The series 4000. (Courtesy Computer Power Systems)

Computer-room air conditioning is a science all on its own. Many manufacturers of air conditioners are designing interfaces into their equipment so that interrelated hardware can be networked together.

The Future

Not long ago I was on an airplane seated next to the marketing Vice President of a major manufacturer of microchips. We struck up a conversation and the subject turned to power. He told me in no uncertain terms that soon no computer would need power conditioning since they were developing smart power supplies.

The smart power supply, he explained, would be able to react in nanoseconds to any variations in power and take the appropriate action. His tone indicated that this new technology was a serious threat to the power industry, and I had better take note of the unsavory direction of my career.

Well, I was somewhat taken aback. But soon I realized that the real implication of what the man had said was cause for great joy. Why? I knew that smart power supplies would certainly not be a quantum jump ahead in cost. The computer industry would never buy a technology that increased cost significantly. We must remember that it is very convenient to blame the utility company for all adverse power conditions. Smart power supplies come perilously close to shifting the power burden back to the computer manufacturer, and who wants that to happen?

What smart power supplies will do is more of what IBM has already built into many of their systems. When a power deviation is sensed, certain action is taken. For example, a signal would be sent that would halt processing momentarily, or prevent a disk write procedure from continuing. This kind of strategy would keep data from being tainted or destroyed by the effects of a transient or low voltage condition.

This sounds like utopia. The practical result of this will be another set of annoying problems for DP professionals. The data may be saved. The process internal to the computer may have been halted in time to protect the work in process, but what about the problems that causes? How long will it take to recover from the action of a smart power supply? What thresholds will be used? Will the cure be more painful than the cause?

As we have stated earlier, the new technology, while saving data, has made recovery much more difficult. As DP managers have discovered this, they have literally screamed for power products that keep their systems from going down.

The advent of the smart power supply will not obviate the need for power products or the friendly electrical environment they provide. If anything, it will create more of a demand for power products. Meanwhile, power products will get more sophisticated. UPS systems, rotary and static, will get smaller. New methods will be used to filter, suppress, and isolate. Every user from micro to mainframe will become aware of the need for protection.

Many advances are in process for the computer. None that I have heard of require less consideration for power. All require better power. Each advance in computing continues the trend: smaller, faster, and more complex.

The computer needs a heftier, higher quality power supply. But that will surely not happen. Are smart power supplies the answer? Maybe we just need to get smart about power. Hopefully this book has helped you do just that.

Glossary

AC, Alternating Current Electrical current which reverses direction periodically, expressed in hertz or cycles per second.

Actual power A term referring to the number of watts of power consumed by a load.

Amp, Ampere The quantitative unit measurement of electrical current.

Ampacity A term used to describe the current handling capacity of an electrical device.

Amperage A term synonymous with current used in describing electrical current.

Antimony An element found in lead acid batteries used to harden the plate material.

Apparent Power The load power as expressed in VA or kVA. This value is usually greater than real power or watts due to circuit reactance. This reactance causes the timing between the voltage and current to vary. Device sizing must be in accordance with Volts times Amps rather than Watts since Volt-Amperes is the apparent load seen by the power handling device.

Arc Sparking generated when current flows between two points of different potential due to leakage through the intervening insulator.

Arrester A device placed from phase to ground whose non-linear impedance characteristics provide a path for high amplitude transients.

Autotransformer A transformer that uses common turns for both primary and secondary windings, thus providing no isolation for input from output.

Balance A term used to describe the even distribution of loads on the legs of a three phase system.

Battery A group of cells connected in such a way that more current and/or voltage is delivered than from one single cell.

Battery, sealed A battery containing gelled or liquid electrolyte that has no opening for water replenishment.

Blackout The total loss of commercial electrical power. Sometimes referring to the length of time power must be off to bring the computer down. Used synonymously with Outage.

Branch Circuit A discrete division of a load that is protected by one fuse or breaker.

Breaker Short for Circuit Breaker.

Brownout A long duration undervoltage condition usually hours or days in length. Brownouts can be caused by heavy usage during peak hours, or they may be planned as an energy conservation strategy.

Building Service Entry That point where commercial power enters the building.

Bus, Busbar A heavy, rigid conductor often equipped with screws or some other means by which a number of smaller conductors are connected to it.

Bypass Line, Bypass Circuit An alternate electrical path around some other device, usually a UPS, that allows for the flow of power to the load. This bypass may make before breaking power to the load or drop power to the load in the switching process. Bypass lines are used for three purposes: to perform maintenance on equipment, to bypass damaged equipment, or to pass fault current to a circuit breaker upstream.

Calcium An element used in lead acid batteries to harden plate material.

Capacitance A term referring to the electrical properties of a capacitor or a circuit that displays capacitor-like behavior.

Capacitive Reactance The behavior of alternating current as it interacts with capacitance encountered in a circuit.

Capacitor A discrete electrical device which has

two electrodes and an intervening insulator called the dielectric.

Cell A combination of two metal plates suspended in an electrolyte which, when connected to an external circuit, causes a current to flow.

Charge Voltage The voltage that must be applied to storage batteries to maintain their maximum charge.

Choke A form of inductor which is constructed to allow desirable frequency signals to pass while acting with high impedance to signals at some undesirable frequency.

Circuit Breaker A resettable device that responds to a preset excess of current flow by opening the circuit thereby preventing damage to circuit elements.

Coax A cable constructed by using two concentric conductors separated by an insulator.

Common Mode Noise Abnormal signals that appear between a current carrying line and its associated ground.

Compensating Winding A winding on the primary of a ferroresonant transformer that is connected opposite to the output winding in order to improve regulation.

Converter A device that changes alternating current to direct current or a device that changes direct current to alternating current can be called by the general term "converter." In this sense, a rectifier/charger and an inverter might be termed converters. The term converter is also applied to any of a family of devices that convert the frequency of the alternating current.

Core The iron structure of a transformer around which the windings are wound. A choke also has a core but does not act as a transformer.

Core Saturation That point at which the iron material, core, of an inductor or transformer will no longer produce more lines of flux when current flow through the windings is increased.

CPU An acronym meaning central processing unit of a computer.

CSA The abbreviation which stands for Canadian Standards Association. This is a Canadian safety assurance agency similar to Underwriter's Laboratories.

Critical Load That portion of electrical/electronic equipment for which power quality is a vital consideration. The term load applies to all current carrying devices on a given circuit or feeder. The term critical load refines the language to include only those current using devices whose operation is considered essential.

Current The flow of electricity in a circuit as expressed in Amperes. Current refers to the quantity or intensity of electrical flow. Voltage on the other hand refers to the pressure or force causing the electrical flow.

Current Balance A term that describes the nearly equal flow of current on each leg of a three phase power system. With this flow balanced the theoretical flow of current in the neutral with respect to ground will be zero.

Cycles Per Second This term describes the frequency of alternating current. Frequency is more properly described using the term Hertz, which is synonymous with cycles per second.

DC, Direct Current Electrical current which flows consistently in one direction.

Delta A term describing a kind of connection in a three phase circuit, often the primary side of a transformer. A delta connection may or may not have a neutral conductor.

Delta/Wye Transformer A three phase transformer with a delta connection on one side and a wye connection on the other. Most often the delta connection is on the primary side.

Dip Another term for Sag.

Disk A memory device using magnetic media for serial storage of information. Disk as a term has expanded into other areas often used to describe the shape of the storage media that is, floppy disk, compact disk, laser disk, or hard disk; or sometimes referring to the way in which the storage media mimics a disk media, that is, RAM disk or bubble memory.

Distortion The waveshape of a signal that is not normal is distorted. Distortion is a term that describes abnormal wave-shapes.

Distribution The way in which power is routed to various current using sites or devices. Outside the building distribution refers to the process of routing power from the power plant to the users. Inside the building distribution is the process of using feeders and circuits to provide power to devices.

Drop-out A total loss of voltage for a short period of time.

Electrolyte The acid or alkaline solution in which the plates of a battery cell are immersed.

EMI, Electromagnetic interference A term that describes electrically induced noise or transients.

Engine Generator A combination of an internal combustion engine and a generator, often referred to as a diesel generator.

Feedback Energy that is fed from the output of a circuit to its input.

Ferroresonance When an iron core inductor is part of an LC circuit and it is driven to saturation increasing its inductive reactance to equal the capacitive reactance of the circuit, it is called ferroresonance.

Ferroresonant Transformers A transformer that uses the principle of ferroresonance to regulate output voltage.

Filter An electronic device which opposes the passage of a certain frequency band while allowing other frequencies to pass. Filters are designed to produce four different results: A high pass filter allows all signals above a given frequency to pass. A low pass filter allows only frequencies below a given frequency to pass. A bandpass filter allows a given band of frequencies to pass while attenuating all others. A trap filter allows all frequencies to pass but acts as a high impedance device to the tuned frequency of the filter.

Flashover Arcing that is caused by the breakdown of insulation between two conductors where high current flow exists with a high potential difference between the conductors.

Flywheel A heavy, wheel-like, piece of metal or steel which acts as a governor to provide inertial force generally found in motor generators.

Fuse A device that automatically self destructs when the current passing through it exceeds the rated value of the fuse.

Gassing The process by which hydrogen gas is produced from the breakdown of the water in an electrolyte solution during battery charging.

Ground A general term referring to the point at which other portions of a circuit are referenced when making measurements. Power systems grounding is that point to which the neutral conductor, safety ground, and building ground are connected. This grounding electrode may be a water pipe, driven ground rod, or the steel frame of the building.

Ground Fault An undesired path for current to flow from a line to ground.

Ground Loop The condition of having two or more ground references in a common system. When two or more grounds have a potential difference between them, current can flow. This flow of current is a new circuit or loop which can interfere with the normal operation of the system.

Harmonic A frequency that is a multiple of the fundamental frequency. For example 120 Hz is the 2nd harmonic of 60 Hz, 180 Hz is the 3rd harmonic, and so forth.

Harmonic Distortion Excessive harmonic content that distorts the normal sinusoidal waveform is harmonic distortion. This can cause overheating of circuit elements and might appear to a device as data corrupting noise.

Hz, Hertz A term describing the frequency of alternating current. The term Hertz is synonymous with cycles per second.

Impedance Measured in Ohms, impedance is the total opposition to current flow in a circuit where alternating current is flowing. This includes inductive reactance, capacitive reactance, and resistance.

Impulse A disturbance of the voltage waveform that is less than about one millisecond. Voltages can rise to hundreds or even thousands of volts in a very short period of time. An impulse may be additive or subtractive (sometimes called a notch).

Inductance This term describes the electrical properties of a coil of wire and its resultant magnetic field when alternating current is passed through it. This interaction offers impedance to current flow thereby causing the current wave to lag behind the voltage wave. This is what's known as a lagging power factor. Reactance is expressed in the unit call the Henry.

Inductive Reactance A term used to describe

the impedance to alternating current offered by an inductive circuit.

Inductor A discrete circuit element which has the property of inductance. It should be noted that at very high radio frequencies a straight wire or path on a printed circuit board can act as an inductor.

Inrush A term used to describe the high current demand of a device when it is initially turned on due to low load impedance before it has reached its normal operating value.

Inverter The subassembly of a UPS that converts DC power into AC power.

Isolation The degree to which a device can separate the electrical environment of its input from its output while allowing the desired transmission to pass across the separation.

J-Box, Junction Box A metal box inside which electrical connections are made.

kHz, kilohertz A term meaning 1000 cycles per second.

kVA, Kilovolt Amperes Volts time Amps is expressed in kVA. Kilovolt amperes are Apparent Power and can be found by dividing kilowatts by power factor.

KW, Kilowatts Real power or the power actually used by the load.

LC An abbreviation for inductance and capacitance that are used in the same circuit.

LED, Light Emitting Diode A semiconductor that emits light when a current is applied to it.

Lightning Arrester A device used to pass large impulses to ground. It is vital that this device be placed upstream from the computer ground.

Line A term used generally to describe a current carrying conductor.

Line to Line A term used to describe a given condition between conductors of a multiphase feeder.

Line to Neutral A term used to describe a given condition between a phase conductor and a neutral conductor.

Load Any electrical device connected to a power source may be called by the general term of load.

Magnetic Field The lines of force that exist around an energized electrical conductor, magnet, or inductor.

Magnetic Synthesizer A marketing term for a certain variety of ferroresonant regulator.

Maintenance Bypass A line that allows power to be routed around a power device so maintenance or repair can be performed on the unit.

MHz, megahertz One million Hertz or cycles per second.

Motor Alternator A device that consists of an AC generator mechanically linked to an electric motor which is driven by utility power or by batteries. An alternator is an AC generator.

Motor Generator A term used synonymously for motor alternator.

MTBF, Mean Time Between Failure A statistical estimate of the time a component, subassembly, or operating unit will operate before failure will occur.

MTTR, Mean Time to Repair A statistical estimate of the repair time for a failed item.

N.E.C., National Electrical Code A set of rules and regulation along with recommended electrical practices put out by the National Fire Protection Association.

Neutral One of the conductors of a three phase wye system is the neutral conductor. Sometimes called the return conductor, it carries the entire current of a single phase circuit and the resultant current in a three phase system that is unbalanced. The neutral is bonded to ground on the output of a three phase delta wye transformer.

Noise An undesirable signal which is irregular yet oscillatory that is super imposed on the desired signal. See common mode noise and normal mode noise.

Normal Mode Noise A noise signal which appears between a set of phase conductors irrespective of their associated ground conductor.

Notch Slang for a negative or subtractive impulse.

Ohm The unit of measurement for resistance, impedance, and reactance.

Ohm's Law The mathematical relationship between Volts, Amperes, and Ohms: Volts = Amperes X Ohms.

Orderly Shutdown The turning off of power to

computer devices in such a way that data is not lost or corrupted.

Oscillation Generally used to mean an electrical phenomenon that produces a number of occurrences above or below a given instantaneous voltage level.

Outage A long term loss of voltage resulting from a localized utility failure.

Overvoltage Similar to a surge but for a longer period of time, over 2.5 seconds.

PDU, Power Distribution Unit A portable electrical distribution device that provides an easily expandable and flexible electrical environment for a computer and its associated peripherals.

Peak The maximum instantaneous measurement of an electrical event.

Phase A term used to describe the timing between two or more events tied to the same frequency.

Phase Balancing The practice of placing equal electrical loads on each leg of a three phase system. See Neutral, Balance.

Phase Rotation The sequence in which a comparable voltage appears in all three phases: A, B, and C, of a three phase system.

Plante' Plate A kind of lead antimony grid used in the construction of battery plates.

Power A general term which means the capacity for doing work. In the electrical environment this is usually measured in watts.

Power Factor Watts divided by volt amperes or the ratio of actual power to apparent power.

Power Line Monitor A measuring device which reports information on the changing conditions of electrical power.

Primary The input winding of a transformer.

Pulsating DC A voltage that periodically rises and falls but does not change polarity.

Pulse Width Modulation Varying the width of a train of pulses by tying it to the characteristics of another signal.

Reactance The opposition to the flow of alternating current in a circuit, usually described as capacitive or inductive reactance.

Rectifier/Charger A subassembly of a UPS that performs the function of converting the incoming AC into DC for driving the Inverter and charging the batteries.

Redundancy The practice of providing backup modules to support a function should other modules fail.

Reflection The wave that is generated when a traveling wave reaches the point at which line impedance changes.

Regulation A term used to describe the action of holding a constant electrical value in the face of fluctuations.

REPO, Remote Emergency Power Off A device that permits the total shutdown of electrical power devices from an exit in the event of an emergency.

Resistance A term describing the opposition of a circuit to alternating or direct current.

Resistor A discrete electronic component designed to produce a DC voltage drop when current passes through it.

RFI, Radio Frequency Interference Electromagnetic signals of a frequency associated with electromagnetic radiation which are coupled to a conductor either directly or as with an antenna.

RMS, Root Mean Square The square root of the arithmetic mean of the squares of a set of electrical amplitudes.

Rotary A term used in describing certain electrical power equipment that functions through rotational mechanics.

Safety Ground A conductive path that bonds all cabinets and conductor shields to the power source ground.

Sag A short term RMS voltage decrease which exceeds an established upper limit for less than 2.5 seconds.

Secondary The output winding of a transformer.

Shield A conductive enclosure or barrier that prevents electrical interference from external sources.

Shunt Trip A type of circuit breaker that can also be activated by a circuit other than the one it is protecting.

Sine Wave A fundamental waveform produced by periodic oscillation that expresses the sine or cosine of a linear function of time or space or both.

Single Phase That portion of a power source which represents only a single phase of the three phases that are available.

Single Point Ground The practice of tying the power neutral ground and safety ground together at the same point avoiding differential ground potential between points in a system.

Surge A short term voltage increase that exceeds established upper limits for less than 2.5 seconds.

Synchronization In this context the term relates to maintaining a constant phase relationship between AC signals.

Tap A terminal on a transformer winding.

Tap Switching The action of changing from one terminal on a transformer winding to another thereby changing the turns ratio of the device to maintain a desire voltage relationship.

THD, Total Harmonic Distortion A term referring to the alteration of a waveshape by the presence of multiples of the fundamental frequency of the signal.

Three Phase An electrical system with three different voltage lines or legs which carry sine waves that are 120 degrees out of phase from one another.

Transfer Switch A device used to transfer the load of a power unit from itself to a bypass line.

Transformer A device used for changing the voltage of an AC circuit and/or isolating a circuit from its power source.

Transient An electrical event of a nonrepetitive nature. The term is used interchangeably with the term impulse; however, the term relates more to the intermittent occurrence of surges and sags.

Transverse Mode Noise Often used as a synonym for normal mode noise, it more clearly relates to noise that is the result of the conversion of common mode noise to normal mode noise after it passes through a transformer.

UL The abbreviation for Underwriters Laboratories, an independent United States product safety assurance agency.

Undervoltage Like a sag but for a longer period of time, over 2.5 seconds.

UPS, Uninterruptible Power System A power conditioning and supply system that provides power during outages.

Volt The quantitative measurement of electrical force or potential also called electromotive force.

Volt-Ampere The unit of measurement of apparent power.

Voltage Regulator A circuit that has a constant output voltage when input voltage fluctuates.

Watt The unit of measurement of actual power.

Waveform The graphic form of an electrical parameter.

Wye A three phase connection with a single common neutral and three phase conductors.

Zero Signal Reference The result of a properly installed ground structure is a constant potential over a broad band of frequencies between the devices that are part of the structure. This highly desirable state is called zero signal reference, meaning the potential between points on the ground reference is equal to zero over a broad range of frequencies.

Bibliography

Bent, Rodney; Lewis, Warren; Clark, O. Melville; Martzloff, Francois D.; Richman, Peter; Tetreault, Maurice; Kalbach, J. Fred. *Surge Protection of Computers and other Electronic Systems*, Madison, WI: University of Wisconsin, [n.d.].

Bobry, Howard. *Understanding Uninterruptible Power Supplies*, EC&M, April, May, June, August, November 1983, February, March, 1984.

Bowyer, Richard N. "Rotary And Static UPS Both Convert DC to AC But Total Costs Vary," *Computer Technology Review, Winter 1985*.

Brill, Kenneth G. *Computer Power Protection Equipment: An Introductory Guide*. California: Atlas Energy Systems, 1977.

Computer Power Systems. *Guide Specification: EDP Site Grounding*, Carson, CA: CPS, [n.d.].

Con Edison. *Electric Power and the Computer*, New York: Con Edison, 1984.

Conwill, Norman B. *A New Concept in Power Distribution* "The Computer Power System", Carson, CA: Computer Power Systems, [n.d.].

Daughtry, Vicki C. and Keller, David. "New Ferro Power Conditioners Deliver Computer Grade Power" *Computer Technology Review*, Summer 1986.

Devore, Tim. "Nonlinear Loads and UPS Systems" *EC&M*, July 1985.

Douglas, John. "Quality of Power In The Electronics Age" *EPRI Journal*, November 1985.

Dranetz. *How To Correct Power Line Disturbances*, Edison, NJ: Dranetz Technologies, Inc., 1985.

Dranetz. *How To Identify Power Line Dsiturbances*, Edison, NJ: Dranetz Technologies, Inc., 1985.

Dranetz. *Understanding Power Line Disturbances*, Edison, NJ: Dranetz Technologies, Inc., 1985.

DWP. *Power Supply for Los Angeles*, Los Angeles, CA: Los Angeles Department of Water and Power, 1982.

EPE. *Power: Problems and Solutions*, Costa Mesa, CA: Emergency Power Engineering, Inc., [n.d.].

Falossi, Aldo. *Data Communications and Interconnections*, Hardcopy Magazine, January 1987.

Goldstein, M. and Speranza, P.D. *The Quality of U.S. Commercial AC Power*, Whippany, NJ: Bell Telephone Laboratories, 1982 (IEEE).

Gould Deltec. *AC Power Handbook of Problems And Solutions*, 3rd. ed., San Diego, CA: Gould, Inc. Power Conversion Division, 1975.

Holt, Wayne E. *The RJ-11 Modular Jack*, Interact Magazine, Feb. 1986.

IEEE. *IEEE Standard Dictionary of Electrical and Electronic Terms*, New York: IEEE, 1977.

IEEE. *The Gold Book: Recommended Practice for the Design of Reliable Industrial and Commercial Power Systems*, ANSI/IEEE Std 493-1980.

IEEE. *The Gray Book: Recommended Practice for Electrical Power Systems in Commercial Buildings*, IEEE Std 241-1983.

IEEE. *The Green Book: Recommended Practice for Grounding Industrial and Commercial Power Systems*, ANSI/IEEE Std 142-1982.

IEEE. *The Orange Book: Recommended Practice for Emergency and Standby Power for Industrial and Commercial Applications*, ANSI/IEEE Std 446-1980.

IEEE. *The Red Book: Recommended Practice for Electric Power Distribution for Industrial Plants*, IEEE Std 141-1976.

Kalbach, John Fredrick. *Interaction Between Computer Systems and Their Power Sources*, Boston, MA: Kalbach Engineering, 1984.

KW Control Systems, Inc. *Introduction To The Uniblock UPS System*, Middletown, N.Y., [n.d.].

KW Control Systems, Inc. *Uniblock Analysis: Reliability and System Availability*, Middletown, N.Y., [n.d.].

Lewis, Warren H. *Electrical Power, Grounding, and Life Safety Systems For EDP Sites*, California: Computer Power Systems, 1981.

MacDonald, Ian. *Solutions to Computer Power Problems: Uninterruptible Power Systems*, Santa Ana, CA: Emerson Electric, [n.d.]

MacGorman, D.R. et al. *Lightning Strike Density for the Contiguous United States From Thunderstorm Duration Records*, Washington D.C.: National Oceanic and Atmospheric Administration, 1984.

McEachern, Alex. *Changing Strategies for using Power Line Monitors*, Foster City, CA: Basic Measuring Instruments, [n.d.].

National Bureau of Standards. *Federal Information Processing Standards Publication 94*, Washington D.C.: U.S. Department of Commerce, 1983.

National Electrical Code, NFPA-70-1981/84, National Fire Protection Association, Boston, MA.

O'Connor, James. "Power's Electrical Reference File" *Power*, October 1953.

O'Neill, Thomas. *Understanding Uninterruptible Power Supplies*, EC&M, April and July 1984.

Paulin, William and Drabkin, Mark. "Series-Hybrid Circuits Protect Sensitive Loads From Power Anomalies" *Computer Technology Review*, Spring 1986.

Rechsteiner, Emil B. "Comprehensive Power Protection Requires A Static or Rotary UPS" *Computer Technology Review*, Spring 1986.

Rechsteiner, Emil B. *Power to Computers; Keep it Clean and Stable!*, Littleton, MA: Frequency Technology, Inc., [n.d.].

Rosch, Winn. *Backup Power When the Juice Stops Flowing*, PC Magazine, September 16, 1986.

RTE Deltec. *AC Power Handbook of Problems And Solutions*, 5th ed., San Diego, CA: RTE Deltec Corporation, 1975.

Salzer Technology Enterprises, Inc. *UPS: Uninterruptible Power Systems and other Power Protection Equipment*, Santa Monica, CA: Salzer Technology Enterprises, Inc., 1986.

Sorgel Transformers. *Sorgel Dry-Type Transformer Study Course*, Milwaukee, WI: Sorgel Transformers, [n.d.].

The Office of Business Research and Analysis. *The Effects of Electrical Power Variations Upon Computers: an Overview*, Washington D.C.: U.S. Dept. of Commerce, [n.d.].

Tremaglio, Don. *Power Line Disturbances and How to Eliminate Them*, Bristol, CN: Superior Electric, 1985.

Westinghouse Architect's and Engineer's Electrical Data Book, Westinghouse Electric Corporation, 1957.

Wirl, Charles. *Inside Wiring*, Data Communications Magazine, September 1985.

Index

AC. *See* Alternating current power systems
Air conditioners, and impulses, 38–39
Allen, George, utility power survey by, 26
Alternating current power systems
    effect of computer systems on, 27–29
    inverters for. *See* Inverters, AC
    line drops in, and overheating, 52
    regulators for, 104–107
    from utility power. *See* Utility power
ANSI (American National Standards Institute), standards by, 16, 22, 23
Antistatic techniques, 50–51
Apparent power, 8–9
Arc equipment, and power disruptions, 38
Arrays, for lightning protection, 47
Auto transformers, 92
    variable ratio, for line-voltage regulation, 104–105
Avalanche diodes, for transient protection, 84–85

"Backup Power" (Rosch), 143
Baluns, for noise prevention, 71, 104
Batteries
    charging of, 121, 123–125
    end voltage of, 140, 146
    for personal computers, 146–147
    recharging of, 124, 140
    for RUPS, 120
    for standby power systems, 128
    for UPS, 123–124, 131–132, 135–140
Bell Telephone, utility power survey by, 26–27
Bent, Rodney, "Lightning and the Hazards It Produces for Explosive Facilities"
    on arrays, 47
    on formation of lightning, 42
    on lightning voltages, 45
Blackouts, 16
Bowyer, Dick, on flywheels, 118

Brownouts, 17, 27
Buildings
    power distribution systems for, 34–36
    structure of, and noise, 63, 72
Bypass switches
    for RUPS, 122
    for UPS, 124

Cables
    buried, and lightning, 45
    ribbon, and noise, 53
    types of, 74–75
Capacitors and capacitance
    and ferroresonant transformers, 107, 109
    and impulses, 25, 38
    and inrush currents, 28
    and noise, 95–96
    and Ohm's law, 7
    and power factor, 9, 38
    and ride through, 25
    and shielding, 57
    and voltage, 8
CBEMA (Computer and Business Equipment Manufacturers Association), and computer tolerances, 22–25
Cells, battery, 135
Circuit breakers, for PDUs, 99
Clamps, for transient protection, 84–88
Clean grounds, 59–60
Clocks, computer
    as noise source, 51
    and power frequency, 23–24
Cluster cabling, 76–77
Coaxial cable, 74–75
Codes, electrical, and grounding, 55, 58–59
Commercial buildings, power concerns for, 36
Common-mode noise, 51–52
    and baluns, 71, 104
    and computer damage, 53

and ferroresonant transformers, 109
and filters, 104
and ground loops, 60
and grounding, 56
and isolation transformers, 93–94
See also Noise
Computer and Business Equipment Manufacturers Association, and computer tolerances, 22–25
Conditioning. *See* Power conditioners
Conduction angle, in switching power supplies, 28, 68
Conductors
  ground, 61
  losses in, 8
  and power factor, 9
  shielding of, and noise, 53
Conduits
  and computer flexibility, 97–98
  and noise, 53, 63, 98
  and PDUs, 99
Connections, as source of noise, 53
Constant-voltage transformers, 107–111
Control, electronic, and M-G sets, 119–120
Cores, transformer, 9
Cost cutting
  and computer facilities, 64
  and PDUs, 100
  and power supplies, 26, 52
  and surge protectors, 86, 149
  and UPS, 130–131, 144, 146
CPS series 4000 power centers, 153–154
Crowbars, for transient protection, 82–84
  grounding and placement of, 88
Current
  ground, and noise, 63
  and inductance, 8
  from lightning stroke, 42
  and Ohm's law, 4, 7–8
  phase-to-phase, 3
  and power loss in wiring, 7–8
Current limiting
  and battery recharging, 124, 140
  and voltage sags, 124–125
CVT (constant-voltage transformers),107–111

Data, wiring for, 72–78
Datapoint Corporation, and microcomputers, xv

DC (direct current) power supplies, and noise, 52–53
Dedicated branch circuits, 39
Dedicated feeders, 34, 37, 39, 73
  and step-down transformers, 62
Delta systems, 3, 33
Depreciation, and PDUs, 101
"Development of a Guide On Surge Voltages In Low-Voltage AC Power Circuits, The" (Martzloff), 81
Diodes, avalanche, for transient protection, 84–85
DIPs. *See* Sags
Direct current power supplies, and noise, 52–53
Disks
  and line conditioning, 149
  and power frequency, 24–25
Distortion
  and ferroresonant transformers, 108–109
  and filters, 104
  and switching power supplies, 28, 51, 68–69, 91
  and three-phase transformers, 91
  and UPS, 144
  in utility power, 16
Distribution, of power
  in buildings, 34–36
  in computer facilities, 97–99
  with PDUs, 99–101
Diverters
  for lightning protection, 47
  for transient protection, 82
Double-shielded isolation transformers, 95
Downtime, cost of, 130
Dranetz Technologies
  definitions by, 16
  line-monitoring meter by, 20
Dropouts, 17
  and computers, 23

Earth ground, and grounding, 55, 59
Electrical Power, Grounding, and Life Safety Systems for EDP Sites (Lewis), 36
Electromagnetic interference. *See* Noise
Electromagnetism, and transformers, 9
Electromechanical transfer switches, for UPS, 130
Electronic control, and M-G sets, 119–120

Electrostatic discharge, 49–51
Electrostatic shields, and isolation transformers, 95–96
Electrostatic transfer switches, for UPS, 130
EMI (electromagnetic interference). *See* Noise
End voltage, of batteries, 140, 146
Engine generators, for UPS redundancy, 130
Environment, power, monitoring of, 153–154
ESD (electrostatic discharge), 49–51

Falossi, Aldo, on network expansion, 74
Faraday shields, and isolation transformers, 95–96
Fault clearing, in UPS, 129–130
Fault return paths, 56–57
Feeders, dedicated. *See* Dedicated feeders
Ferroresonant devices, for power conditioning, 148
Ferroresonant inverter UPS, 125
Ferroresonant power supplies, and power frequency, 25
Ferroresonant transformers, and voltage regulation, 107–111
Fiber optics, and noise, 53, 75–76
Field service, 152–153
  and MTBF, 132–133
Filters
  and electrical isolation, 53
  and power conditioning, 103–104
  RF noise, and impulses, 25
Flashes, of lightning, 42
Flexibility
  and conduits, 97–98
  and PDUs, 99
Flywheels, and M-G sets, 118
Frequency, power supply
  and computers, 22–24
  and ferroresonant transformers, 110
  and induction motors, 119
Fuses, for MOV failure, 86–87

Gas-surge arresters, 83–84
Gel cells, 139
Generators, creation of electricity by, 2–3
Goldstein, M., utility power survey by, 26–27
Green wire
  and grounding, 61
  and lightning arresters, 88
  and PDUs, 99
Grids, signal reference, 62–63
Ground fault return paths, 56–57
Ground loops
  and baluns, 71, 104
  and conduits, 98
  and fiber optics, 75
  and filters, 104
  and noise, 60–61
  and PDUs, 99
Ground planes
  for equipment common ground, 89
  and telecommunications equipment, 72
Grounding
  and earth ground, 55, 59
  and electrical codes, 51, 56
  and fault return paths, 56–57
  and lightning, 45
  and noise, 51, 53, 56, 69–70
  and PDUs, 99
  and personal computers, 69–72
  and safety, 56–60
  and shielding, 56–58
  techniques for, 60–65
  in telephone systems, 71–72
  of transient suppressors, 88–89
Groups, of buildings, power concerns for, 35

Hard disks, and line conditioners, 149
Heat
  and component damage, 52–53, 145
  from lightning, 43–44
  from square waves, 144
Homes, power concerns for, 36
Horizontal buildings, power concerns for, 35
Humidity, and ESD, 50
Hydroelectric power, 11

IBM
  and telecommunications, 78
  utility power surveys by, 26–27
  XT, transfer times for, 143–144
IEEE (Institute of Electrical and Electronics Engineers), standards by, 16, 80
IG. *See* Isolated grounds
Impedance, and Ohm's law, 7

Impulses, 17
   and air conditioners, 38–39
   and capacitors, 25, 38
   frequency of, 27
   in line voltage, 24
   and personal computers, 67
Induction motors, and M-G sets, 118–119
Inductors and induction
   and current, 8
   from lightning, 45
   and Ohm's law, 7
   and transients, 88
Industrial plants, power concerns for, 35–36
Inrush currents, 27–29
   and battery charging, 124
   and ferroresonant transformers, 110
   and tap-switching regulators, 112
Institute of Electrical and Electronics Engineers, standards by, 16, 80
Insulation, for electrical isolation, 53
Intel, 8008 microprocessor by, xv
Interaction, of equipment and wiring, 32
Internal combustion engines, and RUPS, 121
Inverters, AC
   for RUPS, 121–122
   for UPS, 123–127
Isolated grounds, 59–60
   for personal computers, 70
Isolation, electrical, 53, 91–97
   and M-G sets, 117
Isolation regulators, 107
Isolation transformers, 91–97
   and PDUs, 99
   and tap-switching regulators, 111–112
   See also Transformers

Jars, and batteries, 135
J-Box (junction box), and PDUs, 99

Kalbach, J. F., on inrush currents, 28
KVA, 8–9

LANs. *See* Local area networks
Lead antimony batteries, 137
Lead calcium batteries, 137
Lead-acid batteries, for UPS, 131–132, 136–137

Leader process, and lightning, 42–44
Lewis, Warren, *Electrical Power, Grounding, and Life Safety Systems for EDP Sites*
   on high voltage systems, 36
   on noise, 41
   and PDUs, 99–100
Lightning
   and common-mode noise, 51
   creation of, 41–45
   electrical effects of, 45
   frequency of, 45–46
   mechanical effects of, 44–45
   and metal structures, 63
   protection from, 46–48
   sags caused by, 27
   and surges, 45
   and transient overvoltages, 48–49, 79, 82
Lightning arresters
   for lightning protection, 47–48
   for transient protection, 81, 83–84
Lightning rods, for lightning protection, 46–47
"Lightning and the Hazards It Produces for Explosive Facilities" (Bent), 42
Line conditioners, for personal computers, 148–149
Line voltage. *See* Alternating current power systems
Load balancing, and three-phase systems, 68–69
Load switching
   and computer performance, 37–38
   and noise, 37, 51
   and sags, 18, 37
   and transients, 37–38, 79–80
Local area networks
   expansion of, 74
   grounding of, 71
Low-pass filters, and noise, 103

Magnetic coupling controlled regulators, 106
Manufacturers' representatives, and product selection, 152–153
Martzloff, Francois
   "Development of a Guide On Surge Voltages In Low-Voltage AC Power Circuits, The", 81
   "Origins of Transient Overvoltages", 80
Mean time between failure
   of M-G sets, 120

of RUPS, 132
of UPS, 132–133
Mean time to repair, of UPS, 132–133
Metal-oxide varistors, for transient protection, 85–86
M-G sets, 117–120. See also Rotary uninterruptible power systems
Micropower II tap-switching regulator, 111–112
Microprocessors, Intel 8008, xv
Minicomputers, and PDUs, 100
Modularity, and M-G sets, 121
Monitoring, of power environment, 19–21, 153–154
Motor-generator sets, 117–120. See also Rotary uninterruptible power systems
Motors
    induction, and M-G sets, 118–119
    pony, 119
    and sags, 27–28, 37–38
    and surges, 27–28
    synchronous, and M-G sets, 119
MOVs (metal-oxide varistors), for transient protection, 85–86
MTBF. See Mean time between failure
MTTR (Mean time to repair), of UPS, 132–133
Multistage protection, for transient protection, 87–88
National Bureau of Standards, on line voltage tolerances, 23
NEC (National Electrical Code), and grounding, 55, 58–59
Networks. See Local area networks
Neutral conductors
    current in, and noise, 28, 36, 68–69
    and safety, 56
NICAD (nickel cadmium) batteries, 138–139
"No trouble found" service calls, and power supplies, 20
Noise, 41, 51–53
    and baluns, 71, 104
    and capacitors, 96
    and coaxial cable, 74
    and computer damage, 52–53
    and conduits, 63, 98
    and earth grounds, 59
    and electrostatic shields, 95
    and ferroresonant transformers, 109–110
    and fiber optics, 53, 75
    and filters, 103–104
    and green wire, 61
    and grounding, 51, 53, 56, 59–60
    and isolation transformers, 92–95
    and line inductance, 88
    and neutral conductor current, 28, 69
    and neutral wire, 36
    and PDUs, 99
    and personal computers, 67–69
    and RF filters, 25
    and shielding, 53
    and tap-switching regulators, 115
    and twisted pairs, 76
    and UPS, 144
Noise filters, and impulses, 25
Normal-mode noise, 51–52
    and capacitors, 96
    and computer damage, 52–53
    and ferroresonant transformers, 109
    and isolation transformers, 93–94
    See also Noise
Notches, 17

Ohm's law, 4, 7–8
On-line power systems, compared to standby systems, 127–129
Optical isolation, and noise, 53
"Origins of Transient Overvoltages" (Martzloff), 80
Outages, 17
    frequency of, 27
    and M-G sets, 117–118
    and UPS, 140
Overload protection, and ferroresonant transformers, 110
Overvoltage, 18

PDU (power distribution units), 99–101
Personal computers
    backup power systems for, 147–148
    grounding of, 69–72
    and noise, 67–69
    power conditioners for, 147–149
    surge protectors for, 149
    UPS for, 141–147
    and utility power, 67–68
Phase-to-neutral voltages, 33
Phase-to-phase current, 3

Phase-to-phase voltages, 3, 33
Plante' batteries, 137
Pony motors, for synchronous motors, 119
Power, electrical (watts)
 and Ohm's law, 7–8
 and transformers, 9–10
Power bars
 for personal computer grounding, 70–71
 transient suppressors in, 86
Power centers, 153–154
Power conditioners, 103
 compared to protection devices, 147–148
 M-G sets, 117–120
 for personal computers, 147–149
 RUPS. See Rotary uninterruptible power systems
 UPS. See Uninterruptible power systems
Power distribution units, 99–101
Power factor, 8–9
 and capacitors, 38, 51
 and noise, 51
 of synchronous motors, 119
 and three-phase transformers, 91
Power-line monitors, 19–21
Prewiring, for data, benefits of, 74–78
Programmed cycle down, and UPS, 131
Pulse-width modulation inverters, for UPS, 125–126

Radial power distribution systems, 12–13
Radio-frequency interference, 51
 and line inductance, 88
 and shielding, 53, 57
Real power, compared to apparent power, 8
Rectifier/chargers
 for RUPS, 121
 in UPS, 123–125
Redundancy, in UPS, 130–131
Regulation, of voltage, 103–104
 with ferroresonant transformers, 107–111
 with line-voltage regulators, 104–107
 with tap-switching, 111–115
Resistors and resistance
 and Ohm's law, 4, 7–8
 soft-start, and impulses, 38
Resonance, and ferroresonant transformers, 109–110
Response time, and tap-switching regulators, 114–115

Restrictive transient suppressors, 82
RF noise filters, and impulses, 25
RFI. See Radio-frequency interference
Ribbon cables, and noise, 53
Ride through, 25
Ring-wave transients, 80
RJ jacks, for computer terminals, 76
Rolm, and IBM, 78
Rosch, Winn, "Backup Power", 143
Rotary uninterruptible power systems, 120–123
 415 Hz, 123
 compared to static systems, 133
 MTBF of, 132
RS-232C interfaces, and twisted pairs, 77
RUPS. See Rotary uninterruptible power systems

Safety
 and grounding, 56–61
 and phone systems, 72
 and sensors, with PDUs, 100–101
Sags, 17–19
 and computers, 24
 frequency of, 27
 and line-voltage regulators, 104
 and M-G sets, 117–118
 and motors, 27–28, 37–38
 and overheating, 52
 and UPS, 124–125
Saturable reactors, and voltage regulation, 106
SCRs (silicon-controlled rectifiers), in tap-switching regulators, 111, 115
Sealed batteries, and UPS, 131–132, 137–138
Segall, Donald, utility power survey by, 26
Selection, of equipment, considerations in, 151–152
Sensors, and safety, with PDUs, 100–101
Service, 152–153
 and MTBF, 132–133
Shielding
 and grounding, 56–58
 and noise, 53, 57, 77
 and PDUs, 99
Side flashes, from lightning, 45, 47–48
Signal ground, 55
Signal reference grids, 62–63
Silicon-controlled rectifiers, and tap-switching regulators, 111, 115
Sine waves, in three-phase systems, 2–3, 5–6

Single-phase power systems
  compared to three-phase, 2–3
  monitoring of, 20
  voltages in, 33
Single-point grounding, 60
  for personal computers, 70
  and transformers, 62
  and transient supressors, 88–89
Smart power supplies, 154–155
Soft-start resistors, and impulses, 38
Spark gaps, for transient protection, 82–84
Speranza, P.D., utility power survey by, 26–27
Spikes, 18
  frequency of, 27
SPS (standby power systems)
  for personal computers, 141–147
  and power conditioning, 147–148
  and UPS, 127–129, 142–147
Square waves, and overheating, 144
Standards, electrical, 16, 22–25
Static (electrostatic discharge), 49–51
Static transfer switches, for UPS, 124, 130
Static uninterruptible power systems. *See* Uninterruptible power systems
Steam plant power, 11
Stepped leaders, and lightning, 42–43
Step-wave inverters, for UPS, 126–127
Strings, and batteries, 136
Strokes, lightning, 42
Surges, 17–19
  and computers, 24
  frequency of, 27
  from lightning, 45
  and line-voltage regulators, 104
  and motors, 27–28
  protectors for, 149
Surveys, of utility power, 26–27
Switches. *See* Bypass switches; Transfer switches
Switching power supplies
  conduction angle in, 28, 68
  and cost cutting, 25
  distortion from, 28, 51, 68–69, 91
  and three-phase transformers, 91
Synchronicity, in UPS, 144–146
Synchronous motors, in M-G sets, 119

Tall buildings, power concerns for, 35
Tap-switching regulators, 111–115

Telecommunications
  and grounding, 71–72
  and IBM, 78
Three-phase power systems, 5–6
  advantages of, 2
  compared to single-phase, 2–3
  and ferroresonant transformers, 110–111
  load balancing in, 68–69
  monitoring of, 20
  and noise, 28, 68–69
  transformers for, and power factor, 91
  voltages in, 33–34
Tolerances, power, for computers, 22–25
Transfer switches, for UPS, 129–130
Transfer times, for personal computers, 143–144
Transformation ratio, 10
Transformers, 9–10
  auto, 92, 104–105
  and cost cutting, 25
  and electrical isolation, 53
  ferroresonant, and voltage regulation, 107–111
  and grounding, 56
  and inrush currents, 28
  isolation, 91–97
  and noise prevention, 53, 61–62
  reliability of, 91
  step-down, and dedicated feeders, 61–62
  in tap-switching regulators, 111–112
  and transients, 83
  variable-ratio, and line-voltage regulation, 104–105
Transient suppression plates, 63
Transients, 18, 79–82
  from lightning, 48–49
  and personal computers, 68
  suppressors for, 82–90
  and transformers, 28, 83
Transmission, of AC power, 1–2, 11–13
  voltages used in, 8
Transmission cables. *See* Cables
Transverse noise. *See* Common-mode noise
Triple-shielded isolation transformers, 95
Twinaxial cable, 74–75
Twisted pairs, 76–77

UL (Underwriters Laboratories), and codes, 59
Undervoltage, 18
Underwriters Laboratories, and codes, 59

Uninterruptible power systems, 123–132
    batteries for, 135–140
    compared to RUPS, 133
    compared to SPS, 142–147
    MTBF of, 132
    for personal computers, 141–147
Univac 1, xv-xvi
UPS. See Uninterruptible power systems
Utility power, 10
    computer effects on, 26–29
    and computer tolerances, 22–25
    creation of, 2–4
    disturbances in, 16–19
    monitors for, 19–21
    and personal computers, 67–68
    quality of, 25–27
    reception of, 11–13
    transmission of, 1–2, 11–13

Variable-induction regulators, 105–106
Variable-ratio transformers, and line-voltage regulation, 104–105
Varistors, for transient protection, 85–86
Ventilation
    and gel cells, 139
    for lead-acid batteries, 136–137
Vertical buildings, power concerns for, 35
Voltages
    and capacitance, 8
    clamping of, and transients, 84–86, 149
    for computers, ANSI standard for, 22, 23
    distribution of. See Distribution, of power
    from ESD, 50
    high, and power transmission, 8, 36
    from lightning stroke, 45
    and Ohm's law, 4, 7–8
    phase-to-neutral, 33
    phase-to-phase, 3, 33
    regulation of. See Regulation, of voltage
    in single-phase systems, 33
    in three-phase systems, 33–34
    transient, from lightning, 48–49
    utility power. See Utility power

Watts. see Power, electrical
Waveforms, of UPS, 144–145
Wiring
    and current, 7
    for data, 72–78
    and equipment interaction, 32
    for feeders, 39
    for grounding, 61
    problems with, 97–98
Wye systems, 3, 33

Zenith power supplies, transfer time for, 143–144
Zero-current crossing switching, and tap-switching regulators, 113